Looking at Media Studies
New Edition

for GCSE

Julian Bowker

Hodder & Stoughton

A MEMBER OF THE HODDER HEADLINE GROUP

Orders: please contact Bookpoint Ltd, 130 Milton Park, Abingdon,
Oxon OX14 4SB. Telephone: (44) 01235 827720, Fax: (44) 01235
400454. Lines are open from 9.00 – 6.00, Monday to Saturday, with
a 24 hour message answering service. You can also visit our
website: www.hoddereducation.co.uk

British Library Cataloguing in Publication Data
A catalogue record for this title is available from The British Library

ISBN - 10: 0 340 848553
ISBN - 13: 978 0 340 84855 5

First published 2003
Impression number   10 9 8 7 6 5 4 3
Year   2006 2005

Digital artwork by Colin Brown
Typeset by Fakenham Photosetting Ltd, Fakenham, Norfolk.
Printed in Great Britain for Hodder Arnold, an imprint of Hodder
Education, a division of Hodder Headline, 338 Euston Road,
London NW1 3BH by Martins the Printers, Berwick upon Tweed.

Contents

Acknowledgements

This book is dedicated to Fiona and Lily.

The author would like to thank the following:

Students of Varndean College, Brighton – Alex Hill, Anne-Marie Illingworth, Nansi Mellor, Sarah Morland, Judah Shostak-Reilly and Rachel Stone. Staff of Varndean College, Brighton – Caroline Fryer and Martin Sohn-Rethel.

The author and the publisher would like to thank the following for permission to reproduce copyright text and illustrative material:

The Advertising Archives 56; The Advertising Standards Authority 202, 203, 205, 206; All Action 12; Alpha Photo Press Agency 18; Associated Press 14, 101; Audit Bureau of Circulations 42,146, 181; Black Echoes Ltd 14; ©BBC 32, 34, 36, 45, 84; ©BBC Education Publicity 31; ©BBC News Online 174; ©BBC Photo Library 53, 223; ©BBCi/Holby City 162; ©BBFC 38; ©BFI 20, 21, 99, 100, 110, 114, 126 and in the colour section; British Sky Broadcasting Limited 33; BRAD 85, 86; Capital Radio Group Plc/Matt Soper 231, 234; Capital Radio Group Plc/Southern FM 230; ©Channel 4 21; Channel 4/Amanda Searle 172; CosmoGirl! Magazine © National Magazine Company 185 and in the colour section; Emap 40, 41, 45, 186, 187, 189, 193 and in the colour section (further information at www.emapadvertising.com); Emap Performance 86; ©Empics/Michael Ashton 219; Empire Magazine/Peter Mountain 188 and in the colour section; EPA Photo/AFP/Gerard Cerles 218; ©The Guardian 32, 96, 140, 154–5, 242; ©The Guardian/Willem 61; Guzelian Photography 12; HarperCollins 25; ©The Independent on Sunday 3, 43, 81, 158; ITC 206–7; ITN 124; The Kobal Collection 22; The Kobal Collection/Columbia/Sony Pictures Imageworks 115; Life File/Emma Lee in the colour section; ©Microsoft 243; Mirrorpix 138, 153; © Mizz/IPC Syndication 201; Music Week 86; Nestlé 208; ©1996, 1998 Newsweek, Inc. All rights reserved 61; New Nation 153; ©The Official UK Charts Company 2002 76; Press Association 15; PA Photos/European Photo Agency 10; PA Photos/Kirsty Wigglesworth 18; PA Photos/M J Kim 82, 198; PA Photos/SeanDempsey 174; Popperfoto/Reuters 11, 14; ©Predator Publishing Limited/DVD Monthly in the colour section; The Press Standards Board of Finance Ltd 150; © PressWise Trust 151; Radio Times 161; Revlon/Jay Brooks (photographer)/Wieden & Kennedy (agency) 200 and in the colour section; Rex Features/Ray Tang 209; Ronald Grant Archive 7, 18, 21, 22, 24, 102, 105, 107, 108, 109, 110, 119 and in the colour section; Screen International 93, 118; Skint 79; Topham Picturepoint 57; V2 Music Limited 87; Walkers Snack Foods Limited illustrations by Paul Cemmick 48 and in the colour section; www.bloomsburymagazine.com/Thomas Taylor (illustrator), /William Webb (cover design) and ©Winston Link (photograph) 23; www.borobarmy.com 224.

© Crown copyright material (213) is reproduced with the permission of the Controller of HMSO and the Queen's Printer for Scotland

Every effort has been made to trace copyright holders but this has not always been possible in all cases; any omissions brought to our attention will be corrected in future printings.

Introduction

How to use this book

This book is designed to match the requirements of AQA and OCR. Many of the activities will also suit WJEC specifications. To use the book to its best advantage you should obtain the current examination syllabus from the board you are studying. These can be obtained from the addresses at the back of the book. Teachers and centres should also have copies of these.

The book is divided into the following sections:

■ Concept chapters 1–4.
■ Practical production chapter 5
■ Media topic chapters 6–16.

Topics such as Film Promotion, Pop Music, Science or Comedy Fiction Films, Television and Sport, Television Talk shows, Television News, Newspapers, Teenage magazines and Advertising have been set by one or more boards for the timed examination papers. It is therefore worth finding out what the set topics are for each year to help plan your study. Soap dramas are covered in different sections, on pages 44–46 and 53–56.

The chapters can be followed in any order, once the first four conceptual chapters have been read. **Key words** and **technical words** are included in each chapter to highlight key terms. Practical activities, a glossary of terms and resource listings are included to aid understanding and knowledge and to support research.

The questionnaire which follows is designed to start you thinking about what media you use and produce. When you finish the book it might be worth comparing your responses at the start. Completing the questionnaire will provide an ideal opportunity for making this comparison. Activities are designed to be flexible for classroom or individual use – I hope you enjoy them!

Julian Bowker
December 2002

Questionnaire
Media Check-up

This questionnaire is designed to help you assess how much and what type of media you consume. It also may surprise you to discover how much media you produce yourself, when you assess what you produce across the whole range of media. Keep this information for a year and see if it changes during that time. You could also compare your results with someone else in your year or with someone much older or younger than yourself to see what differences you find.

Fill in all the questions by ticking the appropriate answer, unless instructed otherwise.

Age

Surname and first name

Year

1. What media do you watch/ read/listen to? *Circle the appropriate number.*

	No. hours per week						
Television	0–1	1–5	5–10	10–15	15–20	20–25	more than 25
Films	0–1	1–5	5–10	10–15	15–20	20–25	more than 25
Computer games	0–1	1–5	5–10	10–15	15–20	20–25	more than 25
Music	0–1	1–5	5–10	10–15	15–20	20–25	more than 25
Photography	0–1	1–5	5–10	10–15	15–20	20–25	more than 25
Fiction books	0–1	1–5	5–10	10–15	15–20	20–25	more than 25
Non-fiction books	0–1	1–5	5–10	10–15	15–20	20–25	more than 25
Internet – general search	0–1	1–5	5–10	10–15	15–20	20–25	more than 25
CD-ROM – general knowledge	0–1	1–5	5–10	10–15	15–20	20–25	more than 25
Phone/text/email	0–1	1–5	5–10	10–15	15–20	20–25	more than 25

2. Top five

List the top five media by the number of hours you spend on each.

1.

2.

3.

4.

5.

3. Television

a) How many television sets do you have in your house?

None	☐
One	☐
Two	☐
Three	☐
Four	☐
Five	☐
More than five	☐

b) Where are the television sets located?

Bedrooms	☐
Sitting room	☐
Kitchen	☐
Bathroom	☐
Other places (please state)	☐ . . . .

c) What type of television programmes do you like to watch?

	Yes	Don't Mind	Don't Like
Sitcom/comedy shows			
Sport			
Films			
Soaps			
Police drama			
Hospital drama			
Game shows			
Music shows			
Quiz shows			
Reality TV			
Confessional programmes (Oprah Winfrey, Trisha)			
Documentaries			
Advertisements			
News and current affairs			
Cartoons			

4. Film

What type of popular mainstream films do you like to watch? Tick as appropriate.

Horror ☐

Science fiction ☐

Romance ☐

Action ☐

Comedy ☐

True stories ☐

Musicals ☐

Western ☐

Thriller ☐

Fantasy ☐

Cartoon ☐

Martial arts and other (please state) ☐ . . . .

5. Games

What type of computer games do you play?

Fantasy ☐

Races ☐

Other ☐

6. How much media do you produce?

	Once	More than once	Often
Photographs (e.g. holiday snaps)	☐	☐	☐
Video	☐	☐	☐
Computer (letters, homework, photo-scanning, T-shirts)	☐	☐	☐
Music compilations, soundtracks, mixing, etc.	☐	☐	☐
Newsletter, magazine or fanzines	☐	☐	☐
Stories	☐	☐	☐
Web page	☐	☐	☐

Evaluation

1 How many hours per week do you spend using media products?

....

....

2 How many hours do you spend making media products?

....

....

3 What percentage of time in an average day do you spend on all the media you consume and make? (For example, if you have an average of 13 hours awake in an average day)

....

....

4 What conclusions do you draw from your media questionnaire about you and the media?

   i.   I consume more than I thought   ☐

   ii. I make more than I thought   ☐

   iii. I would like to make more media   ☐

   iv. I should consume more   ☐

   v. I might be able to make more   ☐

1 Asking questions
What is Media Studies?

What you will learn

This chapter explains the type of texts studied in Media Studies courses and provides a general introduction to the concepts which will be discussed in Chapters 2, 3 and 4.

You will analyse some cartoons and questions are given to start you off on learning how to analyse images. You are then given general outlines of responses to these questions to check against your interpretation.

KEY WORDS

- text
- languages
- categories
- producers
- audiences
- messages and values

TECHNICAL WORDS

- print run
- layout and design
- tabloid
- broadsheet
- leader
- editorial

What is Media Studies?

Studying the media involves looking, watching, listening and participating in, discussing and producing a range of media products.The study is about more than just the products themselves. It entails investigating the people who made them and thinking about what type of people consume them and what they gain from them.

What is a media text?

A media text is any modern media product which is the object of study. It could be a radio news bulletin, a family photograph or a music CD. The media texts covered in this book are:

- film
- television
- radio
- newspapers and magazines
- books
- computer software
- video
- advertisements
- CD-Rom
- internet

Media studies involves the analysis of the content of media texts, their producers, audiences, the technologies used, the social and economic context in which they were made, and what they mean.

Media Studies concepts

Media Studies concepts apply equally to the making of the product and to its analysis. There are six main concepts which are useful to learn and apply in media studies. These inform the learning activities of analysis, creativity and media culture. Chapters 2, 3 & 4 have been divided into the following three pairs of concepts. For each concept pairing there are some key questions and these questions can be applied to any text.

1 **Languages and Categories (Forms and Conventions)** – What type of text is it and how does it communicate?
2 **Producers and Audiences (Institutions)** – Who made the text, who consumes it and how?
3 **Messages and Values (Representations)** – What is the idea behind the text? What are the ideas in the text? What worth or value does the text have?

In the rest of this chapter the aim is to introduce you to the different media concepts and begin to discuss some of the theories about media texts, production processes and practices, their institutions and audiences.

Languages and Categories (Forms and conventions)

Analysis of the cartoon

1 The image in the cartoon is the wrong way round because the author of this cartoon wanted to make a joke. There is however, a serious point being made, in that paintings can never be exactly the same as the reality on which they are based. Every painting, television programme, film, etc, is only a representation of the real world.
2 A typical cartoon contains:

▮ Fine line drawings.
▮ Caricatures – humorous portraits of people; exaggerated body parts and facial expressions.
▮ A major concept expressed as an unusual visual idea or situation.
▮ A humorous setting.
▮ A caption of dialogue or a short single-line statement.

3 The point the cartoonist is trying to make is that there is no such thing as an accurate version of reality. The painter or the photographer selects a part of the real world and recreates it in their mind before reproducing that idea on paper and placing a frame around it.

┌─ **ACTIVITY 1** ─────────

1. Why is the cactus the wrong way round in the picture within the cartoon above?
2. How do we know this is a cartoon? What are the typical features of a cartoon?
3. What point is the cartoonist trying to make?

Producers and Audiences (Institutions)

Source: *Independent on Sunday*, 14 June 1992

ACTIVITY 2

1. Who made this cartoon?
2. Why was the cartoon produced?
3. What type of person will have read it?
4. In what type of media text, and where in that text, would you find this cartoon?
5. How did this cartoon reach its intended target?
6. What is the cartoon saying about all newspaper editors?

Note: The phrase 'to cry crocodile tears' means to pretend to cry, while secretly not having any feelings.

Analysis of Cartoon

1 The person who drew the cartoon is called Riddell, as they have signed it in the top right-hand corner. Getting the final image to the public is the work of several other people who were also involved in the process of reproducing the image. The picture editor of the newspaper, *The Independent on Sunday* (IOS) commissioned the cartoonist to draw it. The cartoon is then scanned into a computer and positioned on a page of the newspaper by a layout designer. Finally, the image is reproduced a few hundreds of thousands of times as part of the newspaper's print run. A print run is the number of copies printed.

2 The newspaper wanted a cartoon that could tell the story of tabloid newspapers' (see Chapter 9) overuse of Diana, Princess of Wales to sell their papers. An IOS editor then decided to create a cartoon mocking the national press' apparent declaration, that from then on, they would not intrude on Diana, Princess of Wales's private life.

3 The typical reader of *The Independent on Sunday* is a reader of broadsheet newspapers (see Chapter 9) and is usually educated. They are likely to have political views: and reader political party affiliation ranges from liberal Conservative, Liberal through to democrat Labour.

4 You would normally find a cartoon like this on the front page or inside the home pages of a serious broadsheet newspaper. The cartoon might be next to a leader column or editorial on the inside home pages or on the front page next to the main article.

5 Newspapers are usually passed from the printers to the wholesalers who distribute them to local depots. The newspaper shops (retailers) then receive the number of copies they hope to sell, based on previous sales. The public then buy it from the shops.

6 The image contains the following: a chart showing rising circulation figures, an editor depicted as a crocodile crying with a mischievous grin on its face; a desk covered in small format newspapers (*The Sun*, *The Express*, etc.) and a large desk chair. The meaning of the whole image is a comment on the ruthless way the tabloid newspapers used the stories about Diana, Princess of Wales's private life to sell copies.

The number of papers sold rose when Diana was the subject of the newspaper. When the story was tragic, such as the information about how unhappy she had privately been in her marriage to Prince Charles, the papers pretended to be sorry – the crocodile tears. However, the fact that the newspapers still used the information to sell copies implied that they may not have been truly sorry.

Occasionally questions were asked about the harassment and intrusion of the press into her private life, simply to get a picture of Diana. Several newspaper editors did express their sympathy for Diana, Princess of Wales, but one must question their sincerity when so many papers had been sold in the months when Diana was placed in the spotlight.

It is possible to comment on the IOS's cartoon that the serious newspapers used the stories which the tabloid's created in order to sell their own newspapers.

Messages and Values (Representations)

LOOK AT THOSE LETHAL WEAPONS

NOW DOESN'T THAT MAKE YOU WANT TO GO OUT AND KILL SOMETHING?

ACTIVITY 3

Study the image below and answer the following questions:
1. What do the images on the cave wall illustrate?
2. Do you agree with the statement, 'Now doesn't that make you want to go out and kill something'? Give reasons for your answer.
3. In your opinion, for what reasons did cave people draw images on walls?

Analysis of cartoon

1 The images on the wall are typical of paintings discovered around the world of cavemen killing animals. They depict pre-historic humans hunting animals.
2 The point of the cartoon is to state that violence is a part of society and that paintings are not the direct cause of violence – pictures tell us something about how humans live their lives. The statement, 'Now doesn't that make you want to go out and kill something' is meant to be sarcastic. In the real world, people are not usually driven to violence by simply looking at pictures – the aggression and the need to hunt depicted in this image is illustrating a social factor that already exists.
3 This question raises other issues. Why do humans need art or some form of expression? How is violence represented in fiction and factual media texts?

Effects of media images

It has been argued that 'the media' (usually television) causes violence in society. This is part of what is known as the 'effects' debate. The effect television has on society has not yet been conclusively proven. It is possible to argue that depicting violence in art is a positive experience. It is a form of fantasy and therapy; catharsis. We can see the consequences of violence if we see the effects and dangers dramatised in front of our eyes. In reality, it is too long ago to prove what cave dwellers thought when they drew or looked at such drawings. Perhaps we can say that these scenes served as a mirror to their hunting activities, as a source of comfort, or to instil a sense of superiority over the animals in their successful kills.

2 Languages and Categories (Forms and Conventions)

How do media forms communicate?

What you will learn

In this chapter you will learn about the concepts of languages and categories across various types of media. You will also analyse and create ideas for still and moving images.

KEY WORDS

- text
- forms and conventions
- codes
- signifiers
- denotation and connotation
- anchorage
- genre
- narrative
- *mise-en-scène*

TECHNICAL WORDS

- cropping
- enlargement
- captions
- headlines
- typeface
- close up
- medium and long shot
- track
- zoom

IS IT A FILM?

NO, IT'S CRIMEWATCH UK

ACTIVITY 1

Discuss the difference between a film and a TV documentary.

The languages of the media

In the study of the modern media, we call any media product a 'media text'. Media texts include radio, television, film, newspapers and magazines, music tapes and CDs, advertisements, computer games and books.

From an early age, a child responds to and interprets visual and sound texts. Each medium has a different way of communicating to us, depending on its technology and format. For example, radio news is purely aural, whereas television news combines sound and vision with typed text. We can describe each medium's method of communication as a 'media language'. Like the world of many cultures and languages the modern media exists in a variety of forms.

We gain information and ideas from newspapers quite differently than we do from television. Newspapers are made from paper; they consist of newsprint and are laid out in columns with computer word processed type, and they also contain electronically reproduced photographs. A reader of a newspaper can pick it up and read it in any order, as selectively as they like. Television programmes are electronically broadcast via air waves or by cable. The transmitting signal consists of sounds and images which are sequenced and shaped into a combined visual/sound narrative. Unless we use a remote control we therefore watch the television in a fixed sequence.

The language of each medium is learnt at a very young age by repeated reading, viewing and listening. By sharing ideas with others about what we have experienced we make sense of these different media languages. In the early days of film people were very alarmed to see trains appearing to come at them from the screen. Today we are rarely surprised if we see half a person appear on the screen – we do not think, as did some of the early film viewers, that the person's legs had been chopped off.

Each media language has what are known as a set of codes, forms and conventions.

Fig 2.1   William Shakespeare's Romeo and Juliet

Codes

The use of slow motion in films is an example of codes. A slow motion action sequence, as in the film *Chariots of Fire*, is code for a moment of fantasy and wonder. Throughout that particular film there are slow motion sequences depicting 'heroic' competitive running, and these scenes are set to grand orchestral music. In *William Shakespeare's Romeo and Juliet* when Romeo (Leonardo di Caprio) is knocked down, the use of slow motion indicates Tybalt's resolution to attack Mercutio – the tragedy is sealed.

ACTIVITY 2

Discuss the films you have seen slow motion used in and what it was used for.

Another example of a code is in drawn cartoons where the convention of using italics marks indicate that the subject is moving through the air.

ACTIVITY 3

Obtain a comic or a cartoon strip. What conventions are used such as moving through the air? For example, a happy dog or an aerated character.

The way we learn these codes is curious as children are not taught to 'study' television or cartoons with the same intensity that they are taught to learn to read books by being read to or instructed at home. Somehow through familiarity, we pick up what each medium's language is and what the codes mean.

Conventions

A typical television soap opera convention is a cliffhanger. This dramatic moment often takes place at the end of an episode, where we are given an important piece of information, such as when a new character appears announcing: 'I am your long lost brother'. The surprise leaves the audience in suspense, waiting to find out what happens next – and they have to wait until the next episode is broadcast.

A convention of a newspaper front page is to have the most important piece of news announced in large typeface with a short headline, for example, 'Prime Minister Resigns!' A typical convention of an hourly radio news programme is to have a sound of a clock bleeping or a pre-recorded piece of dramatic music to indicate that the words we are about to hear are important and serious.

Media languages: How does each medium communicate?

ACTIVITY 4

Discuss the following questions. If you wish, draw and annotate your responses to the questions.

1. Film – What types of images and sounds do we usually expect to see and hear if the film is a thriller and danger is present?
2. Television – What is the difference between a typical studio set for a television news programme and a game show? List or sketch out differences in who is present, the layout, the studio set and props.
3. Magazines – What is the difference in looks (i.e. form) and content between a front cover for a fanzine and a music magazine like *Mixmag*?

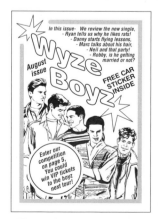

Fig 2.2   *Example of a commercial fanzine*

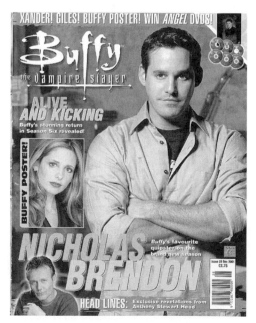

Fig 2.3   *Example of a cult TV fanzine*

Big bands with costly promotional back up will have a fanzine. A fanzine or 'Zine' is then produced on a very low budget, made at home by the fans. A very small number are distributed amongst friends and clubs. There a variety of types of fanzines – specialist music and football 'zines' are common. We can describe a zine as being non-mainstream or an alternative to the mainstream product. cult TV fanzines, such as *Buffy the Vampire Slayer*, also support marketing and audience interests.

Form

As well as different kinds of media, within each medium there are different forms of the same product or text. For example, all newspapers consist of printed text, photographs, headlines and captions, columns, pugs ('ears'), headings and sub-headings.

The form of newspapers

There are two main forms of newspaper: tabloid and broadsheet. A tabloid usually has a four column width and a broadsheet has a seven column width. A tabloid is A3 size and a broadsheet is twice as long.

Historically tabloids tended to be simpler to read and aimed at an 'easy read' audience, with large photographs and more pictures.

Fig 2.4   Tabloid

Fig 2.5   Broadsheet

Tabloids tended to be less 'wordy', while broadsheets often had a higher word content and were targeted at the more literary reader.

In recent times more newspaper editors have chosen to use the tabloid form. This is perhaps because the tabloid form suits a magazine style of content and is easier to hold and carry about. The *Daily Mail* and the *Daily Express*, for example, which used to be termed as broadsheets, are now often described as 'tabloids'. Most Saturday and Sunday newspapers now have tabloid or magazine supplements, even if the main paper is a broadsheet.

Image analysis

The photographic image is the major component of newspapers, magazines, CD covers, and print-based advertising. Creating an image involves selecting real objects and presenting them in a way that means something to the viewer. To appreciate this the viewer has to be able to interpret visual signs and symbols.

There are four aspects of analysing an image:

- Analysis involves explaining what the images selected and represented from the real world mean.
- Analysis also involves studying what words have been used to accompany the image and how their content, style of lettering and layout changes its meaning.
- The analysis of images involves looking at how images are presented technically to create effects.
- Analysis of images also involves identifying where the image is placed, who has placed it there and for whom?

Symbols

ACTIVITY 5

Discuss in pairs and write down or draw and annotate your responses to the following question:

What ideas do you associate with the following images?

1. red ribbon
2. red poppy
3. red nose
4. red rose

It is possible that you discussed the association of AIDS World Day with the red ribbon; Armistice Day with the red poppy, clowns and Comic Relief for Africa with the red nose and romance, or perhaps the Labour Party, with the red rose.

Signifier and signs

Each of the images mentioned previously mean something else, aside from their meaning as real objects. A red rose is a flower, but is also associated with romance and so is a commonly recognised symbol of this. When objects signify other meanings, then these objects become what are known as 'signifiers of meaning'.

Meaning also depends on culture and country. In Japan or Brazil, a red poppy would not have the same meaning as it does in the UK – why do you think this is?

ACTIVITY 6

Draw or describe objects which are signifiers of:

1. American culture
2. New York
3. British nationality
4. Youth culture

Discuss what your images are and explain what they signify.

Fig 2.6   Before the World Trade Center was destroyed in a suicide attack, it represented successful icons of American business culture.

Icons

The word icon is another term used to discuss the ideas associated with pictures and photographs of people and objects. Literally, an icon means 'to resemble', from the Greek. Paintings of Christ in the Eastern Christian Church were often painted onto panelled wood and displayed in churches for worship. Different religions have their own icons to pray to. However, in many religions creating a likeness is viewed as blasphemous, and taints the god-like with the human.

In modern Britain, an icon is more likely to refer to a pop star, a soap celebrity or royal family figure. An icon is someone or something worshipped by devoted admirers or believers. The icon is usually given a special significance verging on the religious or cultish.

ACTIVITY 7

Discuss the following:

1. Diana, Princess of Wales, when she was alive and after she died, became an icon for people in Britain. In your view, what is Diana, Princess of Wales an icon of?
2. What associations do the Danger Mine signs and the trainers create? How do the Danger Mine signs and trainers relate to Diana, Princess of Wales?

Fig 2.7   After the destruction of the World Trade Center, films with a theme of destruction or terrorism in New York were postponed.

Source: Popperfoto/Reuters

Fig 2.8   *Modern iconography*

Source: © Guzelian Photography

Icons in culture

In recent film and pop culture history Marilyn Monroe (50s and 60s), Debbie Harry (70s and 80s) and Madonna (80s and 90s) have all been icons in the shape of sex symbols. They have all become icons of female sexuality in different ways, in different decades.

One major reason why these women have become so important is because their images have been mass-produced and circulated so frequently.

Icons as objects

We can also use the word icon to describe objects. For example, in the Western film genre there are a number of typical images of real objects. These are not simply parts of the scenery, but over many years films have

Fig 2.9   *David and Victoria Beckham: icons of their era.*

Source: All Action

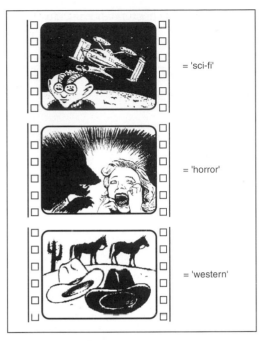

= 'sci-fi'

= 'horror'

= 'western'

Fig 2.10   Using icons to describe films:
            sci-fi, horror and the western

ACTIVITY 8

Discuss and research images of icons in the music or film industries.

1. Who in the music, film or celebrity world would you describe as being contemporary icons?
2. Ask an adult who they would describe as their five most significant twentieth century icons from the world of politics, sport or pop culture.
3. Identify four icons of American culture.
4. Identify one person who defines themselves as a rebel in the film or music industries.
5. What iconography would you expect in
   a) American High School teen drama
   b) James Bond films?

come to signify what we recognise as a western: the gun, the hats and boots and spurs, cacti, the horse, the desert and rocky outcrop and the tumbleweed.

Examples of icons in a science fiction film are futuristic technology and settings, space crafts and robots. All of these icons have become well established over the years. In film studies the word 'iconography' is used to cover a whole collection of icons belonging to a particular type of film genre, be it the Western, the science fiction movie or the horror film (see Figures 2.10). Stars also become icons for certain genre: Sigourney Weaver in *Alien* or *Mr Bean*.

Recognising the image

What can you recognise or identify when you look at an image? A famous line drawing tested people to see what they thought they were seeing. Look at Figure 2.11 and see what you can recognise. What is this an image of?

It is possible that you saw the line drawing as a duck or as a rabbit. This illustrates two points:

1 Images can sometimes contain more than one meaning.
2 What they associate with the image will depend on that person's background and experience.

An image that has the potential to mean several things is said to be 'polysemic', that

Fig 2.11

is it has many meanings. Advertisements in particular often contain several meanings. Even newspaper photographs about real events are capable of having several meanings. The photo in Figure 2.12 was taken on 20 April 1998, at an event held to mark the occasion of Israel's 50th anniversary. It was printed in *The Guardian*. The image of the Israeli national flag combines the image of war with the innocence of the boy. The flower symbolises peace. To a Palestinian, this peace may not be associated with the Israeli flag.

Fig 2.12   *An image with many possible meanings*
Source: © Associated Press Ltd.

Facial expression, posture and gestures

We can analyse images of people and how someone looks in terms of their facial

Fig 2.13   *What point of view is represented here?*
Source: Popperfoto/Reuters

expression, body posture and gestures with their hands.

Photographic image analysis

Study the picture below of Armand Van Helden. It was taken for the front cover of *Inside Trax*, a garage, house and club supplement to *Echoes*, the 'Black Music Weekly'.

Fig 2.14   *Armand Van Helden*
Source: Black Echoes Ltd.

ACTIVITY 9

a Describe the expression on the face of Armand Van Helden in the photograph.
b Describe his pose and posture. How natural or posed do you think he is?
c Analyse the hand gestures and clothes.
d What angle is the photograph taken from and why?

Denotation

Fig 2.15   Clare Short: image denotation and connotation
Source: The Press Association

The image of Clare Short, International Development Secretary, (Figure 2.15) conveys several ideas associated with the objects featured:

▌ Weapons of war – landmines.
▌ Sign with a skull and cross bones.
▌ She is wearing protective clothing usually worn where explosives or guns are involved.
▌ The sea is in the background.

This description of ideas contained in the image is known as denotation. If we then start to draw some conclusions about what these objects mean and interpret the image and the ideas that are associated with it – these are connotations of the image.

Connotation

In Figure 2.15, the manner in which Clare Short is holding up the landmines suggests that she considers them to be objects which are offensive. She knows the photographers are looking at her and the way the image is composed suggests that she has co-operated with them. In other words, she has not been snapped without her permission, rather the reverse.

In fact, Clare Short has set up the whole photographic event to draw attention in the newspapers to the world problem of unexploded landmines. Referring back to the late Princess of Wales' campaign against landmines, you will recognise the protective clothing is the same as Diana wore when she was drawing attention to the same issue. Clare Short's serious facial expression suggests that she is unhappy about the landmines. The familiar danger signs of the symbol of the skull and cross bones indicates that these are indeed very dangerous objects.

When the image in Figure 2.15 was printed in *The Guardian*, in October 1997, the original caption below the image gave us to understand that the sea behind is in Brighton; the southern coastal location where the Labour party conference was held in 1997. At this event, the issue of the world's sites of unexploded landmines was discussed. In the light of this information we can recognise that where Clare Short is standing is not the location of the mines she is holding up.

Image in context

ACTIVITY 10

Create three fictional captions to place under the image of Clare Short for each of the following:

a a film poster
b a local newspaper article
c a government health warning to be displayed on billboards

Discuss for each example how the meaning of the original image and words has changed, i.e. not the words but the image itself.

Anchorage

'Anchorage' is the term given for placing words next to an image. The words convey the meaning of the image. Very few images appear in commercial advertising or government information promotions without words attached. In the captioning activity on the previous page you were fixing the meaning of the image in three different ways, even though the image itself remained the same.

Image: techniques analysis

Following are three examples of how a student has changed the Clare Short image and the context of the images. You will now see that the image's meaning has been fixed in three different ways. The converted image is no longer polysemic, as with the captions and headings it has a limited range of meanings – it has been anchored.

TASK 1

Analyse the techniques and processes used to produce images 'A' 'B' and 'C' (coursework by Anne-Marie Illingworth).

Examine lighting, colour, camera angle and type of shot, and the size and shape of the edited image.

In image 'A' the student has used techniques of cropping, enlargement on a photocopier, captioning and wordprocessing headlines. They have also used different font sizes and typefaces, to suit their sci-fi magazine.

The same techniques have been used in image 'B' for this newspaper or billboard advertisement for a documentary on television.

Image 'C' has not been cropped. Aside from this however, the same techniques have been used for this front page of a newspaper. The name of the newspaper is in a font and typeface which suits a broadsheet newspaper like *The Observer*.

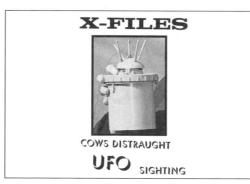

Image A

Image B

Image C

Image production

In this exercise you will crop, format and analyse a chosen image. Select an image from a newspaper or magazine which is interesting and can be divided into two more images.

ACTIVITY 11

Remember to keep the original captions or headings from your chosen image. Now place these three images into new contexts, for example, a newspaper, a magazine or an advertisement.

ACTIVITY 12

Start with the whole image but without the words. Invent new headings or captions, or overlay words on the image. In doing this, you will change the meaning from the original meaning of its original newspaper/magazine context – explain how this has occurred.

ACTIVITY 13

Next crop the image into two more parts. You will now have invented two more different contexts, for example newspaper, advertisements or film poster. You may need to enlarge your cropped image. These new images should be completely different from the whole image idea that you created in Activity 12. Make the image either landscape or portrait, to suit the place where it will be seen.

ACTIVITY 14

Write about each of the three images and their new captions, headings or overlays of printed words, in a critical commentary. You should aim to write about 250–400 words.

Critical commentary

A critical commentary is a piece of analytical writing. A 'commentary' involves explaining the process of how you came to produce your images and what you are trying to suggest (or connote) in their new formats. The 'critical' part of the commentary means you can show that you have reflected on and analysed the process and meaning of the images you have produced. You will also have to explain why you changed the shape and size of your images and how you produced them in their new versions.

Use the following headings to guide your written analysis of each image produced:

1 Analysis of process: these are decisions made in producing different captions, headings, lettering, typeface and fonts, and for cropping and enlarging.
2 Image analysis: this includes the terms denotation and connotation. One must ask what is included in the image and what does this mean? How is the meaning conveyed, for example is it conveyed by signifiers or symbols?
3 Anchorage: how do the captions alter the meaning? What forms and conventions are used in the image?
4 Photographic techniques: analyse the original image, i.e. lighting, colour, camera distance, angle, framing and focus.
5 Institutions: who made the image? How do the two different contexts affect the image content?

6 Audience: who is it targeted at? How many different types of audience might look at these images? How might people react differently to the same images and text?

An example of the commentary from this project is on pages 70–72.

Media Categories

This section deals with identifying various media text categories.

┌─ **ACTIVITY 15** ───────

Discuss the following in pairs:

a Name a television programme. What type of programme is it?

b From reading their titles, do you think the following programmes are fiction or factual? Explain your reasons.
   ∎ *Buffy the Vampire Slayer*
   ∎ *Who Wants to be a Millionaire?*
   ∎ *SM TV Live*

c Now, examine the photographs below – is it possible to tell simply by looking at these, which are factual or fictional? Give reasons for why you think you know.

d What type of fiction programme is Friends?

Categorising media texts

We can usually categorise media texts in at least three ways:

1 Categorisation as the labelling and identifying of the different types of media (radio, television, film, newspapers, magazines, etc.).

2 Media forms can be divided within one medium into genre categories. For example, television can be divided into documentary, fiction or news.

3 Types of film or television genre can be further subdivided into groups. For example, film fiction can be subdivided

into comedy, sci-fi, musical or western. Alternatively, television factual programmes can be subdivided into quiz, soap or sport, for example.

A further subdivision of the above categories is a sub-category where you can describe a cartoon such as *The Simpsons* as a sitcom with a satirical edge.

Television

When you switch on the television and flick across the channels, how do you know what type of programme you are watching? Is it a film, a quiz show, a sports programme or a children's drama, for example? We know how to identify a quiz show because there is a host/ess, there are contestants, a panel and a studio audience. These elements are known as the forms and conventions that have become the accepted shape and format of the programme type.

ACTIVITY 16

List at least two forms and conventions of the following television programmes:

- ▌ Holiday travel consumer advice
- ▌ Saturday morning children's entertainment shows

It is usually possible to immediately identify what type of programme (or media text) it is, as we have seen them before and we recognise the elements which make each type of programme distinctive.

Film

ACTIVITY 17

Introducing this section on film genre are short summaries of four films, for which the titles have been deliberately left out. Try to identify the genre of each film from the descriptions.

a Shakespeare's famous love story meets the busy modern media in this violent and sexy romance depicting the fate of the two ill-fated lovers, Romeo and Juliet. When they meet on Verona Beach, the sands of time trickle out as the ruinous hatred is played out between their two rival families, the Montagues and the Capulets.

b Vincent has a heart defect. It helps him survive in this futuristic world, where geneticists design babies free of imperfection. The future is bright for perfect ones who rule over the invalids. With clever deception, Vincent passes as one of the elite, until a murder is committed and DNA evidence points to him.

c The Musketeers are sworn to fight for each and for France to the death. A mysterious French prisoner leads them to embark on their most dangerous mission ever, to save France from certain downfall. They must be strong to defend their friendship, France, and the prisoner whose identity threatens to destroy not only their lifelong friendship but also the throne the Musketeers have sworn to serve.

d 007's brief is to find out the real truth behind the fastest growing news network owned by the evil media mogul, Eliot Carver. There's also the mysterious business of the wreck of the Naval frigate Devonshire, apparently lost in territorial waters – all in a day's work for Bond, James Bond.

Genre

It is not always easy to find a single word to label a film. You may have found in the previous activity, that you could either explain a film with one word or that you had to use several words to explain the type of film exactly.

The word used to describe different types of films is 'genre'. It originally was used to define books into different categories: such as romance, gothic or comedy. When applied to films the word genre also means type or category.

Modern films often combine genres and create their own unique labels and categories. For example, *Mary Shelley's Frankenstein* (1994) combines horror, adventure romance, science fiction and period costume drama.

Mary Shelley wrote the original *Frankenstein*, a gothic novel, in the nineteenth century. The word gothic is often used to describe a dark, melancholic mood and setting: gloomy castles, shadowy corridors and misty graveyards. The director Kenneth Branagh gave his *Frankenstein* the title *Mary Shelley's Frankenstein* because he wanted it to appear to be a faithful rendition of the original story.

The horror genre

The 1935 *Frankenstein* film directed by James Whale started the type of horror movies we now associate with Count Dracula, haunted castles, bats, vampires, possessed females and reconstructed humans. Although the Hammer horror films with Boris Karloff, Peter Cushing and Christopher Lee are old fashioned, the typical ingredients of a horror film today remain similar and are immediately understood by audiences. Even modern films such as the horror-comedy *Scream* series are packed with moments of suspense and terror, just as we saw in the Hammer films.

The violence usually contains some blood letting, an obsessive scientist or psychotic, an out of control monster and the slave or victim who is controlled or killed by the demonic character who craves power over other people. There is also often a monster who carries out the master's wishes, several exciting and scary chases, and the themes of good versus evil and natural versus supernatural.

Fig 2.16   Mary Shelley's Frankenstein: *horror film*

Source: © BFI

Fig 2.17   Mary Shelley's Frankenstein: *period costume drama*

Source: © BFI

Sub-categories

Today, there are sub-categories of horror films, such as 'slasher' movies. There are also more modern genres such as Kung Fu films. These are created mainly in Hong Kong and use manga animation, which is Japanese.

ACTIVITY 18

Study the titles of the films listed below and research their genres.

a King Kong (1935)
b Stagecoach (1939)

c Star Wars (1977)
d Brassed Off (1996)
e The Full Monty (1997)
f Lara Croft: Tomb Raider (2001)

(If you are unsure of any, try researching in a library or resource centre or on the internet: *Halliwell's Film and Video Guide* and *imdb.com* are useful resources.)

Fig 2.19   Stagecoach

Source: © BFI

ACTIVITY 19

Now that you have studied the titles of the films, look at the film stills pictured here and overleaf. All of the films in the list were box office successes except *Brassed Off*. Make a list of reasons why some films are more successful than others. For example, the film *Brassed Off* is set in Northern England and its theme is unemployment. However, *The Full Monty*, with the same area and general theme, raced away to become the biggest selling film in the UK ever, up to that date, in 1998.

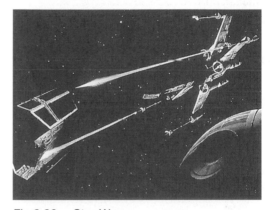

Fig 2.20   Star Wars

Source: © Ronald Grant

Fig 2.18   King Kong

Source: © BFI

Fig 2.21   Brassed Off

Source: © Channel 4

Fig 2.22   The Full Monty
Source: © Kobal Collection

Fig 2.23   Lara Croft: Tomb Raider
Source: © Ronald Grant

ACTIVITY 20

Is there a difference between 'good' and 'popular' films?

Early Film Narrative

In the 1890s Britain, along with France, Germany and America, was in the forefront of experimenting with the new medium of film. UK film pioneers such as Willamson and Hepworth filmed in the open air due to lack of sufficient indoor light or artificial lighting. They used very simple camera shots and angles.

Audiences usually saw the films projected on a large scale onto walls in theatres, music halls or village halls and in disused shops or specially constructed mobile peep shows, where people would have to pay to view.

Music, live stage effects, such as smoke and bombs, and actors would often accompany the moving images. These films tended to be simple drama and used real footage, for example of trains coming into stations, and basic special effects to create illusions. A narrator would often accompany the screening in person to explain what was in the film and make up for the pieces that needed linking together.

Films would sometimes be replayed several times. They were even played backwards for fun, as they were very short. Films aroused a great deal of curiosity in people and in the early years were included as part of the fun of a range of entertainments. As with video games and the Internet today, the potential of films was barely recognised at this time.

Rescued by Rover

Rescued by Rover (1905) by the British film maker, Cecil Hepworth, became a public favourite because it starred a dog as the main character. The dog finds a baby who

Fig 2.24   Rescued by Rover: *a popular film in 1905*
Source: © BFI

has been stolen by a poor woman, and is seen running from scene to scene, linking the different scenes together. As a piece of fiction it is fairly slight, but for the time when it was made it is quite a long piece of film drama, at 6 minutes 25 seconds duration. Perhaps for the audience it held the same kind of curiosity as a piece in a Home Video programme, where members of the public send in videos of the absurd antics of their pets.

Film structure

There is a formula for writing a film script which Hollywood films tend to follow. One page of script equals one minute of film time, and most features run for 90 or 110 minutes. The basic structure of most films breaks down into three acts:

▌ The Set-Up (script pages 1–30).
▌ The Confrontation (pages 31–90).
▌ Finally, the Resolution (pages 91–110).

Between pages 10 and 15 there is a disruption which displaces the normal order of the drama. This event sets the hero or heroine on their quest. By the last act the quest must seem impossible, however, somehow in the final chase scenes (pages 80–110) the hero/heroine manages to find a way out by using force or logic. They succeed in their quest by defeating the enemy and winning the object of their heart's desires.

ACTIVITY 21

Select any film you have liked.
Identify

a) the set up
b) the description
c) the resolution.

Where do stories for films come from?

Ideas for films come from a variety of sources. The main ones are:

▌ Adaptations from plays, short stories and novels (for example, *Great Expectations*, 1946 and 1998).
▌ Fairy stories, myths and legends (for example, *Cinderella* or *Little Red Riding Hood*).
▌ Real life events (for example, *Malcolm X*, 1992, or *Ghandi*, 1982).
▌ Remakes of tv serials into films (for example, *Star Trek*, 1979, or *The Avengers*, 1998).
▌ Original screenplays. For example, *Spice World the Movie*. This was wholly created around the Spice Girls phenomena. The style of the film was similar in spirit to *Hard Day's Night* which followed the Beatles as a successful band constantly hopping from place to place besieged by their fans.

Fig 2.25   Harry Potter and the Philosopher's Stone: *book cover*

Fig 2.26   Harry Potter and the Philosopher's Stone: *film poster*

Fig 2.28   Lord of the Rings: *film poster*

Creating film ideas

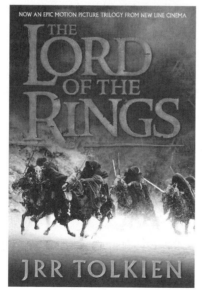

Fig 2.27   Lord of the Rings: *book cover*

ACTIVITY 22

Adaptations

Following is an example of a colourful outline of a film, which would be included in a press pack:

Charles Dickens' classic nineteenth century novel, Great Expectations, is now adapted as a modern-day, sexy and provocative film set in New York and Florida. The story follows the journey of a young Finn Bell, whose father and mother died when he was very young. He is now an artist who hopes to make his way in the world, but this is dramatically changed by three separate strangers: a sinister convict named Lustig (Robert De Niro); the cool and aloof Estella (Gwyneth Paltrow); and the old, wealthy and definitely cracked Miss Nora Dinsmoor (Anne Bancroft).

Write a short press statement for a remake of a classic story by William Shakespeare, Charles Dickens, George Eliot or Jane Austen. Explain the modern settings and the cast.

ACTIVITY 23

Original fairytales, myths and legends

1. Turn the fairy story *Cinderella* into a modern film drama, using contemporary themes and settings. If you want to select and cast famous actors and actresses, try to ensure that they will suit the parts you give them.
2. Read the story of *Cinderella* below and then write a new version. You should try to keep to writing 300 words maximum.

Cinderella lives with her father and two ugly stepsisters. Her stepsisters hate her and make her do all the cleaning and cooking while they lie about having a good time. When an invitation arrives for the prince's ball, the two stepsisters insist that the invitation is for them only and that Cinderella has to stay behind to clean the house. And so Cinderella has to stay behind and do the cleaning, but she wishes that she too could go to the ball. Her fairy godmother appears and grants her wish with one stipulation – that she must leave the ball by midnight.

At the ball, Cinderella is a hit, especially with the Prince, who is entranced. However, Cinderella almost forgets her fairy godmother's warning and escapes just in the nick of time, accidentally leaving her tiny glass slipper behind.

The Prince combs the kingdom looking for the woman whose foot fits the shoe. Finally, after much searching and even interference from the ugly sisters, he discovers Cinderella. They get married and live happily ever after.

3. Now plan the opening scenes of a film version of your story and how you will establish the characters and the settings. Write out in detail what you will see and what dialogue and soundtrack you will hear in the first three minutes of the film.
   a Plot outline (200–400 words)
   b Characters
   c Key elements:
      – Cinderella
      – fairy godmother
      – stepsisters
      – carriage
      – glass slipper
      – 12.00 curfew
   d Treatment
   e Genre – what type of film is it? e.g. comedy – romance, horror – gangster, sci-fi – thriller.

Film language and narrative structure

Films communicate through a series of images and sound combined together. There are camera shots of different sizes and angles and framings. The camera shots are composed by a camera director and artificial lighting is used to emphasise dark and bright areas. The soundtrack consists of speech, sound effects, atmospheric sound and music.

Narrative structure

The narrative structure of a mainstream film usually starts with normality (equilibrium) and then something happens to disrupt that normality (disequilibrium) then the rest of the film is about how normality is once more restored. Some film narratives develop the plot on many levels and can be quite complex.

A simple and often used narrative technique is to have parallel plots running simultaneously so that we see different events and characters occuring in what appears to be the same time. Films today use space and time in a unique way, in contrast to the early days of cinema when it was considered confusing to keep switching between locations and seeing the action unfold in two separate places.

One technique for achieving the parallel plot effect is by editing the film through cross-cutting. Cross-cutting is where the image is switched from one place to another, making the actions appear simultaneous. An example of parallel plot action is when two people talk together on the phone and there is some action going on in the background of each setting.

Big close up
B.C.U.

Medium shot
M.S.

Very long
shot
V.L.S.

High angle
(looking down)

Close-up
C.U.

Medium long
shot
M.L.S.

Over the
shoulder shot

Low angle
(looking up)

Medium close-up
M.C.U.

Long shot
L.S.

Moving subject –
framed with space to
walk into

Tilted frame

Fig 2.29   An illustration of various shot types

Editing

Editing techniques are used to place the narrative in sequence and also to shape time and space. Imagine how a boxing match has to be filmed and then edited to make it feel like we the audience are in the ring with the fighters, as well as including the spectators' point of view. A range of close-ups, medium and long shots are needed to achieve this effect.

Other editing techniques are as follows:

▌ Dissolves – to mix from one scene to another, for example to show that time has passed in the same place.
▌ Wipes – to make a narrative transition from one place to another, for example to move from a scene in London to one in New York.
▌ Cuts – a direct interruption and switch to another place or time, to keep both action and narrative moving quickly and sharply.
▌ Fades – emerging or disappearing scene creates the effect of slowly departing or arriving into the place or mood of the narrative.

Storyboard simulation

ACTIVITY 24

a Invent and present an opening sequence to the film you wrote out in Creating Film Ideas: Activity 24 (see page 25).
b Produce a storyboard of between 6–10 frames of the opening scene(s) of your modern fairy story. Include the following information:

▌ Lighting
▌ Setting
▌ Soundtrack – music, atmosphere and special effects
▌ Speech
▌ Camera angle
▌ Camera shot size

Alternatively, use a digital camera to create a photo sequence.

ACTIVITY 25

Write a critical commentary on your film of approximately 300 words. Discuss the following:

a Genre – what film is it like or unlike?
b Narrative style – is it a flashback, a drama or a mood you have created?
c Camera composition – is there any particular style or point of view conveyed in the way you have positioned your camera?
d Editing – are the shots dissolves or cuts?
e Signifiers – have you used signifiers, for example, urban concrete landscapes and smoke-filled bars for a gangster film?

Extension Tasks

1 **Research** a range of newspapers on the same day and collect examples of photographs, captions and headlines about the same event or persons, which can then be compared. Compare and contrast how much space is given to each item and why you think the amounts vary.

2 **Produce** a storyboard of a title sequence (10–15 frames) for a new crime genre police series. Give a critical account (250 words) of how the sequence would be typical or untypical of current police series.

3 **Produce** a radio advertisement for a film that is about to go its video rental release. Include a short dramatic excerpt from the film, either by taping it or reconstructing the soundtrack. The film can be one that you have made up. Write a commentary (300 words) on the effects used and how the narrative for the advertisement was composed. State who the film is aimed at and where the trailer will be heard and seen.

 Examination Skills

Textual Analysis

Students will need to produce a detailed textual analysis employing a range of technical and conceptual vocabulary and demonstrating a degree of knowledge of forms and conventions, including the importance of categorisation and genre.

All GCSE examination boards' coursework and examination components require a competent ability to analyse all media forms and their genres, for example, the Science Fiction or Comedy Film genres.

Students should have an idea of how to analyse the denotative level of meaning and the connotative level of meaning in still and moving image media. Ideology, explored in Chapter 4, Messages and Values (see page 60), is another aspect which should be tackled.

Knowledge and Understanding

Essays in OCR, AQA and Welsh boards' examinations demand knowledge and understanding of a range of media forms and conventions, in particular film, television news and drama, radio, newspaper, and magazines, and including advertisements and all promotional texts in any medium. Both technical (for example, close-ups) and conceptual (for example, narrative structure) vocabulary should be used to indicate a level of conversance with the medium in both its practical and theoretical aspects.

Practical Work

Students will need to show an understanding of some of the ways meaning is constructed through form. They will need to show competence in their skills of organisation, attention to detail and a polished finish in creative tasks. Critical commentaries will demonstrate the understanding of technical processes and problem solving. Theoretical writing should reflect a sound awareness of how the student product is similar to or different from mainstream and alternative forms and conventions.

3 Producers and Audiences (Institutions)

By whom, for whom, for what purpose?

What you will learn

The aim of this chapter is to develop a knowledge and understanding of the producers of media products and the audiences who consume them. There are various types of producers who own, make, control and distribute media products – these range from the large global media organisation to the one person producer of fanzines. You will also learn about what influences the content and the output of media products and become familiar with different ideas about audiences, for example how they enjoy and gain information and consume mass and niche media products.

KEY WORDS

- institution
- producer
- distributor
- broadcaster
- exhibitor
- point of interaction
- active and passive
- uses and gratifications

TECHNICAL WORDS

- ident
- licence
- subscription
- watershed
- codes of practice
- TV schedules
- pre-echo
- hammocking
- inheritance
- identification

ACTIVITY 1

Discuss the following:

1. Your opinion of the channels listed below:
   - BBC1
   - BBC2
   - ITV
   - Channel 4
   - Channel 5
   - Sky TV (any channel within Sky's package)

2. The types of programmes you associate with each of those channels.

Particular programmes can lead you to either like or dislike a channel. To give an example, many young people used to associate BBC2 with adult programmes such as the Open University, however, during the 1990s programme directors tried to change this image to suit a younger audience by broadcasting more comedy programmes. Would you consider BBC2 to be a fun channel to watch? Whatever your opinion may be, you will no doubt have been thinking about the various channels as organisations, as they all produce certain types of programmes which together give each its identity. These channels belong to media institutions.

Media Institutions

A major media institution is organised around the three different stages of making a product:

▌ pre-production
▌ production
▌ post-production

Pre-production for television documentaries involves people such as researchers and directors preparing the script and finding locations and people to interview. Production involves all the technical staff such as the lighting, camera and sound operators, the interviewer and the director, filming the product. The post-production stage brings in the editors of the images and the sound. One must not forget the publicists who inform the rest of the media about the programme, or the transmission engineers who ensure the programmes are broadcast to the homes of the viewers.

Finance and promotion

Large media institutions have the finance to pay for advertising and the promotion of their company's services and products. They either use their own publicity and marketing departments or employ independent companies to do this.

Idents

An example of promotion on television would be the red coloured scenarios and the logo of the BBC shown frequently between programmes on BBC1. The image of the BBC as multi-cultural, and across ages, abilities and genders is created by the different scenes set in locations around the UK.

This type of moving image sequence is known as an 'ident'. An ident is a short

animation or piece of film which links programmes. It usually consists of a moving image which brands the channel's identity, and usually includes the institution's logo.

ACTIVITY 2

Study the channel logo for the ITV channel in your region. Discuss and make notes on the following:

a What do the image(s) and logo convey about the region and its identity?
b Do you think it is effective? If so, discuss why or why not.

ACTIVITY 3

1. Produce a rough sketch of a design for an ident, logo and soundtrack advertising a new cable community channel which is starting in your district. Write notes explaining the colours, images, graphic style, audience and institution.
   ▌ What is the institution?
   ▌ Invent a name for the logo.
   ▌ What type of audience is the ident aimed at?
   ▌ Will the image reflect who might watch it?
   ▌ Make notes on artwork and ideas.

Consider the target audience carefully before you start on the idea. If people in your audience are over 50 years of age then you will need to create something that is in a style which will appeal to them. If the audience is under 30 years of age then the style of the graphics, music and images will be different again. If it is a family audience then there will have to be something for everyone.

2. Think of the main landmarks in your area (for example, a building, bridge or a park)

The Television sector

The television sector in the UK is divided into two types of institutional operations: public and commercial.

Public
The BBC

The BBC is an organisation which has grown into a large institution over seventy years (since 1926) to provide programmes which 'educate, entertain and inform' the British public. The organisation is run by an executive committee of ten people and they form part of a management committee of a

and perhaps incorporate one or more of them into the overall image created in question 1. Consider the type of programmes you might have on the channel and whether you want to reflect their content in the ident. Will the letters of the logo move and change? The images and logo will only be on screen for a maximum of 10 seconds, therefore it will need to be simple and striking. What music will accompany the image?

Press release

Press releases are another way of raising the profile of a media institution in the public mind.

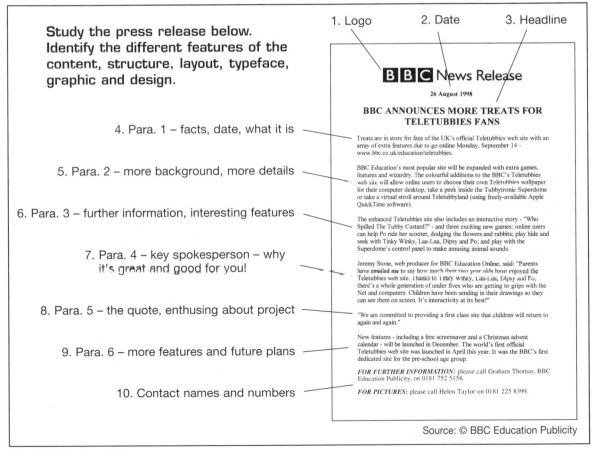

Study the press release below. Identify the different features of the content, structure, layout, typeface, graphic and design.

1. Logo   2. Date   3. Headline

4. Para. 1 – facts, date, what it is

5. Para. 2 – more background, more details

6. Para. 3 – further information, interesting features

7. Para. 4 – key spokesperson – why it's great and good for you!

8. Para. 5 – the quote, enthusing about project

9. Para. 6 – more features and future plans

10. Contact names and numbers

BBC News Release

26 August 1998

BBC ANNOUNCES MORE TREATS FOR TELETUBBIES FANS

Treats are in store for fans of the UK's official Teletubbies web site with an array of extra features due to go online Monday, September 14 - www.bbc.co.uk/education/teletubbies.

BBC Education's most popular site will be expanded with extra games, features and wizardry. The colourful additions to the BBC's Teletubbies web site will allow online users to choose their own Teletubbies wallpaper for their computer desktop, take a peek inside the Tubbytronic Superdome or take a virtual stroll around Teletubbyland (using freely-available Apple QuickTime software).

The enhanced Teletubbies site also includes an interactive story - "Who Spilled The Tubby Custard?" - and three exciting new games: online users can help Po ride her scooter, dodging the flowers and rabbits; play hide and seek with Tinky Winky, Laa-Laa, Dipsy and Po; and play with the Superdome's control panel to make amusing animal sounds.

Jeremy Stone, web producer for BBC Education Online, said: "Parents have emailed me to say how much their two year olds have enjoyed the Teletubbies web site. Thanks to Tinky Winky, Laa-Laa, Dipsy and Po, there's a whole generation of under fives who are getting to grips with the Net and computers. Children have been sending in their drawings so they can see them on screen. It's interactivity at its best!"

"We are committed to providing a first class site that children will return to again and again."

New features - including a free screensaver and a Christmas advent calendar - will be launched in December. The world's first official Teletubbies web site was launched in April this year. It was the BBC's first dedicated site for the pre-school age group.

FOR FURTHER INFORMATION: please call Graham Thomas, BBC Education Publicity, on 0181 752 5158.

FOR PICTURES: please call Helen Taylor on 0181 225 8399.

Source: © BBC Education Publicity

Fig 3.1   Press Release

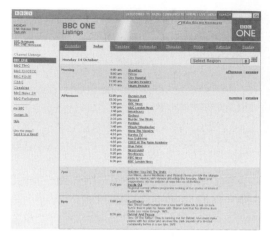

Fig 3.2   BBC Online

Source: © BBC

further five directors. Overseeing general policy is a body of 12 governors.

The BBC's channels 1 and 2 do not have advertising between programmes and the organisation is financed largely by a licence fee raised from the public. The BBC has other channels: BBC News 24, BBC Choice, BBC Prime, BBC Four and BBC World.

The increased competition from ITV and the introduction of Sky TV and Channel 5 has led to a decline in the BBC's share of the total number of people who watch the television. The BBC aims to hold onto around 30% of the ratings despite all the new digital channels.

Commercial

Channels 3 (1955) and 4 (1982) belong to the Independent Television network (ITV) and represent the commercial sector. Their revenue comes largely through advertising. Channel 5 (1996) is the most recent channel and it too is dependent on advertising. All of these channels are also required by law to provide certain public services, broadcasting news, community issues, information and debate. As with the BBC, these channels are terrestrial channels – they can all be received by a standard aerial attached to a high point near the television set, which receive signals from land based transmitters.

Satellite and cable

The other commercial channels are satellite channels, such as Sky TV, and require special

SHARE OF TOTAL TELEVISION AUDIENCE 2001

Channel	
BBC	38.2%
ITV	29.3%
Channel 4	9.9%
Cable	8.9%
Sky	6.1%
Channel 5	5.6%

Fig 3.3   Audience figures

TELEVISION AUDIENCE % VIEWING SHARES 1996–2000

Channel	1996	1997	1998	1999	2000
BBC 1	32.5	30.8	29.5	28.4	27.3
BBC 2	11.5	11.6	11.3	10.8	10.9
ITV AND GMTV	35.1	32.9	31.7	31.2	29.3
Channel 4 AND E4	10.7	10.6	10.3	10.3	9.9
Channel 5	–	2.3	4.3	5.3	5.6
Satellite and cable	10.2	11.8	12.9	14.0	15.0

Source: The Guardian Media Guide, 2002/Steve Peak and Paul Fisher

Fig 3.4   *Sky: the magazine*

Source: British Sky Broadcasting Ltd.

dishes to be received, as they transmit via satellites in space thousands of miles above the earth's surface. A cable line is sometimes also used to feed whole communities although these are linked centrally to a satellite reception point. These non-terrestrial channels do not have to provide any public service programmes as they were allowed freedom from the regulations as set out in the Broadcasting Act of 1990. They are financed by advertising and subscriptions.

Subscription television means that the viewer pays a fixed amount of money for specific channels or even single programmes, such as important football matches.

Mass Media Content

Factors

There are seven major factors that affect the content of any mass media product, such as television. These are as follows:

1 Ownership and finance – who owns and pays for it?

ACTIVITY 4

Study the video cover of the Teletubbies below. Note down your answers to the questions posed in factors one to five listed above and overleaf. Then compare your answers to the sections which follow.

Teletubbies characters and logo © and TM 1996 Ragdoll Limited.
Licensed by BBC Worldwide Limited.

2 Production – who actually makes the product?

3 Distribution – who delivers the product and in what form (e.g. broadcast, video rental or sale)?

4 Exhibition/Broadcast/Point of interaction – where is the product consumed, and technologically, how does the consumer receive it (e.g. cinema, television, newspaper)?

5 Controls – what rules and constraints exist concerning suitability for public consumption, and who decides on these controls?

6 Promotion and marketing – what methods are used to inform audiences about the content of the product and how to buy it? Who does the promotion and the marketing?

7 Audiences – how socially, personally, and technologically do audiences use, select, enjoy or reject the products they receive, purchase or consume?

Ownership

If you study the cover of a Teletubbies video you can see that the BBC own the video. The BBC letters are designed into a logo and it is positioned on the top right of the front page. The BBC is clearly associated with the Teletubbies programme which is broadcast on the terrestrial UK television channel BBC2. The BBC paid for its production and distribution.

Production

If you look closely on the back page of the video you will find that the BBC did not actually make the programme. It was made by an **independent** company called Ragdoll, for the BBC. Ragdoll is a company that specialises in children's television

programmes. Ragdoll have been very successful with Teletubbies, which now has worldwide popularity and high commercial profits.

Distribution

One commercial section of the BBC, which sells and distributes products is BBC Worldwide Limited. BBC Worldwide licenses the video from Ragdoll, who then earn further money from the sales.

Exhibition/Broadcast/Point of interaction

Teletubbies programmes are initially broadcast on air twice a day, every weekday morning on BBC2. Once they have been broadcast they are then duplicated to be sold in the form of a video. Teletubbies videos can be bought in a range of shops, including supermarkets and newspaper retailers.

Controls

On the back of the video cover, there is a 'Uc' certificate issued by the British Board of Film Classification (BBFC), who decided that the video is suitable particularly for young children. The spine of the Teletubbies video cover also states that it is a 'Children's Video', so there is a clear message that this is for young children.

Internal controls

No television programme maker can ignore certain rules which exist both within the BBC and outside it. Within the BBC there is a code of practice called *Producer's Guidelines (1996)*. These guidelines cover such areas as the depiction of violence, sex or bad language on television and radio.

ACTIVITY 5

Study any video (film/TV) cover. Discuss and make notes in answer to the following:

1. Who made the film/programme and who distributed it?
2. Are they the same company or different ones?
3. Find out what you can about the company/companies (try the local library or resource centre or the Internet). What else do they make or sell? For example, Blockbuster video hire shops, MTV and Paramount Film Studios and Nickleodeon are all owned by Viacom, who are also well-known as film distributors. Viacom is in fact part of a much larger company owned by an American family, Redstone, whose US operation is called National Amusements.

For information, institutions like the BBC have many departments dedicated to the production of television. These cover television, radio and a range of genres such as news, comedy and sport. There are also several departments which deal with matters such as finance, copyright, education, digital developments and administration.

The Watershed

There is a period of time called the 'Watershed', which is 9pm. All programme makers must ensure that no bad language, graphic sex or violence is contained in a programme broadcast before this time. The period of time leading up to 8.30pm–9pm is considered to be family viewing time.

The BBC has a well-established policy of making 9pm the pivotal point of the evening's television, a Watershed before which, except in exceptional circumstances, all programmes on our domestic channels should be suitable for a general audience including children. The earlier in the evening a programme is placed, the more suitable it is likely to be for children to watch on their own. However, the BBC expects parents to share the responsibility for assessing whether or not individual programmes should be seen by younger viewers.'

Source: BBC Producer's Guidelines, BBC, 1996

Taste and decency

The following quote is taken from the *BBC Producer's Guidelines (1996)*.

The BBC is required in the agreement associated with its Charter not to broadcast programmes which 'include anything which offends against good taste or decency or is likely to encourage or incite to crime or lead to disorder, or be offensive to public feeling'. The BBC seeks to apply this requirement to all its broadcasting, whether to a domestic or international audience.

Taste and decency raise sensitive and complex issues of programme policy for the BBC. We broadcast to a much more fragmented society than in the past; one that has divided views on what constitutes good taste. People of different ages and convictions may have sharply differing expectations. Research suggests that while people have become more relaxed in recent years about the portrayal of sex and sexual humour they remain concerned about the depiction of violence.

BBC Producer's Guidelines, BBC, 1996

Audience loyalty

Television schedules are printed in the newspapers every day. Creating a running order of the programmes is a fine art which programme directors organise. Many thousand of pounds can be gained by the channel if advertisers see that their product will be watched by their audiences. For the BBC, the importance of audience figures lies in justifying the licence fee to the taxpayer.

Scheduling techniques

In television, once the viewer has sat down and decided to watch a programme there are three techniques which schedulers use to keep audiences loyal to their channel:

1 **Hammocking** is when a less interesting programme is placed between two more interesting programmes.
2 **Inheritance** is where a viewer will stay with the same channel because they simply do not want to change to another channel.
3 **Pre-echo** is where viewers switch on early for their favourite programme, so they end up viewing a preceding programme which they might not have otherwise have watched.

Programming bodies and agencies

Further controls on television and radio programme makers come from government bodies, agencies and pressure groups, social opinion and commercial factors. These include:

▮ **ITC** – Independent Television Commission
▮ **BSC** – The Broadcasting Standards Commission
▮ **Oftel** – The Office of Telecommunications
▮ **ASA** – The Advertising Standards Authority
▮ **IRA** – Independent Radio Authority
▮ **VLV** – Voice of the Listener and Viewer
▮ **BBFC** – British Board of Film Classification
▮ **PCC** – Press Complaints Commission

ACTIVITY 6

Look up a recent Case Study on the Internet from one of these bodies, and do a short presentation.

Independent Television Commission (ITC)

The ITC is responsible for licensing and regulating Channels 3, 4, and 5, public teletext, cable and satellite services. In the year 2002 all the regional ITV licences come up for renewal. Each company must show that it has fulfilled certain quality criteria if they are to be renewed over others who want to buy the right to broadcast in that area.

Current licence holders may be asked if they have produced enough local news or information services to the community.

For example, in 1998, there were complaints about a documentary on drugs smuggling called *Connections*, produced by ITV's Central and Carlton companies. The documentary makers who produced the programme paid people to pretend they were drug smugglers. This sort of practice is considered to be unfair and cheating the public. The ITC made the companies issue an apology in the papers and on the television, and also fined them £2 million.

The Broadcasting Standards Commission (BSC)

The BSC was set up in 1996 to produce guidelines which all programme makers must follow. These are called 'codes of practice'. If a viewer complains, the BSC has to decide if the producer has broken a code of practice.

The Office of Telecommunications (OFTEL)

The Office of Telecommunications is in charge of monitoring telecommunications which include telephone lines, cable and satellite. Now that the Internet has become more widely used, OFTEL's role in television and Internet communication covers more than just the technical and financial markets.

As more people are linking the use of their telephone line to their computers and televisions, there are new controls and freedoms for OFTEL to monitor. The name of the new organisation will be OFCOM. Telephone lines are capable of transmitting signals cheaply which can then be converted back into images and sounds, and the use of this form of communication is used by many media institutions to relay their products and services (for example, cable TV, online television and image, or sounds and text such as cartoons and music).

The future of the control of the Internet and the role of the media institutions using these forms of networking is monitored by OFTEL. OFTEL is a government body whose aim is to decide whether the companies who control the lines are operating fairly between each other and in the best interests of the public.

Advertising Standards Authority (ASA)

The ASA regulate the advertising industry. If any advertisement causes offence and there is a complaint then an investigation is made by ASA. For example, Bennetton was reputed to have upset many people because it used a man dying of AIDS to advertise its clothes. Tango, a fizzy orange drink, advertised people surprising other people and ambushing them with a can of drink, with a voice saying, 'Have you been Tangoed?'.

This was subsequently deemed too dangerous by the ASA in case other people imitated it. The authority has a right to make the advertiser withdraw the advertisement.

Independent Radio Authority (IRA)

The Independent Radio Authority monitors the licences for radio stations and ensures that quality criteria are maintained.

Voice of Listener and Viewer (VLV)

VLV is a lobby organisation of unpaid enthusiasts who believe in the public's interest being served by the television and radio media. They produce small leaflets and write to the BBC when it is appropriate about programme content and the running of the institution.

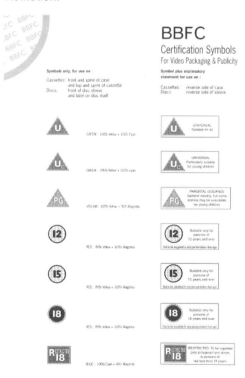

Fig 3.5   BBFC Classification Symbols

Source: © BBFC

British Board of Film Classification (BBFC)

Other media industries pay their own governing bodies to create guidelines for controlling the content. In the film industry, for example, each distributor pays the BBFC to certificate their films for showing in cinemas, or video rental and hire.

Press Complaints Commission

The Press Complaints Commission was set up to investigate the complaints made about newspapers who may harass or go into people's private affairs, intrusively. In 1998, the 14 year old daughter of a woman who had served a prison sentence discovered through the newspapers that her mother was Mary Bell. Mary Bell had murdered two children many years previously. The daughter's mother had been paid by a writer to sell her story, which was then serialised in *The Times*. When the press found out about the payment the mother and daughter were tracked down.

In theory, newspapers are not supposed to intrude and expose children under sixteen years of age to the spotlight of the media. In the latter case a press 'pack' of hounds hot on the chase of a story meant that the PCC guidelines were ignored. Furthermore, unless someone is prepared to pay for the legal pursuit of the case, then the PCC is limited in how it can act. The PCC did however comment on the case, and they declared that, though regrettable, the press were not at fault for allowing the child to be caught up in the media coverage.

British Videogram Association

The British Videogram Association oversees the certification of the videos for hire and sale, in association with the BBFC in its capacity as the classifier of the certificate.

ACTIVITY 7

Discuss the following scenario:

A councillor is rumoured to have helped to sell off council property to his friends, in exchange for money. Is it fair that the press should be allowed to interview him against his will in the following places?

1. In an NHS hospital.
2. Outside a school gate, where he picks up his children.
3. In a restaurant or café.
4. On a walking holiday.

Media products
Mass media

Mass media products are intended for a large population and can be shared as a film in a cinema or in the home on the video.

Many media products are designed for mass consumption across all the social groups which already exist in society. A mass media product is designed to appeal to a wide range of people spanning age, gender, class, race, etc. The contemporary mass market is often targeted at the family audience. For example, there are jokes in *Shrek* that are for adults and there are silly noises that are for children.

Niche media

Niche media products are targeted at an existing group, for example, by age, gender, race or lifestyle. A niche product is aimed at a specific interest or social group, for example, a motorbike magazine is aimed at motorbike enthusiasts. Another example is business television news which is aimed at the financial market.

Alternative media products

Some media products are made for non-commercial reasons. These can be intended for the public benefit, for alternative cultures such as 'zines or take the form of music loaded onto the Internet for free use. These products are created by enthusiasts not institutions, and they are interested in the product for its content, more than for its ability to sell. Their distribution is very small and often limited.

Audiences

The word 'audience' carries with it the picture of a group of people assembled together in a space like a cinema or theatre to listen or watch a performer on stage. With modern media this idea is no longer a fixed one.

Members of an audience in a theatre or cinema come into the hall, sit down and laugh, cry or are silent. It is essentially a captive audience – all share the same moments of

drama on the stage or screen in front of them. In the case of modern media (television, cinema, videos and video hire, magazines, newspapers, Internet on-line, CD ROMs and mobile phones) there are now hundreds of public places where we can see or hear media products. We can also watch television or read a magazine or listen to a walkman on our own due to technological advances.

An 'audience' ranges from the individual watching a video in the bedroom, to the passer-by seeing an advertisement on the side of the bus, to the group watching a large screen projection of a music video in a club, to the student with a walkman secretly listening to a favourite piece of music in the classroom.

EastEnders and *Coronation Street* regularly reach over 17 million people from all walks of life but there are also products which are targeted at specific audiences by age, class, gender or racial groups. Most media products can be seen or bought in many different venues, for example the *TV Times*. Magazines, comics and male and female interest magazines may be aimed at small

Discuss

Compare these Elle Girl and More profiles. Discuss the following:

1 What are the target ages of each magazine?
2 What lifestyle does each group have?

Editorial
Ellegirl is the first fashion and shopping magazine for girls. Sweet, stylish and spirited, Ellegirl is very much diffusion ELLE (the MiuMiu to her Prada) and has remixed it's "older sister's" award-winning blend of gorgeous fashion, A-list celebrities and feel-good lifestyles for a teenage readership. With its glamorous but useful content and groundbreaking design, Ellegirl has quickly distinguished itself from the rest of the teen magazine market and has a dedicated readership who love "this amazing magazine with life-saving style tips for girls who want to be happy." Being a teenager has never looked so fabulous.

Readers' Lifestyle
Target audience 12–17 year old girls witha core of 14–16. The Ellegirl reader loves to dress up and is the leader (& the one that wants to be) in her class. She is a fashion fanatic and brand conscious. A suburban babe with big aspirations!

Editorial

more! is the UK's biggest selling young women's magazine every fortnight. Full of humour, more! is a worldly-wise companion promising useful advice and first person reports that ring true for every young woman, more! deals with sex in a fun, informative and saucy (but never coarse) way, celebrating men with its Men Unzipped section and its Centrefold.

more! is all about aspiration-it is Davina McCall not Gwyneth Paltrow. Every fortnight its readers get accessible, affordable but glamorous fashion and beauty coverage. It is a sexy, sophisticated and saucy package.

Readers' Lifestyle

The more! reader is sexy, cheeky, sussed, warm, feisty and gossipy. She is in her early twenties, in her first job and wants a man like David Beckham. She loves shopping with her mates and is incapable of going out without her mascara. She is going on holiday to Ayia Napa or Ibiza this year and loves clubbing (foam parties, not the serious stuff). She is a sexy, sophisticated and saucy type, just like her favourite magazine-more!

sectors of the market. For example, *more!* is a magazine targeted at women aged 21–23 yrs, who are either in further education or employment.

Other media products can be defined as alternative, such as independent music labels which can only be found in specialist shops, sold by mail order, on the Internet or in street markets. They do not use the conventional methods of promotion adopted by other media, such as posters or magazine advertisements. These products exist through word of mouth and playing concerts. Alternative products also serve a small section of the total market, a niche (see page 39).

Definitions

The definition of an audience depends on who defines it.

- Industry: circulation and readership figures and target readership.
- Industry: constructed audience.
- Government: demographics.
- Advertisers: segmentations (lifestyle and aspirations).
- Social scientists: values.
- Social scientists: passive/active.
- Social scientists: identity.

Circulation and readership

What is most important to owners and producers of media products is whether they sell or not. The audience is first and foremost a buyer and a consumer and the financial wellbeing of most newspapers and magazines depends on how many people read the product.

ACTIVITY 8

Study the list of newspapers in Figure 3.6.

1. Which daily newspaper has done the best since January 2001?
2. Which newspaper (daily or Sunday) has sold the most newspapers?
3. Which newspapers have sold the least copies?
4. What are the circulation figures for this month? The ABC website (www.abc.org.uk) has this information. Have there been any significant changes for any newspapers?

	January 2002 (excluding bulks)	January 2001 (excluding bulks)	% change	January 2002 (including bulks)	Aug 01– Jan 02	Aug 00– Jan 01	% change
Dailies							
Sun	3,502,697	3,624,563	−3.36	3,502,923	3,467,969	3,611,500	−4.25
The Mirror	2,136,958	2,113,705	1.10	2,164,576	2,143,300	2,174,164	−1.42
Daily Star/The Star- Republic of Ireland	705,861	637,826	10.67	706,554	721,913	640,034	12.79
Daily Record	573,672	593,138	−3.28	584,290	584,879	601,956	−4.50
Daily Mail	2,388,157	2,441,398	−2.18	2,489,264	2,392,435	2,337,385	2.35
The Express	894,099	943,898	−5.27	991,560	886,452	973,561	−8.95
Daily Telegraph	968,771	975,890	−0.73	1,013,653	972,401	972,235	0.02
Times	673,085	686,618	−1.97	711,295	671,901	674,152	−0.33
FT	453,244	458,292	−1.10	475,475	453,471	453,019	0.10
Guardian	397,435	400,708	−0.82	411,386	402,184	388,928	3.41
Independent	193,239	197, 075	−1.95	224,655	198,513	196,705	0.92
Sundays							
News of the World	4,086,409	4,024,011	1.55	4,086,621	4,032,723	4,026,699	0.15
Sunday Mirror	1,816,150	1,801,843	0.79	1,845,860	1,795,864	1,851,813	−2.92
People	1,360,983	1,458,535	−6.69	1,389,778	1,351,341	1,465,143	−7.79
Sunday Mail	679,380	696,576	−2.47	692,366	686,862	710,625	−3.34
Mail on Sunday	2,290,177	2,330,545	−1.73	2,342,860	2,310,296	2,240,097	3.04
Sunday Express	813,487	841,873	−3.37	834,999	829,007	897,186	−7.60
Sunday Times	1,385,293	1,378,710	0.48	1,405,430	1,374,097	1,346,857	2.02
Sunday Telegraph	751,968	763,889	−1.57	784,069	777,940	770,167	1.01
Observer	424,003	410,262	3.35	449,806	442,643	412,148	7.40
Independent on Sunday	190,310	215,229	−11.62	231,869	198,646	212,735	−6.62

Fig 3.6   National Newspaper Circulation

Source: ABC

BRAD

The *British Rates and Data Handbook (BRAD)* is used by advertisers to decide which journals and magazines to put their advertisers in. Circulation figures published in *BRAD* show how many readers buy a particular magazine, and the readership figure gives an estimate of how many people read it. The reason for the extra number for readership is that if a magazine is placed in a household, dentist or waiting room, more people will read it. The target readership in the case of a magazine like *Just Seventeen* is 'girls between the ages 11–19 who are fashion conscious, sussed in outlook and style leaders within their peer groups'. This type of definition of target readership is created by the magazine to encourage advertisers to place their advertisements in it.

Constructed audience

In order to make an audience feel part of a like-minded community a magazine may adopt a style of clothing and make-up, or use an advertisement which creates a particular image for its readers. For example, the 'Rachel haircut' in the American situation comedy *Friends* programme became popular for a time. Subsequently, many magazines published images of women wearing the 'Rachel' hairstyle. Readers then identified with a hairstyle they already had themselves or that they recognised as being fashionable.

Advertisers on television then started to use the 'Rachel' hairstyle to promote their product. Again, by using familiar images which audiences already identify with the individual is in turn constructed by the fashionable images of the moment. The producers can therefore be said not only to have targeted their audience but also to have actively constructed them.

Defining Audiences
Demographics

The Government has defined the population into what are commonly known as demographic groups.

The definitions in Figure 3.7 are used to define what type of tax or social benefit people are entitled to. Advertisers and media producers also look at the demographics published in *BRAD*, for their own research, to define what types of people might buy their product.

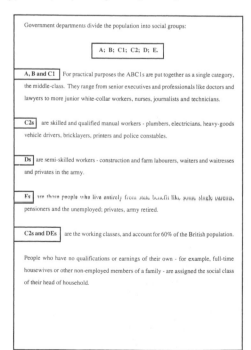

Fig 3.7   Demographic groups

ACTIVITY 9

From the article below study how new ideas for labelling people are invented all the time.

Do you think you fit into any of the categories mentioned?

So, are you a Mouse Potato or a Cybersnob?

New definitions: fact or fiction?

Source: © *Independent on Sunday*, 2 February 1997/Charles Arthur

---

Segmentation

Advertisers use their own categories of people in addition to the categories of demographic groups. These groupings can vary enormously but one model is the one which divides people into seven segments: the succeeder, aspirers, carers, achievers, radicals, traditionals and the underachiever. These descriptions are thought to provide information about a person's attitudes and psychological character. By splitting people into these groups advertisers attempt to estimate whether their audiences are likely to spend money on their products. For example, if your family spends a great deal on holidays every year it will be worth a company trying to target you when selling holidays. They can do this by researching which type of magazine you are likely to buy.

Social values

Another way of defining the audience has come from social scientists who want to provide information to their clients. These are usually commercial clients who want to target their media entertainment products to sell. In addition to class labels, there are also people's attitudes to consider. Possible attitudes include:

▮ Traditionalist – keep things the way they are.
▮ Materialist – have something now; pay later.
▮ Hedonist – to play now.
▮ Post materialist – to be something later.
▮ Post modernist – to have, to be, and to play.

Active or passive audiences

The traditional view of the audience is one of the 'couch potato', where television supposedly switches off the brain and ruins the art of conversation. Most recent studies have shown that viewers can be described as active in their engagement with television. Many people use the remote control and actively search out the channels they want to watch. People do not, as a rule, spend an evening sat in front of the television; they partake in other activities such as games and conversation. For many people having conversations about television is a very important part of their lives. Discussing ideas or keeping up-to-date on the latest soap opera constitutes a form of activity.

Uses and gratifications

One existing media theory concerns how people use the media for different reasons:

▮ As a diversion from everyday life.
▮ To gain information about the outside world.

▮ To compare themselves with other people.
▮ Companionship.

If you look back at your answers to the questionnaire in the introduction you will see how much and what media you particularly liked. Audiences use the media for different purposes; to satisfy needs and wants. Sometimes watching television can serve as an escape from thinking about work. Occasionally watching television is about informing oneself about ideas and facts on a particular subject.

Audience identity

Another way of categorising audiences is by grouping according to the following criteria:

▮ Gender
▮ Age
▮ Race
▮ Family
▮ Class

A further set of categories are:

▮ Education
▮ Religion
▮ Region
▮ Political belief
▮ Urban or rural background

Amongst academics the idea exists that audiences have varying responses to what they watch. They either accept, negotiate, oppose or reject messages and values which are conveyed to them by television programmes. For example, if the programme is racist or sexist the viewer may dislike it and thus reject it.

Extension Tasks

Coursework Specimen Topic (you should check to see what current topics are). These tasks are not actual previous examination questions but coursework ideas, using the AQA format of exam testing. The questions are the sole work of the author and are devised to match the style, mark allocation and format of the relevant questions from AQA and OCR. To avoid covering ground in both coursework and timed examination, it is essential that candidates check the specified topics set for the year of their examination, by the examination board. For previous examination questions, contact the exam board direct.

AQA + OCR

1 What are the typical features of soap operas? Discuss content and structure, characters and themes.

(20 marks)

2 Why do you think soaps appeal to large audiences?

(20 marks)

3 Study the following:

a A job advertisement for a publicist for *EastEnders*.

BBC Broadcast

Publicist – EastEnders

Marketing & Communications

Salary c.£24,000. Elstree, Herts.

EastEnders is television's number one drama serial. Do you have the experience and ability to implement a publicity strategy to make sure it stays that way? BBC Drama Publicity is seeking a second energetic, motivated and highly creative Publicist to promote the BAFTA-award-winning **EastEnders** to the print, broadcast and online media in a highly competitive market place. Probably with a journalistic background or three years' publicity experience, you will need strong media contacts and proven success in news management. You will be able to demonstrate creativity, determination, discretion, tact and good organisational skills, combined with enthusiasm for creative talent and a passion for the programme itself. You will have a highly-developed news sense, remarkable resilience under pressure, the ability to handle conflicting priorities and a strong sense of humour! This is no nine-to-five job, but is a demanding and rewarding post which puts you in the front-line of programme publicity. You should also possess the ability to deal swiftly and sensitively with difficult issues and to build solid relationships with 40 regular artists, production teams and senior programme executives. (Ref. 30429/G)

---

b A job advertisement for a picture editor for *more!*.

Product: more!
Location: London
Deputy
Production Editor

With at least two years experience subbing on a consumer title and preferably some production experience under your belt, you're ready to take on the challenge of the more! subs' desk.

It goes without saying that you can churn out error-free layouts in no time flat, and that nothing – not even the world's busiest production editor – can make you panic. You'll need to show some management experience as you'll be handling the desk in the production editor's absence. And you'll have the more! sense of humour, demonstrated in endless laugh-out-loud headlines and picture captions.

Send your CV with a cracking covering letter, suggesting three alternative headlines and sells for one of the main features in a recent issue of more!, to Matt Coppock, production editor at the address below or email him at matt.coppock@emap.com. Mark your application 'deputy production editor'.

Identify what knowledge and skills are sought from applicants for each of the two job advertisements **a** and **b**.

(10 marks)

4 A soap opera character is going to be written out (killed off) by the producers of one of the following programmes: *Emmerdale Farm, Coronation Street, Home and Away, Family Affair, EastEnders, Brookside, Hollyoaks, Heartbreak High*. You are responsible for marketing and publicity relations with the press, television and radio, and for the online media campaign. **Select** one of the soaps listed.

Either

Invent and design a front page of a listings magazine like the *Radio Times* or *TV Times*, (one side of A4) announcing the imminent departure of the soap character, this week.

Or

Produce a ten image storyboard of a TV advertisement, announcing the departure of a soap character.

(35 marks)

5 Write a 100 word memo to the Executive Producer of your soap explaining:

- Which media you are going to use for your campaign and why.
- What your main images mean.
- The purpose behind any wording or slogans you have used.
- Who and what you are going to promote? Where and for how long, and how much are you going to spend?

(15 marks)

 Examination Skills

Knowledge and Understanding

Knowledge of press releases and their format, structure and style are essential to answer these questions. A knowledge of soap forms and conventions is also important: how do characters get introduced into a series and how do others get phased out? What types of media publicity would be appropriate to let the public know what is going to happen? The composition of the press release should follow the structure of the example given.

A good analysis of the two job advertisements in Question 3 will

demonstrate an awareness of certain skills of promoting and organising under pressure and with other people. The memo in Question 5 should contain understanding of scheduling, cross media publicity and the importance of simple and perhaps controversial means of attracting publicity, for example the manner of their departure or death.

Textual Analysis

Examiners want to see evidence in Question 2 of knowledge of storylines and the way soap narrative is structured, types and stereotypes of the main characters and technical effects.

Practical Work

In the examination, practical activities include: creating storyboards, radio jingles, front pages for magazines and letters summarising key points. The skills required involve the ability to sequence ideas visually and aurally; and to select and to summarise and present information in report or letter form.

Messages and Values (Representations)

What is the meaning and why?

What you will learn

In this chapter you will study the concepts of representation, stereotypes, ideology and realism. How do media texts convey ideas, values and messages about places, people and events? What are the typical ideas and values of the media texts we consume? How do we judge if a media text, like a soap, is realistic, accurate or effective? What judgements might other people make? On whose behalf is the text speaking? How, for example, are images of the British nation created and received abroad? You will also explore how messages can be obvious or hidden in media texts through the production or analysis of specific media texts.

KEY WORDS

- messages
- values
- representation
- selection and construction
- ideology
- types
- archetype
- stereotype
- bias

TECHNICAL WORDS

- slogan
- reconstruction
- edit
- crop
- photo-opportunity
- series
- serial

What are we looking at?

A teacher went into a class and showed the children a poster of S Club 7 and asked the class what it was they were looking at. Some of the class said they were brilliant; others said they made them feel sick; others said nothing at all. The teacher then asked them again what it was they were looking at and someone again said: 'S Club 7'. Grinning slyly, the teacher said: 'I asked you what you were looking at? You are all wrong – it's a poster of S Club 7!'.

Unless the viewer is very young, most people learn very quickly that, for example, the

figures in the children's programme, *Teletubbies*, are part of a television screen image and cannot actually be touched or hugged. The real material used to create the television image is filmed, edited, mixed with sound and formatted. Then it is transmitted into the home via electronic cables or airwaves.

There are three main points to consider before evaluating the meaning of media texts:

1 Media texts can only refer to real subjects whether they exist in reality (for example, news) or as fiction (for example, soaps). They are representations or recreations simulating reality.

2 All media texts are the products of several

production stages involving different technical processes: selection of material, recording, editing and presentation.

3 People respond to media texts differently with regards professional quality, accuracy, truthfulness, realism or its artistic merit.

Representation

It might seem strange to talk about making food at the start of a section on media representation but there is a similarity with the process of media production.

Crisps are made from potatoes: finely cut up and fried. Rice crispies are made from rice: boiled, dried and oven-baked. Both these processes create something new from their original. The products are a different shape, texture and form than their raw original. Yet, they are still recognisable from their original state. In some ways this is what happens to a scene when it is converted by chemicals from film negative into a photographic image. Similarly, a voice is converted into a radio news presentation by electronic recording, editing and play processes.

There is obviously a crucial difference between making crisps and making a media product. Media products carry meanings – meant for the eyes, ears and brain, i.e. via images, words and sounds, whereas food production is meant for oral consumption.

Usually we think of advertising as a billboard poster, a television advertisement or a radio jingle. But the use of advertising and design media to produce visual messages and eye-catching colours and memorable slogans is typical of modern packaging on food products. Packaging, along with all the television and magazine advertising, encourages people to buy a particular brand of food.

But imagine no packaging on a packet of crisps. Imagine there is only a transparent

Fig 4.1   Walker's Crisps: front of packet (see colour section)

Fig 4.2   Back of Walker's Crisps packet (see colour section)

Fig 4.3   M&S Handcooked crisps (see colour section)

bag of crisps to hold the contents, or a transparent bag of cereal rice crispies and no box.

What would be missing from how we would normally confront these products?

How do you normally decide which brand of product to buy?

Are you in any way influenced by how products are packaged?

Do you prefer less packaging and buy only supermarket branded baked beans, for example? Or are you only interested in its calorific value or taste?

┌ ACTIVITY 1 ──────────────

Take two packets of crisps and compare their packaging (see Figures 4.1, 4.2, 4.3 and the colour section).

Using denotation and connotation analysis (see p. 15) bring out the differences and similarities in the meaning of the packaging images, words and messages on two different brands of crisps.

Textual analysis	Walker's Crisps	Marks and Spencer's Crisps
Denotation What is in the picture: words and text, colours and layout design?		
Connotation What do the different elements mean and what ideas do you associate with the content?		
Messages and Values What do the packaging connotations add up to as a message? What does it say about the value of these crisps to you? e.g. your attitude to life, lifestyle or beliefs.		
Form and Style Comment on the graphics, the style of typeface, and the layout		
Audience Who is the demographic group: age, class, gender, race etc?		

Here are some pointers as to what you might have said. Compare them with your own answers and add whatever you think is relevant to your own list.

Textual analysis	Walker's cheese and onion crisps	Marks & Spencer's handcooked crisps
Denotation	E.g. Famous footballers, Michael Owen and Gary Lineker, who appears on a quiz show, *They Think It's All Over*, both featured in a series of advertisements for Walker's crisps. 'Walker's Crisps' is in a red and white banner wrapped around a yellow sun shape. Blue background has yellow and red colouring. Lineker is wearing a grey suit with a red tie.	Black and white photograph of girls tipping out the potato harvest – early twentieth century. French? Buckets and boxes are used to carry the potatoes giving it a homespun quirkiness. The packet is mainly grey, white and black. 'Handcooked Crisps" is set in a grey banner. You can see the crisps in the packet through the cellophane. The circled logo is red plus an orange star shaped mark surround the words are in white, 'cooked in sunflower oil'.
Connotation	Fun, 'jokey' spoof news items showing sports celebrities Owen and Lineker enjoying the press limelight. Lineker is represented as the fool character who doesn't mind a joke – 'Cheese and Owen' – Lineker is the 'cheese' with his cheeky smile – a sporty and youthful image. 'New. Best ever flavour' implies an extra quality has been added to suggest value for money. 'Walker's Crisps' banner wrapped around the yellow sun shape, indicates a purity and glow from the sun-shaped crisps.	The associations created by these images and words are that M&S crisps come from real potatoes and are genuine. The use of black and white usually connotes realism and authenticity, ie this actually happened. The real image of unnamed and unfamous school-age female potato-pickers from some time in the rural past connects us to the idea of the real taste of the land and its produce, untainted by factories and chemical additives. The 'salt and crushed black pepper' is in large typeface to draw your attention to the fact that the seasoning is also fresh

	The back of the crisp's packet suggests a newspaper style report continuing the idea of a media event. The idea that Owen would give Lineker a lift is meant to be a joke on Lineker who is always being teased on his television appearances on *They Think It's All Over*. It all adds jollity to the image of the crisps.	and unprocessed with chemicals. 'Handcooked Crisps' suggests the idea of carefully selected items prepared by humans and not machines and harmful mechanical processes. The separate logo with the words 'Cooked in sunflower oil' again suggests natural products and again indicates purity and healthiness.
Messages and Values	If you eat Walker's Crisps you will be in with the sporting crowd, knowledgeable about football and the media, you are fun-loving and understand a joke. You like bright colours and fun, trendy images and people. You don't mind where your crisps come from as long as they are 'good value' – 'best ever taste' and taste 'good'.	If you eat Marks and Spencer's crisps you are guaranteed a high quality, selected product. You will expect high standards of selection and you will be given the genuine healthy article. You like understated colours and prefer to see the product before you buy it – through the cellophane panel. The ingredients are all good for you and you are being treated with 'good' organic products. Even the salt and the pepper is the most healthy type you can get. You are prepared to pay a higher price to get this 'added value'.
Form and Style	Cartoon style caricatures of Owen and Lineker are accessible like pop art and funny and light.	A black and white, nearly forgotten world of the natural environment captured by the old photographs – realism is implied. Serious, sombre and genuine, as though the potatoes are something special like a photograph collector's rare items.
Audience	0–40 Social groups C1, C2 D and E, white male	20 upwards. Social groups A and B. White, European, across genders.

ACTIVITY 2

Discuss a soap or a film that has been unrealistic. Give reasons.
Discuss a soap or film that has been realistic. Give reasons.

Selection and construction

The images we see and listen to in a documentary or soap is a selection of what was originally recorded as prerecorded television is edited. The final product is literally a re-presentation of the original subject. The process of filming, recording and editing film or news bulletins involves the selection and reconstruction of the original material. This process means that real life is literally re-presented in another shape, to fit news media technology and programme format.

Crimewatch UK

Crimewatch UK is a public service television information programme that reconstructs crimes in the form of a drama. It aims to alert the public to actual crimes that have occurred. The programme makers hope the public will come forward if they have witnessed or know something about crimes shown on the programme. *Crimewatch UK* includes reconstructions of crimes, and uses actors to recreate the event. The programme does not show all the details of the violence or the methods used in the crime. The reason why these aspects are not shown is to ensure that the programme is not too sensational and to avoid giving ideas on how to commit certain illegal crimes or violent actions. The reconstructions usually contain the actual word 'reconstruction' so that viewers do not believe they are watching a police drama series such as *The Bill*.

ACTIVITY 3

1. Produce a rough sketch of a typical family high street studio portrait photograph. List all the elements of colour, lighting, facial expressions and body postures you would expect to see.

2. Produce a rough sketch of an untypical family portrait, entitled 'the family as it really is'. Again, list all the elements of background, props, lighting, body posture, facial expression you would expect to see.

3. Study any photographs of you taken at home. Which ones would you be most happy and least happy to show to other people. Explain your reasons.

Stereotypes

Stereotypes are fixed and customary ideas that we grow to accept as being normal. Consider stereotyped views of teachers. Female teachers are sometimes thought of as wearing glasses, as are librarians. Male teachers are often thought to wear corduroy trousers and Marks and Spencer jackets. Other people's views of Media Studies students and teachers may also be stereotyped, however, one should ask the question: do they all look the same?

Archetypes

Archetypes are fairy tale or universal types. Vladimir Propp, a Russian anthropologist, noted that there were certain features of action and character types which appeared in all of the fairy stories he studied. An example of a film is *Lord of the Rings*, where archetypal characters and a fantasy story line combine high action adventure with dialogue. Typical archetypes include the old wizard, the hero, the tempter and the princess.

Actresses like Barbara Windsor, who rules her family in *EastEnders*, play the strong matriarch.

Ian Mckellen plays a wise wizard in *Lord of the Rings*. Among the younger members of a film or television drama, you may find a prince or princess.

Soap Operas

ACTIVITY 4

Discuss and write down your responses to the following questions:

1. How are people, places, events and ideas represented in soap operas?
2. Which soap is the most realistic? Give reasons for your answer.
3. Which soap is the most unrealistic? Give reasons for your answer.
4. Compare your answers with those of other people. Did you find other people's answers different and/or persuasive?

Fig 4.4   *Barbara Windsor:* EastEnders

Realism in soaps

Realism in soaps works on the basis that:

- The story line is told in the order of events of a normal day, i.e. there are no flashbacks or flashforwards.
- The place looks like a real location. Sets are built to look like markets, streets, shops, etc.
- The community of people appears to be like ones that exist in real life, for example pubs, shops and cafés.
- The events which occur are based on domestic reality and focus on key life events, for example, relationships, conflicts, births, marriages and deaths.
- The real world events, such as Christmas, Easter or Valentine's day are worked into the script so that the soap community appears to live a life parallel to that of its audience.
- Several soaps, such as *Brookside*, deal with contemporary issues over several episodes. For example, AIDS, incest and battered women relate to issues present in the real world.

Critics of soaps say that the realism appears only on the surface. They claim that the world of the soap never precisely matches the real world for the following reasons:

- The range of age groups is unlikely to always meet in the same place, for example the same pub in *EastEnders*.
- The characters change their personalities too suddenly to fit the story line properly.
- The number of traumatic events that occur in some characters' lives is too unlikely.
- The plot requires long-lost brothers and relatives to suddenly appear, and in some cases characters who have been 'killed off' come back to life (for example *Dallas* and *Neighbours*).

The same critics of soaps may argue that the realism is not concerned with whether the set looks natural or if the characters are consistent.

The focus of the soaps on the portrayal of a mixture of everyday and dramatic events and how people interact is the heart of soaps' appeal. Audiences identify with other people's problems and successes, and experience a period of escape from their own lives that is both enjoyable and satisfying.

Series and Serials

The soap community's lives are brought to the audience in a dramatic format called a serial and therefore, theoretically, the show will continue to run and run. In contrast, a series will stop after several episodes. It follows that, if characters are to have a short screen life, in a series they are more likely to be involved in dramatic events.

Stereotypes in soaps

Stereotypes of fictional characters are invented for soap operas such as *EastEnders*. In soaps we are presented with a set of representations of attitudes, actions and characters' personalities. Typical female and male characters in *EastEnders* are as follows:

Women:

- Motherly, tough and wise (Pauline Fowler, Peggy Mitchell and Pat Butcher).
- Eccentric old woman (Dot Cotton).
- Young and irresponsible (Janine Butcher).
- Brassy and warmhearted (barmaid).
- Independent business woman, but emotionally dependent on men (Melanie Owen and Laura Beale).

Men:

- Wise old man.
- Businessman obsessed by work (Ian Beale).
- Middle aged crisis failing business (Roy Evans, Frank Butcher).
- Violent and yet brutish appeal (Grant and Phil Mitchell).

- Foolish teenager (Robbie Jackson).
- Dreamer (Ricky Butcher).

EastEnders caused some newspaper debate when an Irish angle was introduced to the programme. It represented one of the Irish characters as a hard-drinking good-for-nothing, and provoked angry reactions from many viewers in England as well as Ireland.

Regions and soaps

ACTIVITY 6

Discuss the following:
There are now numerous soaps in the UK, some of which are imported.

1. What regions of the UK are represented in the soaps in the list in Activity 5 (for example, London's East End, in *EastEnders*).
2. What regions or areas of the UK are not covered in our soaps?

ACTIVITY 5

1. Study another soap and make lists of types of male and female characters. Add to the list of types and stereotypes made for *EastEnders* previously. Use the following soaps as a guide:
   - *Hollyoaks*
   - *Neighbours*
   - *Emmerdale Farm*
   - *Brookside*
   - *Heartbreak High*
   - *Coronation Street*
   - *Family Affairs*
   - *Pobol Y Cwm*
   - *Home and Away*
   - *Quayside*

2. Can you identify male or female types that are common to both *EastEnders* and your soap? Are there any stereotypes?

Place in soaps

In the opening sequence (the title sequence) of all soap operas there is usually a sequence of images to show the typical background and environment that the characters inhabit.

ACTIVITY 7

Select two soaps and contrast the types of place they represent. For example, the camera angle in *Brookside* starts with high shots of key landmarks in Liverpool and then circles with mixed shots, eventually panning down to Brookside Close. The same occurs with the title sequence of *Coronation Street* in Manchester.

Soap simulation

You are an independent company with some success in dramas and game shows. ITV would like to replace the Australian soap, *Home and Away*, which has been broadcast on the channel at 5.30pm for some years. Write a proposal for a new UK-based soap using the instructions which follow.

ACTIVITY 8

1. Devise a setting for a new soap opera that is based in a different town or region than any other you have seen. Write a short paragraph explaining the setting and key locations of the soap.
2. What is the name of the soap?
3. Write an outline of six or seven of the characters who will appear in this new soap.
4. Write a description of the story line of the opening programme in order to attract your audience.
5. What will be your audience and what will your soap contain that can be of interest to them?
6. You have been encouraged by the Government to introduce the idea that smoking is bad for you. Write a scene in which the main characters cover this topic.
7. Create a title sequence which shows where the soap is set and what type of characters will be seen in the programme. Remember to describe the music.
8. Invent the name of the company who has produced it.

Messages and values: Is the media text accurate, truthful and/or real?

It is possible to examine three spheres within which media products operate:

- Government: propaganda or public information
- commercial
- alternative.

Propaganda

In the Second World War (1939–1945) meat products were in short supply. The Government encouraged people to grow their own vegetables and posters were displayed in prominent places. Figure 4.5 shows a typical British working class male looking happy about growing vegetables.

Fig 4.5   *Government propaganda or public information is used to persuade people*

Source: The Advertising Archives

Propaganda campaigns are direct pronouncements by the Government to their 'people', telling them to do something. In Singapore, the Government often has public behaviour propaganda, for example, to not spit or to be courteous to customers. In Britain, the Government uses the Central Office of Information (COI) to convey their message. 'Don't drink and drive' campaigns, tax return reminders and television licence evasion warnings are some examples of Government information promotions. In these campaigns, the message is usually very direct and clear.

The state and ideology

If you look closely at the picture in Figure 4.6, you will see that it is a picture of a street scene and a large poster in the background.

In the poster there is picture of a child reaching out to the man to the left of centre. There is a female and a male adult on the right-hand side who are holding the child up. There is writing in Chinese and in English – it states that 'Family Planning is a Basic National Policy of China'.

Below the poster people are looking at the wall displays and one man in the foreground is also carrying a child in a wicker basket.

Fig 4.6   *Billboard for one child families in China*

Source: Topham Picturepoint

The message of the image is that you should trust the doctor to look after you on behalf of the state. If you do this then everybody will be happy, judging from the smiles on all their faces.

In China, there has been a policy since the 1970s that couples can only have one child per family. As the population of China has increased phenomenally these controls were introduced. The poster is part of a campaign to drive the message home. The idea for the design for the poster came from an artist, but the idea of a national Family Planning Policy came from the Chinese Government.

State control of messages and values is easy to identify, however in the western hemisphere most messages about products are commercial. The aim of advertising in the western world is to sell something for money.

Bias

A person who brings you a product is also a person who has a point of view. Every media product that is broadcast and distributed has been produced by someone, for some purpose. Therefore, audiences should always look to see if there is a personal viewpoint expressed by the director, the script writers or journalists. Alternatively, it is worth seeing if there is an owner who would like certain information left out or kept in.

Often we only need to know who is the main force behind the advertisement. If it is Cadbury's or Coca Cola, for example, we know that the message is to buy their product. These messages are obvious because the products are well-known and have a long history of advertising and promotion. However, all media products also convey ideas about society, some of which the makers are aware of, others which are not consciously expressed.

Radio: Case Study – social and commercial

ACTIVITY 9

Read through the script 'Shoot Drivers', for London Transport's invitation to discuss a traffic problem.

Read through the script 'Clothes Shop' for Kit Kat.

How are the advertisements different? How are they the same?

Listen to radio advertisements: write your own 20 second commercial or local government information advertisement.

Radio advertisement for London Transport

Title: 'Shoot Drivers'

Location: on the streets of London; sounds of cars and buses etc.

Interviewer: Excuse me, should we shoot drivers who go in bus lanes?

Voice 1: Oh, yes – good idea.
Voice 2: Of course!
Voice 3: No, no way!
Voice 4: A bit harsh.
Voice 5: A fine is a step in the right direction.
Voice 6: We're fining them enough.
Voice 7: We should, we should shoot them really.
Voice 8: No!
Voice 9: I quite agree with that.
Voice 10: I think it is a great idea.
Voice 11: Shoot them.
Voice 12: You have got me there!
Voice 13: No!
Voice 14: Why not?
Voice 15: Totally immoral.
Voice 16: It's a step in the right direction.
Presenter's voice: Ken Livingstone (Mayor) wants to introduce cameras to shoot drivers to go in bus lanes – rubbish or reasonable – please let us know what you think phone 0800 019999.

Creative: Dominic Gettins & Ollie Caporn; Agency: Euro RSCC Wnek Gosper; Producer: Nicola Evans; Sound, Neil Harrington; Copyright: London Transport

---

Radio advertisement for Kit Kat

Title: 'Clothes Shop'

DIRECTORY ENQUIRIES: Which number do you require?
MRS BROWN: Hello, yes, it's a clothes shop.
DIRECTORY ENQUIRIES: Name?
MRS BROWN: Mrs Brown.
DIRECTORY ENQUIRIES: No, the name of the shop.
MRS BROWN: Ah yes . . . it's something fashion.
DIRECTORY ENQUIRIES: Do you have a location?
MRS BROWN: Oh, now that I do know. It's near the traffic lights opposite the bakery.
DIRECTORY ENQUIRIES: Do you have any other information?
MRS BROWN: Oh yes, they sell sandals and I think it's closed on Wednesday afternoons.
DIRECTORY ENQUIRIES: Could you be a bit more specific?
MRS BROWN: Yes, there was a big ginger cat in the window, and it barked.
MALE VOICEOVER: Have a break, have a Kit Kat.

Creative: Kieran Knight and Max Clemens, J. Walter Thompson; Producer: Daniel Heighes; Sound: Wave; Copyright: Nestlé.

Refer to Chapter 15 for further work on Radio.

Even the news, which is supposed to be neutral, can be said to be biased in favour of the majority view of the people in the country. Those people who choose not to live in houses or wear clothes or speak like the BBC news presenters may feel their point of view is not represented. Alternative groups such as *Undercurrents* produce their news on video and distribute by mail order. The typical content of their videos is of protests and demonstrations about the environment, animal rights and pollution. This kind of presentation could be seen to be biased towards the makers' viewpoint.

Alternative values

Non-commercial products and non-governmental organisations with little money have a low chance of success of reaching a mass audience because they have no access to exhibition or points of interaction with the public. Free publicity can be gained by performing 'stunts'. Campaigning agencies such as *Greenpeace* and *Amnesty International* put their money into specific projects. *Greenpeace* has a history of daring stunts such as climbing Big Ben or beseiging whaling ships to gain free publicity about 'green' issues on the news. *Amnesty International* uses strong messages in their photographs to shock people into awareness of abuse of human rights, cruelty and political imprisonment issues.

Added value

In advertisements it is usually obvious what you are being sold. The aim is to persuade the consumer to buy the product. The slogan or catchphrase will be visible or pronounced loudly by the presenter or narrator.

The images of the product are presented to give an idea of what the real product is, but also shown is a lifestyle or a benefit – an 'added value'. If you buy X you will also get Y. Alternatively, if you buy X you will save money. Financial gain is the main message of this aspect of advertising.

Social value

Values about society also are packaged into advertisements, soaps, game shows and news, in fact any type of programme or medium. For example, the 1998 Heinz soup advertisements show a lorry driver returning home to his meal after a cold and long day, and suggest that a soup eater will have a secure home and a warm, family life. These are what are known as values, what society thinks is worth having. Values convey society's ideas about a range of important aspects of everyday life: identity, gender, age, race, family, class, material wealth and politics.

The messages in television advertisements are often spoken by an unseen voice, by a presenter or written on the screen. In televised government health warnings the voice is often direct in telling the viewer what to do, for example, 'Don't Drink and Drive'. These words are usually also printed on the screen or the poster to add impact.

Ideology

Through studying its media it is possible in any country to understand the way its people think about the family, religion, education and political beliefs. The values of the business woman in the city of London will be different from those of the business woman in the Jordanian city of Amman. The main difference is likely to concern religion. In Jordan, the main religion is Islam in comparison to Church of England or Catholic in the UK, for example. This means that the way in which the citizens of both countries make or consume the media will be different. Even if the advertisement is for *Coca Cola* and the basic messages are the same, the reading of the image used may be different.

Ideology and advertising

Another example is the hair product *Wash and Go*. This product combines conditioner and shampoo in one bottle. The American advertisements depicted happy and busy working women going for exercise workouts at the gym, and then using the product. The setting of the television advertisement in a changing room, was indicated by lockers behind the women, thereby depicting the changing room as a typical place for social activities which relate to having to wash your hair. The women in the advertisement were seen with the product and the 'story' works by showing that other women observe that the happy-go-lucky women are using this product and leaving early because they have taken less time to wash their hair.

When the advertisement was shown in Russia, the advertisement did not have the same happy, sporting associations for those who watched it. In Russia, a room with lockers in the background was associated with communal workplaces, prisons and cramped, squalid settings. The idea of a happy, sports loving, working city woman with a few minutes to spend cleaning her hair in a lunch break did not convey well in Russia.

Association

The reading of images depends on the individual's background and the associations the audience has with the image before they look at it. As with the students who responded to the *S Club 7* poster by saying whether they liked them or not, everyone makes judgements. These judgements are the audience's opinions and are a question of taste and personal values.

Whatever the content or the ownership of the product, audiences are potentially able to make of it what they will.

'On behalf of'

It is a common phrase to hear someone in films or in television programmes involving lawyers or business people say that they are representing someone else. Similarly, the production of media products is often carried out 'on behalf of' someone else by advertising companies or corporate film and video companies. This does not mean that the message is neutral or without values. The important factor to establish is whose message is being presented, why, and to whom.

Successful awareness campaigns depend on having the finance to repeat the advertisement frequently with a simple but identifiable message. In many cases the aim is not to interest the consumer, for example, in the film industry the promotional aim is to raise awareness of the product's existence.

National identity

What is the image of Britain abroad? In 1996, according to the Americans, British pop and all things British were considered cool (see Figure 4.5).

However, by July 1998, after the World Cup which included media reports of British citizens involved in violent fights outside football matches, the British image was seen to be declining (see Figure 4.6).

Britishness

Study the images in Figure 4.9 originally published by the French daily newspaper *Liberation* of what British people appear to look like to the cartoonist, Willem.

Discuss

Discuss the following:
1. What images of Britain are suggested by the depiction of the characters in Figure 4.9?
2. What elements do you think are true?
3. Are there any positive or negative images?
4. What images of British people are missing?
5. Do you feel you are represented in these images of Britain?

Fig 4.7   The rise of the British image
           abroad in 1996
                                    Source: *Newsweek*

Fig 4.8   The decline of the British image
           abroad in 1998
                                    Source: *Newsweek*

Fig 4.9   Britain as others see us – is this a true/fair representation?
                                    Source: © The *Guardian*, 2 January 1999/Willem

Fig 4.10   Cows burning on funeral pyres following an outbreak of foot and mouth disease: image of Britain 2001

Messages and values simulation

Specimen examination question: AQA

These tasks are not actual examination questions. The questions are the sole work of the author and are devised to match the style, mark allocation and format of the relevant question papers from AQA and OCR. They are designed for examination practice. The tasks are designed to follow the examination paper timings and mark allocations. It is essential that candidates check the specified topics set for the year of their examination, by the examination board. For previous examination papers contact the examination board direct.

Paper 2 controlled text (4hrs)

You are an advertising company and you have been asked to draw up a rough idea of a promotion by the Central Office of Information (COI). Your target is the European family audience; demographic groups ABC1 and C2. The time the advertisement will be broadcast in

European countries is 6 pm–9 pm. You will have to pitch your idea to the COI to win the contract. The pitch should consist of a short, written presentation and the production of a storyboard.

The brief: Produce a television advertisement encouraging Europeans to buy either British fruit and vegetables or British beef. Either advertisement should include images of a range of different types of British people. Ensure that you cover the range of social groups by: gender, race, class, age and disability.

TASK 1

Explain the representations of social groups in one or more magazines or television advertisements that you have studied.

(40 marks)

TASK 2

Read the brief at the beginning of this exercise.

a Draw up to ten frames for your storyboard of the promotion.
(20 marks)

b Annotate the storyboard with sound, including voice-over and soundtrack, camera angles and movement (see Chapter Two: Languages and Categories).
(10 marks)

TASK 3

Write a commentary on the storyboard created in Task 2 explaining what messages you have tried to convey.

(15 marks)

TASK 4

Explain in a letter to the COI what other marketing strategies and values you have decided to use and promote.

(15 marks)

 Extension Tasks

1 **Collect** three or four magazine advertisements which include male models and three or four that include female models. These should be adverts for products such as food, cars, clothes and perfumes. **Compare and contrast** how men and women are represented in terms of:

▮ Denotation and connotations.
▮ Images of men and women – types and stereotypes.
▮ Lifestyle and aspirations.
▮ Presentation of content, slogan and catchphrases.
▮ Difference and conformity to the 'norm'.
▮ Target audience (see Chapter 3, audience demographics).

2 **Analyse** the messages of radio advertisements on local radio. What form and structure do the advertisements take? What do the advertisements tell us about families, the state, religion and work? Who are the advertisements targeted at? How do these advertisements construct the audience?

3 **a Produce** a jingle for an advertisement for a new takeaway pizza service, also available on the Internet. The advertisement should include details of how to order by phone or via the Internet. The idea behind the advertisement is that the pizza image on the computer screen allows the purchaser to select from the range of toppings by clicking on the mouse and sending the order by E-mail.

b You should also **consider** the following: audience demographics, representation and sound-bite slogan, and music soundtrack. See if you can **identify** images of America (or another country).

4 **Create** a paper collage of magazine and newspaper images of America. Annotate (write notes next to the images) and **analyse** their connotations. What are the images of? Is there a repetition of the same sort of image? Who has produced these images? **Collect** a number of advertisements from television, newspaper, magazines or Internet to compare.

5 **Redesign** a classic book cover for a youth audience. William Sutcliffe's book, *Are You Experienced?* (Penguin Books, 1998) sold 10 times more when its book cover was redesigned. The new cover included an image of a female belly button, a psychedelic colour scheme and a buckle in the shape of a cannabis plant.

Other examples of 'redesigned' media products include: *Great Expectations* (released as a new version of the film in 1998), *Vanity Fair* and *William Shakespeare's Romeo and Juliet* (1996). **Explain** in your commentary the ideas behind your representations, audience targeting and format and layout decisions.

6 **Produce** a poster, press release and a

television campaign (storyboard) for your own 'Don't Drink and Drive' campaign. The target audience is males in the 40–55 yrs age group. Research has shown that this age group is the most likely to ignore these types of campaigns. How will you research where to place your advertisements and posters? What images will be most effective?

7 **Produce** an advertising campaign to launch a new drink for the 16–25 year old market. **Design** an advertisement for a magazine. Which magazines will the advert appear in? What mix of media will you use to maximise your campaign and where will it be seen and heard? What is the lifestyle associated with the drink and what else is the consumer of the drink likely to do for leisure and work? **Devise** a bite-sized phrase or slogan, for example, 'Go to work on an egg', which was used for years to promote egg eating.

 Examination Skills

Knowledge and Understanding

There should be an ability to apply conceptual and technical terms such as representations and serial. There should be a strong understanding of the links between producers and audiences, messages and values and audiences and producers.

In making media texts, including storyboards or scripts, there should be an understanding of audiences and producers, codes and signifiers of meaning. Commentaries should be informed by a knowledge of form and content of mainstream and alternative texts. The understanding of the terms 'values' and 'ideology' will inform the best commentaries.

Knowledge of the use of storyboard conventions: wide variety of shot sizes, camera angles and movements, soundtrack and lighting is also useful.

Textual Analysis

Students should be able to denotate, connotate and explain the broader ideologies by interpreting a media product, using technical and key words terminology. The importance of categorisation, genre and representation should also be recognised as these concepts are linked together.

Students should exhibit an awareness of social institutions and values by reference and links to key social groups or institutions (i.e. Church, Government, work/education and family) and how media texts convey ideas about each of these.

The representation of British people by other European countries in their advertisements is often of a bowler-hatted commuter or a fist-waving football supporter. English behaviour, in other European country's news media and cartoons, is still represented as either terribly polite and charming, or thuggish and brutal. The upper class image is not surprising, since films like *Four Weddings and a Funeral* contain stereotypical images of upper class English society, and of pretty postcard pictures of village greens and churches. These images and stereotypes of Englishness are perhaps why the film sold so well around the world.

Practical Work

Constructing a new product or re-working an old product involves the demonstration of an understanding of concepts of representation, audiences and producers. Close attention to visual and aural forms of representation is necessary. Layout and design skills are less important than a broad understanding of the format and typical content of the following: press releases, storyboards, radio jingles, TV news bulletins, print-based advertising, popular television formats, photography, music video, films and trailers, and posters.

5 Practical Production Guide

What type of media production can be done?

What you will learn

In this chapter you will learn about different types of media production, the importance of having an audience, planning, and critical commentary.

Every Media Studies syllabus includes practical assignments for coursework. There are full-scale productions and there is practical work, which involves a low level of technology.

- **Production work** is the production of media texts for specified audiences using appropriate equipment and resources.
- **Practical work** means activities such as storyboarding and scripting, which are a necessary part of the production process.

Professional versus amateur

Examiners do not expect students to produce magazines, video and radio products to the same level of expertise as the professionals. If you are fortunate enough to have colour desk-top publishing, inkjet or laser printers and television or audio-recording studios, then this will improve the quality of your finished products. However, no student is marked down for not having these facilities. It is important to state in your writing what equipment you used so that an examiner can make a judgement about how well you have managed with the equipment you have available.

Criteria

Examiners are looking for your ability to use the typical forms and conventions of any medium. For example:

- Does your product show awareness of the typical layout and content of a broadsheet or tabloid newspaper?
- Does your video storyboard for an advertisement make sense as a promotion as well as a sequence of images and sounds?

In addition, the examiners are looking for a demonstration of how audiences are targeted. This can be achieved by the way the form and content of the media product has been presented. You will need to provide further evidence of this in the critical commentary.

Practical activity

Producing a storyboard is an example of small-scale practical work. In the real world of television and film, a storyboard is a vital planning format for imagining how the shots and sounds will appear when sequenced together. A storyboard should be well annotated and carefully presented (see Chapter Two: Languages and Categories). On its own, a storyboard does not fulfil the requirements of a complete assignment. A storyboard should be accompanied by, for example, an analysis of mainstream product(s) and a critical commentary.

Practical production

Alternatively, practical work can involve media technology in a larger-scale project. For example, you can use a video camera or an audio-tape recorder to record a news bulletin presentation. The AQA production assignment is intended to incorporate the use of a larger scale practical and technical element.

Example production sheet

Subject: 'Film 2002 with Jonathan Ross' style television film review

Medium: Video (television)

Names of people in group: Funmi, Kamaljit, Jo, and Matt

Equipment and materials needed: Video camera, chairs, posters, editing facilities.

Treatment: We are making a 'Film 2002 with Jonathan Ross' style review of the latest Indian/Pakistan/Hong Kong film video releases. The video sequence will be about five minutes long and will include our views on one film in particular and a general overview on several Asian (mainly Indian) films. The presenter will act in the style of Jonathan Ross, but will be female. The guest panel who will comment on the films will be one Pakistani, one Indian, one Hong Kong Chinese student and one Caucasian. We aim to show what films are on offer to the community in which we live which are very popular but are not much talked about on programmes like 'Film 2002 with Jonathan Ross'.

The camera work will be hand-held and the editing will involve lots of unusual angles and fast pans. The panel will have strong opinions which should differ greatly. The edited version will have clips from the films we have been talking about.

Dates for recording: January 20th and 27th

Date for editing: February 3rd and 10th.

Date for critical commentary deadline: February 20th

Select medium: Video for television

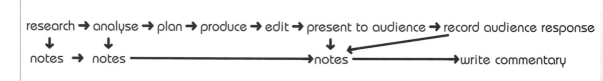

Fig 5.1   Diagram of the production process

Critical commentary

All individual and group practical products need to be explained in a critical commentary. For any media product produced for mass media consumption or for an individual's Media Studies practical production assignment, the same questions can be asked. The critical commentary should explain the process of producing the product (30% of the words). The major part of the commentary (70% of the words) should cover the areas raised by the following questions:

Critical commentary and planning questions

Question	Concept area
■ **Why the product is produced?** (e.g. an advertisement is used to promote and sell another media product, such as a TV programme)	Messages and Values
■ **What format is chosen?** (includes visual and/or aural elements, e.g. documentary)	Languages and Categories
■ **What form, style and design ideas are presented?** (e.g. *T4:* youthful presenters, colourful sets, loud and brash music, bright strong graphics, jerky camera with deliberately exaggerated zooms and pans, short, comical, briskly presented items)	Languages and Categories
■ **Who exactly is it targeted at?** (e.g. *The Priory:* ABC1s aged 15 to 24 males and females)	Producers and Audiences
■ **How is the audience constructed?** (i.e. included in the mode of address or the positioning? *SM TV Live:* Friendly, chatty, youthful presenters who use jokes which a younger audience might not understand. Puns, jokes and games, competitions, music and films for younger audience.)	Producers and Audiences
■ **Is the product effective and successful with its audiences?**	Producers and Audiences
■ **Is the producer satisfied with the end result?** What would they do to improve it?	Producers and Audiences
■ **Who is the producer?** (e.g. an advertising agency called Believe, or a newspaper called *Eyewash*?)	Producers and Audiences
■ **Who financed the product?** (e.g. the company Microsoft, by a sponsor, by actual sales or by the Government?)	Producers and Audiences
■ **What ideas do you associate with the signifiers?** (e.g. dark clouds over castle signifies horror genre)	Messages and values
■ **What attitudes and values about society and people does the media product contain?** (e.g. advertisement depicting sunlit breakfast cereal in perfectly tidy kitchen with two smiling children and mother and father suggests an ideal family event)	Messages and Values

Coursework requirements: by examination boards

Each examination board also has an end of year timed examination paper. Check your specific syllabus for details. Note also that individual examination syllabus requirements may change so check these yearly.

Practical work

OCR specifications

Candidates undertake **one** of the following briefs, either individually, or as member of a group (maximum group size is five candidates)

Audio-visual media

1 An opening title sequence for a new television programme in a genre chosen by the Centre (maximum two minutes), on video, with an accompanying storyboard.
2 A photo-storyboard or video (maximum one minute of trailer for a new film in a genre chosen by the Centre), using original images.
3 An audio sample for a new radio programme (maximum five minutes), in a genre chosen by the Centre, with an accompanying sound script.

Print-based media

4 A sample for a new teenage or children's magazine, to include the front cover, contents, double-page spread and a double-page spread article, using some original photography.
5 An advertising campaign for a new fragrance, to include a brand name design, and two full page magazine advertisements and a billboard poster, using original photography and graphics.
6 A front cover and main inside article on a topic of local interest for a local newspaper, using original photography.

ICT-based media

7 Four web pages for a new entertainment website aimed at teenagers, using some original photography and graphics.
8 A website promotion for a first release by a new music band, to include band biography and information (four pages),

including some original photography and graphics.

AQA specifications

Coursework
Section A: 3 assignments of 700–800 words (can include practical elements)

Section B: Practical production and supporting account

WJEC specifications

Coursework
3 pieces (400–600 words each), including one essay, one pre-production and one practical production piece with evaluation.

Pre-production involves practical preparation for the main production. For example, storyboard, treatment, synopsis.

Example of a critical commentary for an assignment

(Refer also to the images produced by a student on page 16 of Chapter Two: Languages and Categories.)
This extract from a critical commentary explains the meaning of the source image as well as one of the three products the student made from it, by cropping the photograph and placing it in another context.

The image originated from the front page of *The Guardian*. The article was about an item of topical interest involving the late Diana, Princess of Wales. This came to light at the Labour Party Conference a month after her death, in 1997. When Clare Short had a picture taken at Brighton beach she was representing the Government's view of dangerous weapons which she feels should be outlawed.

The image denotes a middle-aged woman holding up two objects. These objects look very much like lethal weapons used in a war situation. There is a sign next to the woman which is indicating that there are dangerous mines around. In the background there is what looks like the sea.

The image connotes that the woman is campaigning against dangerous mines. This might indicate that there are unexploded mines around the coast of Brighton although they are not. Her expression suggests sternness and hostility. She is disapproving very strongly of the weapons. Her posture and the way she is holding the weapons suggests that she feels very strongly and doesn't really want to hold those weapons. This is because she is holding the weapons far enough away from her body so she feels safe. Her hands are only holding the weapons tight enough not to drop them. Her clothes connote safety and protection. The sign is red, this usually connotes danger.

The words anchor the picture by giving it some kind of meaning. For example, we can get some feed back from the picture, for example we know it is about dangerous mines and that the Labour Party have promised to sign the treaty on banning landmines. The campaign is for outlawing dangerous weapons and Diana, Princess of Wales was associated with it.

The picture is representing a very strong and in depth topic. By the way Clare Short is holding the objects, along with her facial expressions, you immediately get the impression that it's a very serious matter which is undergoing a great deal of investigation.

Anne-Marie Illingworth

Invented image and context of image A (Chapter Two: Languages and Categories)

Image A denotes an unusual object which looks like a designer beaker or jam jar. This is mainly because the object has what seems to be a bottom and a lid. The only difference is that the top part of the object is very strange and unusual.

The image could be an object for a photographic competition or a piece of abstract art work. This is partly because there is a hand in the background holding the object up. This also could connote an unidentified object.

The photographer wanted to aim specifically at the object and not at the person. This is shown by a close up on the object. This allows the picture to have a much more specific meaning or aim. The camera position obtains a front on view of the object and gets a good concept of the picture. The lighting throughout the picture is very pale and really only gives us a bold outline of the object. Because of the way the picture has been photographed we don't really know if the object is round, flat or square. I feel by the picture being in black and white and blown up (using a photocopier) so that it loses detail, you get a feeling of uncertainty about the precise details of the images.

The captions of the picture are designed to create a feeling of mysteriousness. This was done using objects which have not been proved to exist. You would expect to find this type of article in a space magazine or an *X-Files* magazine. The new image which I have created has been changed considerably from the original image. I have done this by taking the original dangerous references away and introducing a feeling of sci-fi-mystery.

The audience which I have targeted the magazine article for will range between 12 to 26 years of age and possibly upwards, because the subject matter appeals to the unknown fans, of this age group.

Technology used: photocopier, enlargements, word processor with range of fonts incorporated.

Anne-Marie Illingworth

Production
Examples of typical productions are:

1 Make a 30 second television advertisement for a new perfume, directed at 25 to 35 year olds.

Write a critical commentary explaining the research, the process of production, ownership, the form and content, and audience of the advertisement.
2 Produce a first edition cover and contents list for a new music magazine.
Write a critical commentary explaining the research, the process of production, the campaign to launch the magazine, ownership, the form and content, and audience of the advertisement.

Guidelines for producing a Video

There are three stages in the process of making a video: pre-production, production and post-production (see Figure 5.2).

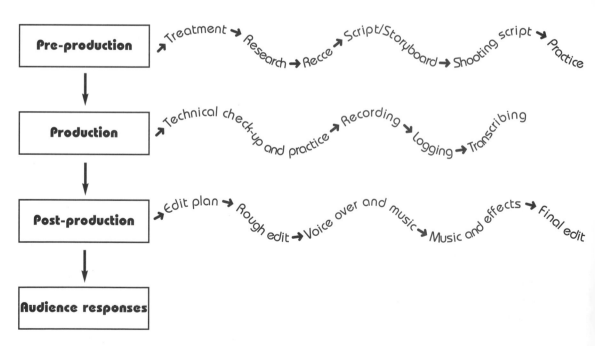

Fig 5.2   Guidelines for producing a video

Pre-production
Treatment

The success of a video depends on planning out as much as possible of the filming and the editing before starting. You need to share and brainstorm ideas. Once you have decided on the content of the video, you must decide on how you will treat the subject matter. You should write a short summary explaining what your video is about, at what time of day the programme will be shown, and what format and style it will take. This summary is otherwise known as the 'treatment'. The treatment should include:

▐ A brief outline of the piece.
▐ Who might take part in it.
▐ What places or events you will include.
▐ The style and tone of your piece.
▐ The format.

Concepts

Remember to answer these main questions:

▐ Who is it for and when will it be shown? (Audience)
▐ Who made it? (Producers)
▐ What do you want to say? (Messages and Values)
▐ What forms and conventions do you want to use? (Languages and Categories)

Research
Fiction

If you are making a drama or a fictional video then you will need to write a script. This details the structure of the programme. A script will show the order of the programme's elements and contain: questions, speech drama, location settings, props and sound effects. See AQA's pro-forma for a script, in the Appendix. These blanks are what you will be provided with in the examination.

Factual

If you are making a factual programme, you will need to think more about how to organise your interviewees and record questions that make sense. You will need to write a script showing the content of the video sequence.

Storyboard

A storyboard is a series of sketches of each frame of the film you are going to write. Storyboarding allows you to plan how to film the shots in each section of your film. It can be tempting to simply pick up the video camera and shoot whatever is in the frame. You need to become familiar with how to use the tripod and experiment freehand with the cameras. However, it is important that you have a clear idea about how many shots you will need to film each section from your idea. You will need to make decisions about:

▐ tripod or hand-held camera
▐ shot size
▐ shot angle
▐ shot movement
▐ shot background and foreground
▐ props and clothes

Pre-production check list

1 Check that everyone knows what they are doing and that they are committed to turning up and bringing their props or piece of equipment to the place where you are videoing.
2 Check you can use all your equipment before you go out. Check also that your equipment works. Check the batteries are fully charged up. There is nothing worse than finding out you have no power left.
3 Check you have enough video tape.
4 Arrange to meet at the location half an hour before videoing starts.
5 Try to rehearse the camera movements and shots without recording, so you have a practice run.

6 Allow ten seconds running in time, once you have pressed the record button. Allow ten seconds running out time, once your scene has finished. (By carrying out the previous two instructions you can edit two sequences together so they lock securely onto the control track, without jumping and ruining the edit.)

Mikes

Test out the sound before you start. If you are using the built-in microphone, make sure you are not too far away from the speaker or actors or actresses. If you are using a hand-held mike, make sure you are pointing it in the right direction, to avoid picking up any irritating noises.

Recording

Make sure your tripod is level and make sure the microphone is working. Be brave enough to record more than one take of the same shot. This covers you in case one of your takes does not turn out well.

Post-production
Logging and labelling

Once you have shot a scene, make sure you label the tape and log the scene on a logging sheet. This will help later when you are editing, as you will often need to find a particular scene quickly from the tapes you have videoed.

Edit plan

Once you have filmed, view your material and make a list of the sections you want to edit together, specifying counter numbers. This paper edit should briefly describe the sequence, the tape and the duration of the piece.

Edit the sequences according to your paper edit. Show your rough edit to friends and teachers. Gain reviews and responses from different audiences, at home and at school.

Write these responses down to include them in your critical commentary. Finally, edit and change anything you think is not what you really want.

If you have the technical facilities, place music and titling over appropriate sections. Place credits at the end, remembering to include any special thanks to people who helped.

Guidelines for producing a radio programme

The process of producing a radio programme is very much the same as for video. All of the stages of video pre-production, production and post-production can be followed. The main consideration in radio is in finding the best sounds to create atmosphere, how much sound is needed and how the presenter makes the medium exciting, live and immediate. The script layout can follow the format opposite.

Many students choose radio because it is in some ways an easy medium to carry around and obtain material for. Radio can use music, sound effects, different locations and a range of opinions in depth. However, it is important to check that you have the facilities to achieve what you want. Most schools and colleges have audio-cassette recorders and some have full mixing desk facilities. If you only have an audio-cassette recorder then you will have to record all your sound 'live'. Any music and speaking will have to be faded in and out as you go along.

Treatment

The treatment should include:

▌ A brief outline of the piece.
▌ Who might take part in it.
▌ What places or events you will include.
▌ The style and tone of your piece.
▌ The format.

Sound	Dialogue	Other information	Timing
Intro: music fade out	This is your only real local alternative radio station bringing you views and news which are different. Oh yes, and there's music as well as chat and gossip. Today, we have in the studio three experts on alternative fashions and why we can't get enough of the style and fit of clothes that we really, really want. If you want to phone in your opinions on fashion, avoid the queue get in your view now by phoning this number ...	Laughter in background	9 secs
Music starts to fade up			13 secs 10 secs total

Fig 5.3   *Sample radio script*

Concepts

Remember to answer these main questions:

▌ Who is it for? (Audience)
▌ When will it be broadcast? (Audience)
▌ Who made it? (Producers)
▌ What do you want say? (Messages and Values)

The forms and conventions may vary according to whether it is, for example, Radio 1, Kiss FM or a local independent or alternative radio station.

Magazine or newspaper front cover production

(Refer also to Chapter Nine on Newspapers and Chapter Twelve on Magazines for layout and content)
The layout and design for a newspaper and flatplan usually takes the form of a series of roughs, showing headlines, spaces where the photographs fit in and the column divisions where the text is allocated space.

Producing a web page

A web page is basically a word-processed page with links. HTML (Hypertext Mark-up Language) is the code which allows these links to be made.

Software resources: Adobe PageMill, Microsoft Front Page, Claris Home Page, Netscape Communicator, Internet Assistant.

Plan on paper the layout of image and text for your page on paper. Consider the following:

▌ Who is your audience?
▌ Write, draw and gather content.
▌ Format.
▌ Assemble page.
▌ Publishing the page.

Scan in your images or use a digital camera. Save the images in JPEG format. Type in the text for your web page. Arrange the layout of the page according to how you want it to look and then save your page as a web page (this may involve saving as 'web page' or as 'HTML').

To publish on the Internet, you will need to run some FTP software (File Transfer Protocol).

Next let people know what your URL is – this is the address of your web page.

Which medium?

Finally, have you chosen the right medium? Selecting the right medium for the right topic depends on the following:

▌ Who will consume it?
▌ Is the topic best suited for that medium?
▌ Financially, is it more viable for one medium or the other?
▌ Is the subject local, regional or national?

Decide which medium suits the following tasks:

1 A documentary followed by a phone in chat show on whether genetically modified foods should be sold in shops. National audience, mainly over 15 year olds.

2 Underage drinking. In-depth interviews with local people about attitudes to under age drinking. Regional and local, 12 year olds and upwards.

3 A campaign to build a new bypass or to pedestrianise a part of a town or city. Regional, over 35 year olds.

4 A consumer guide to 'what's on': reviews and previews about entertainment in the area. Local, youth, 15 to 24 year olds.

6 Music industry

Jingle bells, jingle all the way

What you will learn

This chapter covers the music industry, its promotion of the product, the role of the music press, radio playlists, television music shows, videos and internet sites and the criteria for making a hit single at Christmas.

KEY WORDS

- mainstream
- youth culture
- street credibility
- genre
- indies
- image
- major
- unique selling point
- segmentation
- synergy

TECHNICAL WORDS

- chart
- play lists
- point of sale
- dance
- rap
- techno
- drum 'n' bass
- garage
- artists and repertoire

What is mainstream popular music?

Is it Radio 2 or Radio 1; Kiss FM or Virgin, television's *Top of the Pops* or magazines like *Smash Hits* or *New Musical Express*? Is it today's popular bedroom-produced techno music or club-based dance/rap music?

When people refer to 'mainstream pop music' they usually mean one of the following:

▌ The modern, chart music that is played on Sunday's 'Official Top 40' chart show on BBC Radio 1.
▌ Television's *Top of the Pops (TOTP)* on BBC1.
▌ The Pepsi chart show on Channel 5.

The charts are mainly youth oriented, for the age group 10–25 years. *TOTP* is broadcast at 7.30 on Friday evenings, so many over 25 year olds also watch the programme. It could be argued that Radio 2 is more of a popular music channel as it appeals to a wider age range of people. Its programming targets people who grew up during times when the popular music of the day was different: 1930s and 1940s big band, 1950s jazz music and rock and roll, pop's great explosion in the 1960s and 1970s, and new romantic and punk in the 1980s are all examples of music broadcast by Radio 2.

Mainstream chart-based popular music is the music also heard on local radio stations such as Radio 1 and on television, in clubs and in dance venues. Music that is first played on the Sunday charts show on the radio is then often used in other venues throughout the week.

Albums

Title	Artist	Label
1 WORLD OF OUR OWN	WESTLIFE	RCA
2 GREATEST HITS – VOL 2	MADONNA	MAVERICK
3 DREAMS CAN COME TRUE – GREATEST HITS	GABRIELLE	GO BEAT
4 GOLD – THE GREATEST HITS	STEPS	JIVE
5 THEIR GREATEST HITS – THE RECORD	BEE GEES	POLYDOR
6 ECHOES – THE BEST OF	PINK FLOYD	EMI
7 THE STORY SO FAR – THE VERY BEST OF	ROD STEWART	WARNER BROS
8 FEVER	KYLIE MINOGUE	PARLOPHONE
9 ENCORE	RUSSELL WATSON	DECCA
10 SOLID BRONZE – GREAT HITS	BEAUTIFUL SOUTH	GO DISCS

Singles

Title	Artist	Label
1 IF YOU COME BACK	BLUE	INNOCENT
2 QUEEN OF MY HEART	WESTLIFE	RCA
3 EMOTION	DESTINY'S CHILD	COLUMBIA
4 BECAUSE I GOT HIGH	AFROMAN	UNIVERSAL
5 FALLIN'	ALICIA KEYS	J
6 FREE	LIGHTHOUSE FAMILY	WILD CARD
7 UGLY	BUBBA SPARXXX	INTERSCOPE
8 RAPTURE	IIO	MADE/DATA/MOS
9 THEY DON'T KNOW	SO SOLID CREW	RELENTLESS
10 HEY BABY	DJ OTZI	EMI

Fig 6.1   *Official UK Top 10 Singles and Albums, November 2001*
Source: © The Official UK Charts Company 2002

Youth culture

Youth culture as a marketable idea began with the growth of the popular music industry during the 1950s, when rock and roll was born. Electrified blues and swing music were combined, and the background of today's popular music came into being. Youth culture developed as a reaction by teenagers against their parents. Images of youth enjoying music separately from parents became commonplace. Rebellion in films was focused on icons such as James Dean, star of *Rebel Without A Cause* (1954). Rebellion and youth culture were packaged together and sold back to its own youth audience. Teenagers could buy related consumable goods, such as drinks, cars, records, concerts and films. Various rock and roll stars, especially Americans, were created in the process: Elvis Presley and Bill Haley and the Comets being just two examples.

Street credibility

Yesterday's 1960s rebels, for example The Rolling Stones, have become today's superstars and are now enjoying renewed street credibility. To be considered non-mainstream the artist or band has to have an attitude that is not concerned with selling products. The term street credibility applies when the artist does not seek to promote image above content. The fans respect the artist or band for the music, despite the promotional excess they may have thrust onto them. In gaining street credibility the artist is therefore often difficult to categorise in terms of the genre of their music. The content of the music tends to avoid mainstream categories of music.

'Indies'

Bands who sign up to indie labels (for example, Beggars Banquet or Mushroom Indie) can be more concerned with content than image. They are also currently more likely to be heard in record shops, on independent radio stations, at clubs and concerts and on the Internet. A few selected mainstream DJs may plug indie bands, however they are restricted by the policy of the mainstream stations to play what is in the week's popular chart listings.

Indie bands usually have to work with small distributors and labels to get their product sold. Other methods of selling records include:

▮ word of mouth
▮ through mail order

ACTIVITY 1

1. **Write** notes under the heading 'popular music genre'. How many genres of music do you know? What genres do you like? Are they mainstream or at the alternative end of music culture? Create a large

scale wall 'map' of music culture showing music labels and their companies and how they relate to various genres and bands.

2. **Analyse** the covers of two compact discs (CDs) by the same artist or band, using denotation and connotation techniques of analysis (see Chapter 2). Use the headings and prompts below to discuss your CD covers and music.

   a **Image**. Look at the visual imagery and the graphics used in the packaging of the music product. You might compare two CD covers by the same artist to show how they have common themes or how they have developed a new image or style. What ideas do the images denote and connotate (see definitions in Chapter 2)? Are there any key signifiers? Is the band included in the image and if so, how are they represented? If they are not included in the cover image, why not? What graphics and typefaces have been used? Do they convey a style or image?

   b **Musical style**. What type of music does your artist/band play? Is the artist or band mainstream or at the alternative end of music styles? What image and attitude do the band's members appear to have from the way they look? Note their dress, body language and facial expressions.

   c **Audience**. Who is the audience aimed at? Note the age and gender.

   d **Institutions**. What is the label and the parent company? For example, Sony is the parent company for Creation record label. Who is the distributor?

Image
Promoting a band

To promote a single, with a few notable exceptions, you need an image. If you are

interested in selling your record to more than just your friends and local people, then the idea of your music and the band have to be portable and travel widely. This can only be achieved by projecting the image you wish to present. The scale on which you can do this depends on your budget.

Major companies

The major record companies can afford to spend a great deal of money on promotion and they have staff employed to fulfil various roles in different departments. An example of a record company structure is given over the page in Figure 6.2.

Two examples of promotional activity within a company are the Artist and Repertoire, and Strike Force departments.

Artist and Repertoire

The artist and repertoire (A&R) department searches out, develops and nurtures a company's talent. To develop a band's image they make sure the band wear the appropriate clothes and sometimes modify the musical arrangements to make them sound more professional. The A&R department will look after their safety at concerts and handle press interviews. A&R also act as talent scouts looking for new bands and fresh talent for the market.

Strike Force

The strike force department promotes sales of records, tapes, and compact discs. They will visit music shops to make sure the music is prominently displayed. They will arrange special offers, special artist appearances and highly visible shop displays, for example using stands and cardboard cut outs of the record or the band. This is called point of sale marketing; meaning at the place where the customer makes the actual purchase.

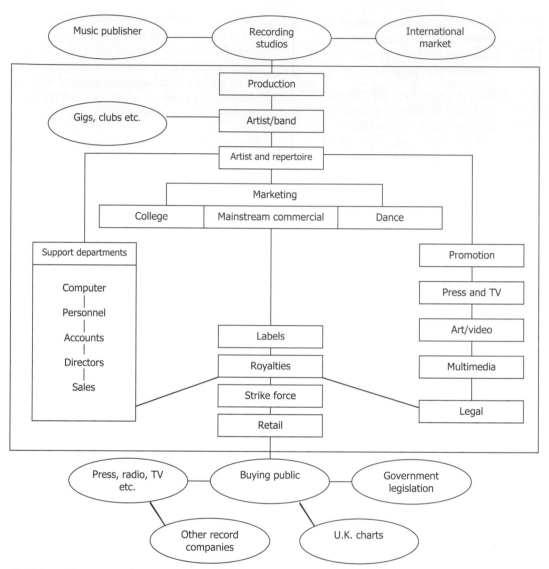

Fig 6.2   Structure of a record company

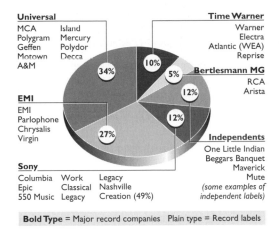

Universal
MCA   Island
Polygram   Mercury
Geffen   Polydor
Motown   Decca
A&M

Time Warner
Warner
Electra
Atlantic (WEA)
Reprise

Bertlesmann MG
RCA
Arista

EMI
EMI
Parlophone
Chrysalis
Virgin

Independents
One Little Indian
Beggars Banquet
Maverick
Mute
*(some examples of
independent labels)*

Sony
Columbia   Work   Legacy
Epic   Classical Nashville
550 Music Legacy   Creation (49%)

Bold Type = Major record companies   Plain type = Record labels

*Fig 6.3   Major record companies and
labels*

Other sources

Indie labels often have to rely on word of
mouth, radio or the music press to give them
strong record sales. Small indies, where only
a small office runs the label, are particularly
weak financially and have to use a major
company to distribute their products. The
bigger indies have a stronger reputation as
they are associated with certain types of
artists. However, even they will collapse if
their major artist either decides to quit the
music business or becomes unsuccessful.
For example, Factory Records closed when
New Order folded in the early 1990s.

Following is a profile of an indie record label
(as promoted by itself).

Skint Records are based in Brighton.
Skint's big brother label Loaded,
began in 1990 and specialised in
releasing a wide range of house
music, under the guidance of JC Reid.
One Monday morning in 1993, DJ
and Journalist Damian Harris joined
the fold and began to build the mighty
and eclectic Skint empire. Fatboy
Slim's 'Santa Cruz' was the label's first
release.

Damian (Midfield General) is Head of
A&R, JC and Tim are the 'Boss-Type
Blokes' and Danny is the Production
Manager. Andy does loads of different
stuff including handling all of Skint's
mail order selection and Dave handles
the licensing. John is the video
commissioner and Gareth deals with
the live side of things and the famous
Big Beat Boutique, a Brighton club
night that has been heaped with
accolades from the popular music and
club press.

Skint also features on the dance
section of The Knowledge, as the
label's roster includes a glorious
wealth of club-orientated acts such as
Fatboy Slim, Cut La Roc, Midfield
General and REQ.

Source: Adapted from www.theknowledge.com

Fig 6.4   Skint Records

Advantages of signing to independent
labels:

- Contract is often 50% share.
- More artistic freedom.
- More care and attention to band's wishes.
- More street credibility.

Advantages of signing to a major label:

- An advance payment is often given, and a
royalty (which is a percentage of every CD
or record sold).
- Promotion will be much more widespread
and effective, with a greater amount of
money and personnel behind the
campaign.
- Greater investment in production and
distribution costs.
- Better international market possibilities.

The music industry

EMI crisis

At the end of March 2002, record label EMI announced 1,800 job losses. EMI is home to a clutch of extremely successful artists, including Robbie Williams and Kylie Minogue.

The general decline at EMI reflects a worldwide decline in record and ticket sales. Two reasons for this are:

▮ Artists disagree with companies over royalties and contracts

▮ Internet piracy and the downloading of music online.

There are three forms of copyright revenues for which a royalty is collected:

PPL (Phonographic Performance Limited) – Every time a song is played on radio or TV they collect X amount of money and give it back to record companies.

PRS (Performing Rights Society) – Every time a song is played in a bar or hairdressers etc a certain amount of money actually gets paid to the person who played the song.

MCPS (Mechanical Copyright Protection Society) – this money goes back to the music publishers, the people who own the actual songs e.g. Michael Jackson gets it because he owns the rights to a large percentage of The Beatles' songs

Music industry statistics

▮ The British music industry is worth £2.5 billion a year, of which £1.25 billion is generated abroad.

▮ The industry employs 115,000 people. (Source: IFPI (International Federation of Phonographic Industry)).

ACTIVITY 2

Survey and quantity analysis

1. Conduct a survey of a class or at least a sample of 20 people in the same age range (half girls and half boys).
   a Find out how many bought a single last year.
   b How many bought an album of the same artist?

2. Create bar charts showing:
   a The breakdown of boys' and girls' consumption
   b Answers to how many bought an album as well as the single.

3. Comment on the figures you have collected:
   a Is there a link between any of the figures?
   b What is a typical pattern of consumption for boys and for girls?
   c Does purchase of singles lead to purchase of albums by the same artist?

▮ Piracy costs an estimated £6.25 billion a year in sales and lost royalties. Most of the piracy involves illegal duplication of tapes and takes place in Russia, Thailand, China and the Far East.

▮ Eighty per cent of all albums sold in the UK are either pop (32.4%), rock (25.9%), dance music (13.3%) or R&B (8.5%). Classical music accounts for 4%, folk music 1.1% and jazz 1%.

▮ Dance music provided 13.3% of all albums and 27% of all singles sold in 2000. There are an increasing number of artists such as Moby, Leftfield, Basement Jaxx, Moloko, Air and Groove Armada who are establishing long careers in a business market usually associated with 'track' rather than 'artist led'.

▮ Both vinyl formats (12" singles and LP) combined sale was worth more than cassette albums and singles put together in the first quarter of 2001.

- Sales effects of the BRIT awards show sales rising dramatically: U2 sales rose by 178% in the two weeks after they were on the 2001 show. Sonique, Craig David and David Gray all showed increases of over 75%.

The average cost of a CD is £13.99 and can be broken down into the following:

- Songwriter publisher   0.68p
- Artist's royalty   £1.61p
- Manufacturing   0.65p
- Distribution   0.72p
- Retailer's margin   £4.67p
- VAT   £2.08p
- Profit pre-interest/tax   0.65p
- Miscellaneous overheads   £1.32p
- Other artists/repertoire costs £1.61p

Who buys music products?

- Men buy almost twice as many albums as women (9.2 a year on average, compared to 5.9)
- Almost half of all money spent on singles (45%) is spent by people under 20.
- Almost half of all money spent on albums (45%) is spent by people between the ages of 20 and 40.
- Buyers aged 12–14 spend more money per year (£94) on albums than buyers aged 30–39 (£85).
- We buy 25% of our albums on Saturday.

Source: BPI Statistical Handbook 2001

Who buys singles?

The percentage of people who bought a single last year can be broken down according to sex (Adapted from *BPI Yearbook*, 2001):

- Men – 51.2%
- Women – 48.8%

and according to social group:

- AB – 11.3%
- C1 – 27.8%
- C2 – 24.9%
- DE – 36.0%

Radio

Listen to Virgin, Heart FM, and Radio 1.

A music critic once complained that there is crude sexual stereotyping involved in the way in which radio programmes are constructed. Discuss this statement. Do you agree?

In the *Independent on Sunday* on 25 January 1998, Matthew Sweet accused various radio stations of either being 'lads' stations full of sexism and Mike and the Mechanics, or 'cosy chats' for girls and Celine Dion (see Figure 6.5). He claimed that Virgin FM has advertisements for breakfast bars, cough sweets and cars, whilst Heart FM has advertisements for fitness centres, healthy breakfast cereals and 'Ladies Nights' in clubs.

FOR GIRLS
Capital gold MW 1548: proper "choons" from the Sixties, Seventies and Eighties for retired rock chicks who aren't too proud to get down to Leonard Skynner as they hoover. Listeners: thirtysomethings who never had that much taste in music in the first place
Heart FM 106.2: lots of solo songstresses, lots of chart, plus keynote golden oldies from Katrina and the Waves and the Eagles. Non-crunchy and Gallagher-free. Listeners: office girls; teenagers; suburbanites
Melody FM 105.4: slushy love songs, showtunes, the Carpenters. Radio 2 with ads, only less challenging. Listeners: new-borns and the hard of thinking

FOR BOYS
Virgin FM 105.8: Britpop, Mike and the Mechanics, Aerosmith, Steve Winwood, plus irritating indie pop from the Lightning Seeds et al. Listeners: New lads and old bores
Jazz FM 102.2: Otis Carmichael, er, Fats Backgammon, that sort of thing. Frankly, it's a mystery to you and me. Listeners: polo-neck wearing, chess-playing, purist jazz bores who tune in to complain about commercialisation and jazz-funk fusion
XFM 104.9: Very alternative, very cutting edge, very indie, very hard work. The John Peel show for the chemical generation. Purveyor of fodder to the review pages of the *NME* and *Melody Maker*. Listeners: erstwhile fans of the Cure; disaffected youth; depressives

Fig 6.5   Are all radio music channels either for boys or girls?
Source: © *Independent on Sunday/Matthew Sweet*, 25 January 1998

ACTIVITY 3

1. Listen to two or three of each radio channel's advertisements and note down who you think they are targeted at.
2. Would you say the advertisers are more interested in one section of the population than another? Discuss.
3. Research your local radio station(s). Analyse the music content and define its audience. Does the advertising reflect any age or gender group? If so, how does it do this?

Fig 6.6   Three members of the Pop Idol panel of judges

Recipe for success

Following is a 'recipe' for marketing a typical 'boy band'.

1 Auditions (on basis of looks and sex appeal).
2 Training the band to dance, with a professional dance teacher.
3 Clothes and makeover – the 'look'.
4 Songs written by professionals.
5 Music produced by professionals.
6 Sound test on group.
7 Studio recording of songs (with or without band).
8 Tour booked.
9 Single released in advance of the tour.
10 Promotion – TV chat shows, interviews with music and leisure press, daily nationals, local radio, local press, local school performances. Plus press release, CD covers, telephone campaign, record, trailers.
11 Tour.
12 Reviews.
13 Record new album.

If the initial campaign begins to create interest, then a single in the Top 40 must be the first target. This gives the band a passport to massive television exposure. Once successful, the main television programmes to promote the single range from chart shows, to chat shows, to children's entertainment programmes.

TV Chart shows
Top of the Pops

BBC1 Fridays, 7.30 pm (and repeated Saturdays):

▌ *TOTP* is targeted at 10 to 45 year olds.
▌ *TOTP Magazine* has a circulation of 500,000 and its target audience is 10–12 year olds.

Pepsi Chart Show

Channel 5 Thursdays, 7.00–7.30 pm:

▌ Targets 10 to 25 year olds.

General TV entertainment

▌ *RI:SE*, Channel 4, weekdays 7.00–9.00 am family programme.
▌ *The Saturday Show*, BBC1, Saturdays, 9.15–12.00 noon, 8 to 15 years age group.
▌ *National Lottery Live*, BBC1, Saturday nights 7.50–8.10 pm family programme.
▌ *Late Night with Jools Holland*, BBC2, Saturdays 11.00 pm, 18 to 55 years age group (a more specialist music programme).
▌ *Top of the Pops 2*, BBC 2, Tuesdays 6.20 pm, retrospective Top of the Pops shows.

- *CD:UK*, ITV1, Saturday 11.30 am, pop and videos.
- *S Club 7*, BBC1 and BBC2, teen drama plus songs.
- *Zee Music*, Satellite TV, daily, Asian music channel.
- *B44*, Music, Satellite TV, Asian music channel
- *Kerrang*, Satellite TV, heavy metal rock channel.
- *Ibiza TV*, Channel 4, Wednesday, fly-on-wall documentaries on the Mediterranean dance scene.

Music video TV channels

The Box, VH1 and MTV are all channels dedicated to nonstop music, including videos of the bands. Videos of bands help sell them when they cannot perform in person.

When bands like The Rolling Stones were on tour it was too tiring to return to London to mime their records on *Top of the Pops*. Instead, they filmed some footage of themselves at the bottom of Beachy Head and used it to play over the soundtrack. In the 1970s, the Queen video of *Bohemian Rhapsody* became known for its technical inventiveness, as did Peter Gabriel's animated 'Sledghammer' video.

When MTV started broadcasting continuous music videos in 1982, it created a new life for many bands who were able to picture themselves in many countries. Some bands, who had no fans in their own country, were able to build up followers abroad.

Music videos

Music videos tend to fall into three categories: **performance**, **narrative** and **abstract**. The most common type of video is where the band is seen on stage, and their live **performance** has been edited. The **narrative** style of video is where the band

perform with their instruments, but also appear informally, sometimes even acting some of the lyrics. If the video contains a solo artist then the individual may be the centre of the storyline, for example Madonna or Michael Jackson. The third type of video is where the band only appears minimally and the entire sequence is an **abstract** interpretation of the lyrics.

ACTIVITY 4

Textual analysis: select two music videos by one artist and answer the following:

1. Identify what type of video it is according to the categories described previously.
2. Explain how the video communicates its ideas visually. Does the video focus on the artist or on the song? What image(s) does the video seek to portray?
3. Consider also where the video is set. Does the setting relate to the lyrics?
4. How does the editing and camerawork link in with the rhythm and pace of the music? Is this effective?

Radio play lists

Play lists are the lists of singles that radio stations draw up, to repeat throughout the week. The 'P' list contains the top 8–10 records; the 'A' list is the next twenty and the 'B' list is the next twenty singles after that. The influential 'Top 40' Sunday afternoon show on Radio 1 plays them all in ascending order. During the week DJs on Radio 1 ensure that the 'P' list has more plays than the 'A' list, which in turn has more plays than the 'B' list.

RADIO 1 play list

Of approximately 250 singles released each week, only around 55 are play listed on Radio

1. 60% of the network's output is play list material, mainly during the daytime. Following is a statement about Radio 1's selection methods:

> Each record is chosen on musical merit and they are judged individually, not according to who the artists are. These decisions have nothing to do with the band or, as has been suggested, an artist's age. However, as part of Radio 1's obligation to provide a distinctive service, the network does support new artists and new music, and it is a contemporary music station.'
>
> Source: BBC Information

ACTIVITY 5

Research the popular music output of Radio 1 and discuss:
Do you think the play list tends to favour one type of artist or age group?

DJ, MC and club music

Much music is created in clubs and the role of the disc jockey (DJ) has changed dramatically in the last ten years. With music created by remixing old records and manipulating vinyl records, DJs have become artists in their own right. Dance music has also allowed the audience to concentrate more on group participation than on the spectacle of the performer on stage. With the rise in so many different types of music, the music industry is finding it hard to sell a single type of music to the whole audience.

Segmentation

With so many different genres the music industry is now like an orange with many segments that are attached together but do not connect. This defines the term 'segmentation'.

The music press

The music press are often useful for increasing interest in a band but in many of the biggest promotional campaigns the press has not made much difference. *Smash Hits* has probably made the biggest impact in recent years in increasing interest through its large scale posters of artists that can be pinned up on the wall. *Q*, *Select*, *NME* and *Melody Maker* offer more in-depth interviews and reports. For fans of the specialist genres, such as heavy metal, there are magazines such as *Kerrang* or *Hot Metal*.

The campaign for relaunching Meatloaf in 1993 avoided using any music press. Instead they reached their audience of 25–45 year olds through the national dailies and Sunday newspapers. News of bands tours, interviews and background to the bands provide details that fans can obtain exclusively from the magazines. However, with the rise of the fanzine, the Internet and teletext, more information can be obtained by other means. This poses the question: does the music industry need music press or does the music press need the music industry?

The look

The front covers of music magazines do provide additional publicity coverage for bands. News retailers effectively provide space for the faces of bands to be seen by the public. Photographs of the artists tend to involve portrait shots with the artist looking straight out at the viewer. The images are usually well lit and the straplines (the words in bite size sentences) summarise the point of the article inside the magazine.

Award ceremonies

The major award ceremonies are the high points in a promoter's year. At these events all the world's media meet and the opportunity for free publicity is great. If an artist/band is nominated for an award then more attention is granted and sales are generated. Some major awards are:

■ Brit Awards UK (early February)
■ Grammy Awards USA (late February)
■ Mercury Awards UK (September)

Sales Effect of the BRIT Awards

The 2001 Brit Awards show (sponsored by Mastercard) was broadcast on 27 February. The TV audience for the show measured at 8.62m with a 32% audience share, with 61% of those watching being aged 16–34.

The effect on album sales for performers, award winners and some nominees was extraordinary. For example, U2 album sales rose by 178% in the two weeks following the show. Sales of 'Parachutes' by Coldplay increased by more than 130%. Sonique, Craig David and David Gray all recorded sales increases of over 75% on average, award winners' albums increased sales by 47%, whilst those of performers rose by 56%.

Source: bpi.org.uk

Study these profiles of two different music magazines. They appear in BRAD (British Rates for Advertising Data). The data about editorial profile and target readership is presenting the magazines' view of themselves. What current artists/bands do you think each would cover?

1. Mojo
Est: 1993
Publisher: Emap
Frequency: Monthly
Price: single copy £3.50
Editorial profile: Monthly specialist music title. In-depth coverage of legendary musicians past and present.
Regular features: Music (blues, classical, country, general, jazz).
Circulation: 96,837 (1 July–31 December 2001)
Adult readership: 207,000 (2.1 readers per copy)
    Female readership: 57,000
    Male readership: 150,000
Target Readership: 25 to 44 year old ABC men with a core of 30 to 40 year olds. Upmarket, urban, stylish and passionate about music.

2. Smash Hits
Est: 1978
Publisher: Emap
Frequency: Fortnightly
Price: single copy £1.90
Editorial profile: All the latest news and gossip from the world of pop.
Regular features: Music, general style & fashion, entertainment, cinema and film technology.
Circulation: 200,212 (1 July–31 December 2001)
Readership: 769,000 (2.7 readers per copy)
    Female readership: 544,000
    Male readership: 226,000
Target readership: 11 to 15 year old girls.

Mojo – *projecting the artist's image*
Source: © *Mojo*/Alpha Pictures

Smash Hits: *the front cover of a popular magazine is great free publicity*
Source: Smash Hits/Emap Performance

Music sales

Hit singles at Christmas

In a typical year top chart singles can sell between 60–100,000 copies. At Christmas, the figures can be ten times as much as this.

Over Christmas 1996, The Spice Girls' '2 Become 1' single sold 495,000 copies. Yet the January 1997 hit, 'White Town' by Jyoti Mishira, sold only 26,000 copies to achieve top of the chart status. Over Christmas 1984, Band Aid sold 800,000 copies of 'Do they Know it's Christmas'.

The Christmas market is the most difficult of all. According to Selina Webb, editor of *Music Week*:

'Normally, a record company would send out a club mix a few weeks before release, and get radio plays, and have a good idea of how a record would do. But not even the most confident of companies would dare predict what will go to the top at Christmas. People who buy records now don't do so at other times of the year'.
Source: *Music Week*, 22 November 1997

Techniques for chart topping success at Christmas:

1 Release the single on the Monday before the final Christmas chart, as the first week of sales is all important.
2 Find a link with a worthy cause, or a television programme like *EastEnders*, or a band with a huge fan base, like the Spice Girls.

Fig 6.7   V2: Website

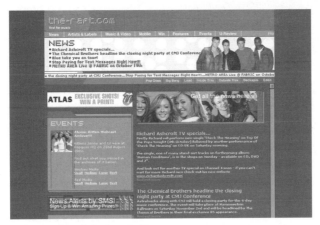

Fig 6.8   The Raft: independent label website

3 Make sure Woolworths is targeted as they are the biggest base for family shoppers.

4 Provide incentives to retailers to sell more copies:

▪ Give aways (for example, ten free copies for each one sold).

▪ Sell 30 copies and get three albums free.

▪ Lower price.

Some of these practices are on the edge of legality. It is important to remember that record companies are *not* allowed to do the following:

1 Supply dealers with records by another artist free of charge or upon specially favourable terms.

2 Cause records to be bought as anything other than genuine consumer purchases.

3 Interfere with sales recording equipment.

4 Offer money or other benefit(s) to a dealer.

5 Use a non-related or excessive gift to encourage record sales.

The number of records sold in the first week will determine its popularity and the sales figures after that week.

Synergy

Celine Dion's single, 'My Heart Will Go On' was reputed to have sold over 1 million records worldwide. The printed music sold over 200,000 copies. As the song is the main soundtrack theme for the film *Titanic* (1997), the music has had a massive public promotion. This cross-media form of advertising is called 'synergy'. Another example of synergy was when the film *Philadephia* (1993) boosted sales of the hit single of the same name, by Bruce Springsteen.

The official UK singles chart

The Chart Information Network (CIN) compiles the main singles chart used by the BBC, *Music Week*, and others. CIN uses sales returns sent electronically from more than 4,500 shops, including specialist chains such as HMV and Virgin. There are also more general shops such as Woolworths and WH Smith and supermarkets such as Asda and Tesco who contribute figures. Independent outlets such as Tower Records and Andy also make up 1,300 of the contributing shops. Each week a sample is taken from 80% of these shops and weighed to 100%, based upon criteria including store turnover.

The electronic process for producing the singles chart:

1 Two types of computer at the cash desk collect sales data: Epson and Electronic Point of Sale (Epos) units. The Epson terminals are used less, since they require a sale to be recorded separately from the cash transaction and so can distort true sales figures. With Epos, money must change hands for a sale to be recorded. With both systems, barcodes are recorded and any sales data stored electronically.

2 Each night from 11.00pm to 4.00am a central national computer telephones each shop, allowing data to be downloaded automatically.

3 Security checks are carried out to identify any sales cheating.

4 Chart positions are announced every Sunday at 1.30pm. Each title is awarded a final sales position, based on total sales and calculated by computer. The BBC has first broadcasting rights and the UK Top 40 is played on Radio 1. This is just 18 hours after the last sale has been logged.

Singles to albums to profit

The expense of promoting a single to become a hit is a largely offset by enticing the audience to buy the artist's album, which is where the real money is made.

Press releases

A press release should be designed to fit onto one side of A4 paper so that it can be faxed and easily read. Typically, press releases include the following:

▌ Logos and addresses of the production label and the distribution company.

▌ Introductory paragraph stating the main news, for example, 'On release in two weekends' time, the new single from D'siree is destined to become the chart hit ...'. A single sentence outlining the song's themes and qualities may be introduced at this point.

▌ The second paragraph will probably be shorter and provide more information about the cast, the USP or the artist's previous history of performing or songwriting records.

▌ The third paragraph will talk about other aspects of the single, such as the production team, other musicians and the technical crew.

*Fig 6.9   CD cover artwork, Silver X, by
Nansi Mellor: original photograph
of fictional artists duo, combined
with computer graphics*

▌ The fourth and final paragraph will enthuse about the single's qualities and invite the press to obtain further information about concerts or a video. A quote from the producer, a reviewer or another authoritative voice will also liven up the text.

▌ A contact name, fax and/or telephone number and E-mail number are also essential.

Unique Selling Point (USP)

The unique selling point of an artist describes most important feature of a single's promotion.

USP: possible selling points

1 It could be the sexiness of the boy or girl band, in which case the looks of the band would be featured most prominently.

2 It could be how loud the music is, so the band would be featured playing their instruments very loudly, with very specific straplines to accompany the image.

3 It could be the rebelliousness of the artist.

4 It could be the mysterious, romantic nature of the songwriting, therefore the images of the artist or landscapes would be in soft focus.

ACTIVITY 6

Discuss
You are a photographer and you have to convey the USP given to you in your brief, by the agent for the artist or band. How will you compose, light and background your shots?

Promotional campaign

Plan a promotion campaign to support one of the following artists or bands for the Christmas Number One spot in the charts. Choose from:

1 A new, manufactured two boy and two girl band – one asian, one afro-caribbean, one white and one Kurd.

2 A French indie drum 'n' bass band playing 'Jingle Bells' in French.

3 An *EastEnders* star's debut song.

4 Linton Kwezi Johnson singing 'I Love my Turkey (Don't Eat Him)'.

5 Your choice.

Read the relevant sections of this chapter and study the information to decide what is the best plan for your campaign.
Note: You will have to create song titles, some words and names for your artists.

TASKS

Task 1
Outline your step-by-step campaign to reach the Number One *Top of the Pops* spot at Christmas.
(20 marks)

Task 2
In your campaign, list the unique selling points of your artist.
(5 marks)

Task 3
In two columns, list possible weaknesses and strengths of the artist or the campaign.
(10 marks)

Task 4
Produce a press release to send to press, television and publicity agents.
(15 marks)

Extension Tasks

1 **Analyse** two or three videos by a manufactured artist or band who is concerned with their star appeal. Consider:

a Star performance.
b How the lyrics link to the images.
c How the music links to images, camerawork or editing speed, and rhythm.
d What is your verdict on the effectiveness of the video? Explain your reasons.
Compare these videos with an artist or band which does seem to be manufactured. Use the same questions as before.

2 **Produce** packaging for a band of your own invention. Choose following formats:

  ▮ A CD cover, back and front.
  ▮ Featured on the cover of a magazine (include straplines, etc.).
You will need to create an image to sell the music. What kind of signifiers can you use for

this? You will need to take a photograph and find people to appear in it. Draw a sketch first. Include details of your artist or band's facial expression(s), gesture(s), body posture and dress. Include also a background, a foreground and props. Take photographs, scan the images into a computer and add text and graphics.

3 **Produce** a press release for the band to coincide with a new song release or tour. Write a commentary of 300 to 500 words explaining your intentions behind the main messages, the unique selling point, and the audience and institutions (invented).

4 **Analyse** the lyrics of a band or artist, with a view to its suitability for a video in which the artist does not appear. Turn the lyrics into a storyboard, showing where lyrics match the images and sound. Write a commentary on how you would expect the images to convey the artist's ideas and sell the product at the same time. Imagine that the video might appear on MTV.

5 **Produce** a one minute radio jingle for an evening dedicated to one music genre, for example, hip-hop, jungle or soul. Use excerpts from songs, mix with a voiceover, interviews and comments to promote this unique evening. Select an appropriate radio channel and identify the audience. Write a commentary on the intentions, audience, sponsors and institutions involved.

 Examination Skills

Knowledge and Understanding

In essay questions about the music industry, it is useful to have a working knowledge of majors and independents. Be aware of how they are organised, of their promotion campaigns and their relationship to other media, for example videos. There should be emphasis on the idea of an image as the heart of the construction of the mainstream and independent band – the unique selling point. Focus also on the different ends of the music business – mainstream as products for businesses, and music with fun or messages attached for the independent end of the spectrum.

Textual Analysis

You will have to be able to analyse how meaning is constructed in images of bands and associated ideas that carry the band's style and attitude (CD covers, videos, press releases, posters). Videos convey ideas about lyrics, stars, and band's performances. Distinguish between the various types of videos, for example, band performs; band plays a part in the narrative of the video; band does not appear and the video is an abstract visual interpretation of the lyrics. Commentaries on practical work should show an ability to stand back from the process and analyse images in terms of signifiers and meaning. This can be difficult if the band is completely the work of the student's imagination, but the aim is to explain how the content of the images convey meanings via association or suggestion.

For example, an analysis of a magazine cover might be:

The solo artist is wearing glasses and clothes which connect them to a street level of credibility. The hip-hop genre of music is associated with rapping words and beat-based music. The artist is photographed against the wall, suggesting the idea of the street-based sounds. The gesture of their foot raised in the air indicates a level of street 'cool' and savvy. It is possible to see this gesture as mixing the idea of kung fu arts and dance. The closeness of the foot in the foreground gives depth and drama to the image as the viewer's eye is drawn back into the picture past the lettering.

Practical Work

Production of images for CD or magazine front covers require an understanding of the following: typical forms and conventions, use of graphics and layout to improve the image and the style; use of cropping, composition using foreground and background, signifiers of expression, body posture and gesture and props as signifiers. Awareness of the difference between manufactured bands and independent bands is also important. How audience (positioning of images) and institutions (label, studio and distributors) are built into the identity of the product is a further area to study. Radio jingles use excerpts from songs and mix with voiceover, interviews and plugs for purchase of records. Skill in combining these elements effectively should be evident.

7 Film industry and promotion
May the force be with you!

What you will learn

In this chapter you will study how films are started, made, promoted and sold. How are films developed through the production process before, during and after filming? Who are the main people involved in making a film successful? Who decides certificate ratings for a film? How are other media products used to brand and promote the film in the market?

KEY WORDS

- genre
- *mise-en-scène*
- narrative
- enigma
- major
- independent
- Art House
- distributor
- exhibitor
- promotion
- marketing
- advertising

TECHNICAL WORDS

- Electronic Press Kit (EPK)
- trailer
- poster
- credit block
- tag (or catch) line
- teaser
- unique selling point (USP)
- press release
- below the line and above the line costs

Review

Reread the sections on film languages in Chapter Two: Languages and Categories to review the terms 'film genre' and 'narrative'. These terms also relate to the way a film is promoted and what audiences expect of a film.

What is the film industry?
Film is a business

All of the films in both the Top 10 lists, with the exception of *The Castle* (Australian), were produced by American companies. The film industry is dominated by Hollywood business. Its main aim is to make money. Hollywood studios employ people with skills in finance, technology, creative arts and science, and America has become the world's most successful country in selling its films at home and abroad. Some films are made by independent companies and if they enter into the mainstream cinemas, they are often helped by major distributors.

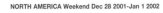

UK/IRELAND Three-day weekend Dec 28–30

Rank	Film/Origin/Distributor	Week	Three-day gross £	Sites
1	The Lord Of The Rings: The Fellowship ... (NZ-US) Entertainment	2	£7,047,220	470
2	Harry Potter And The Philosopher's Stone (UK-US) Warner Bros	7	£2,456,876	535
3	Mean Machine (UK) DIP †	NEW	£1,043,300	313
4	The Princess Diaries (US) BVI	2	£821,923	396
5	Serendipity (US) BVI †	NEW	£461,443	237
6	The 51st State (Can-UK) Momentum Pictures	4	£310,408	241
7	Kabhi Khushi Kabhie Gham (Ind) Yash Raj Films	3	£270,708	35
8	The Others (Sp-US) BVI	9	£201,774	212
9	Christmas Carol: The Movie (UK) Patno	4	£146,576	292
10	Spy Game (US) Entertainment	8	£45,537	41

NORTH AMERICA Weekend Dec 28 2001-Jan 1 2002

Rank	Film (Country of origin Distributor	Week	Theatres	Five-day total $ Dec 28-Jan 1
1	The Lord Of The Rings: The Fellowship ... (NZ US) Now Lino	2	3,359	$56,952,669
2	Ocean's Eleven (US) Warner Bros	4	3,076	$28,168,774
3	Jimmy Neutron (US) Paramount	2	3,151	$22,294,778
4	ALI (US) Sony Pictures†	1	2,446	$20,025,685
5	Harry Potter ... (UK-US) Warner Bros	7	3,186	$16,938,804
6	Vanilla Sky (US) Paramount	3	2,744	$16,362,471
7	Kate & Leopold (US) Miramax†	1	2,452	$14,534,736
8	A Beautiful Mind (US) Universal	2	525	$12,628,870
9	Monsters, Inc (US) Buena Vista	9	1,701	$9,445,443
10	The Majestic (US) Warner Bros	2	2,361	$8,787,653

Fig 7.1

Source: Screen International

ACTIVITY 1

Study the following list of the Top 10 films in the UK and the USA.

1. Which of these films have you seen and why did you, or did you not, go to see them?
2. For which of these films did you see the publicity or merchandise?
3. Judging by the titles of the films, identify the genre of each one.
4. What age group (audience) do you think went to see the first five films in the US Top 10 list?
5. Compare the top box office British ratings with the US box office ratings. Why do you think there is such a difference?

The cycle of production

The life of a film's creative production can be divided into three main stages:

- **Pre-production** is the period when the film is conceived, written into a treatment and screenplay, and when the financial investment, director, cast, technicians, props and locations are planned and found.
- **Production** is the filming process itself.
- **Post production** is the editing process, where sound and image, special effects and titles are added.

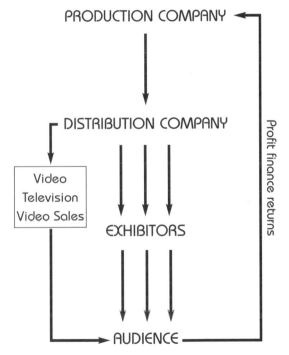

Fig 7.2   Diagram showing the cycle of production

The cycle of money

The total life of a film is much longer than the production process alone. It involves the machinery of an industry that is designed to make money:

- **Pre-production sales** covers the financial investment that is often raised by the sales department, offering the film package to distributors and exhibitors even before the film is made.
- **Production** is the process of writing and making the film itself.
- **Distribution** is the selling, publicising, marketing and print replication.
- **Exhibition** is when the film is seen by the public in cinema theatres.
- **'Sell-through' and TV transmission rights** is a subsequent stage of exhibition and distribution of the film through video hire, video sales, television broadcasting and, for example, aeroplane.

Film making

The pitch of the idea

To make a film you need money. If a producer already has enough money or is an established big name in the industry, then they can go ahead with production. They may however, use an independent production company to actually shoot the film. If the producer is actually an independent company, they will need to convince banks, investors or distributors to lend them money.

Almost inevitably a production team will pitch their creative idea to several potential investors. This means presenting ideas clearly and enthusiastically both verbally and on paper. The hopeful film makers deliver an explanation of their film ideas as sharply and clearly as they can to producers and sponsors.

A good example of a dramatic pitch occurs in a scene in the film *The Player* (1992), a film about Hollywood by Robert Altman. An English scriptwriter, played by Richard E. Grant, approaches Tim Robbins who plays Griffin, the producer, in a chance meeting beside a pool in a Los Angeles hotel.

Imagine the first scene, outside a US penitentiary. It is during the night and there is a demonstration calling for the electrocution of a 19-year-old black man who is on death row. He is guilty. There is a candlelight vigil; the lights twinkle like Japanese lanterns in the rain. It is silent as a black limousine glides up outside the gates and out gets the District Attorney, who is greeted by the prison director's wife. They shake hands and they go in through the gates.

This is the beginning of the pitch for a whole film; it is visual and it is dramatic. To succeed in pitching a film in real life, you will probably have to tell your story hundreds of times. You need to be very persistent, patient and energetic. You also need to 'sell' your idea to the people who will make copies of your film and send it the cinemas and distributors. These people will need to be confident that they can pass your film on to the exhibitors, the cinema owners (who want all their seats occupied by the customers) and the audience.

Your film will become what is known as a 'property' and will be made into a 'package'. Like any other product, the Hollywood 'factory' has to be packaged and presented in order to reach the widest markets. The film script may attract stars, directors, musicians and special effects companies. They will become part of the whole 'package' that the public will see in the publicity before and during the film's cinema release.

Ideas for a film

Firstly, you have to decide what genre of film you want to make. You must have clear ideas about the *mise-en-scène*, narrative and character. It is also important to outline the setting in as much detail as possible.

Mise-en-scène

Mise-en-scène is the placing into the setting of all the elements to be filmed: props, lighting, character behaviour, make-up, sets and anything else that is in the frame of the camera lens at the time of filming. For instance, one might expect the *mise-en-scène* of an adaptation of Charles Dickens' novel *Great Expectations* to include authentic period costume and Victorian buildings, gas lamps and horse-drawn carriages. A typical Dracula horror film might include graveyards, mists, moonlight and lightening-filled night skies.

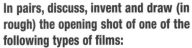

ACTIVITY 2

A more recent film version of *Great Expectations* (1998) had a modern setting, and starred Ethan Hawke, Gwyneth Paltrow, Anne Bancroft and Robert De Niro. The contemporary settings included New York and Florida.

Discuss in pairs: why do you think the setting has been updated to American and modern times?

Setting and genre

Setting is the major element in establishing what the genre of a film is. It would be confusing to set a science fiction film in the wild west of nineteenth century America. Or would it? *Back to the Future Part 3* did exactly that, with time travel. Science fantasy movies can 'travel' across historical periods.

ACTIVITY 3

In pairs, discuss, invent and draw (in rough) the opening shot of one of the following types of films:

a American high school comedy (indicate the type of comedy (for example, slapstick, screwball, farce).

b Agatha Christie murder mystery (indicate the 1930s period).

c Science fiction horror (note: this is a horror film, not a monster movie, like *Godzilla*. What is the difference between a thriller and a horror film?).

You can use one shot only but you may have to draw more than one frame. This could involve a moving camera, zooming or tracking, panning or tilting (see Chapter Two for explanation of camera terms). Explain all the visual elements of the *mise-en-scène*, including the music, sounds or special effects. What signifies an American setting, a thirties period drama or a horror?

Present your opening shot to the rest of the class. Try to also outline the rest of the film's narrative. This will take the form of a pitch: who will buy your idea and is it convincing? Does your class audience think it conveys the genre you chose successfully?

Film marketing

Having successfully persuaded a sponsor to accept your idea, the complete script must be written. This can sometimes take between two and ten years. Before filming can start, the script is used to attract stars and directors to work on it. The script is also used to sell the film to potential distributors, exhibitors and buyers. Marketing a film always starts early on in the process.

Selling the film

It would seem logical to suggest that a film must be made before it can be sold. In fact, many films are sold before they are made. A film production company has to find money to pay the actors and actresses, the camera crew, hire the costumes and locations and pay the director and lab. technicians.

If it is not a big company with financial reserves, it can borrow the money from a financier or alternatively can promise a share of the profits to the distributors or the exhibitors. A distributor such as Miramax will see the opportunity to invest in a film that they like the sound of. They will provide money to the production company

in advance on the basis that they can share any of the profits or have exclusive rights to its distribution. Direct support can be provided in the form of promoting the film, as well as distributing and exhibiting the film.

Marketing campaign

If a film maker is successful in obtaining money, a studio to produce it, a distributor and exhibition outlets, then it will still need to promote the film. A promotion campaign aims to persuade the audience to go and see it. Without this campaign a film maker cannot compete with all the other hundreds of films also trying to reach the audience. Films live or die according to the success of their promotional campaigns.

Once the film is almost finished the marketing campaign swings into action. Marketing a film falls into two categories: advertising and publicity. Advertising is paid for, and consists

Fig 7.3   Nestlé promoting Monster's Inc: *tie-ins and cross business merchandising*

Source: © *The Guardian*/Graham Turner

of press, TV and radio advertising, in addition to posters and trailers.

Publicity is not paid for directly, although it is created by the publicity department and includes reviews, articles and interviews in the media, plus special gala screenings.

Promotions

What does a typical promotional campaign consist of?

▌ Teasers
▌ Posters and radio
▌ Trade press screening
▌ TV and video trailers
▌ Merchandising
▌ Tie-ins
▌ Special events – galas and stunts

There are several media products that are used to promote a film: Electronic Press Kits (EPK), trailers, advertisements, news publicity and advertising merchandise such as T-shirts, games and toys.

Following is a typical promotional campaign for a summer blockbuster (a Hollywood action film with a major star). As an example, this schedule is based on a film released on 1 August, during children's summer holidays.

Further publicity is continued during the screening of the film around the UK (August to September).

Discuss

Discuss and write an explanation of the impact each of the strategies in Figure 7.4 has on the publicity for the film (see example given for trade press screening).

Teaser trailers in cinema	November
Teaser posters in cinema	November
Teaser posters in cinema	February
Trade press exhibitor screening (alerts exhibitors to content of film)	February
New trailers in cinema	March
Cardboard cut out 'standees'	March
Publish book of the film	March
Banners for foyers	April
Release single of the film	May
New trailers	May
Actors and actresses, director start to appear on TV and radio chat shows	June–August
Press invited to preview film	July
Billboards	July
Television teaser trailers	July
Press advertisements	July
Photographs of filming, specially selected for certain media papers and magazines	July
Gala evening in London's West End to premiere the film, plus stars and celebrities	July
General release	August

Fig 7.4   Typical promotional campaign and strategies

Tie-ins

Tie-ins are related products that are often connected to characters or figures in films, such as *Star Wars* toys or *Men In Black* guns. Many non-film companies like to join the film's publicity trails to sell specifically tailored products. For example, *The Lost World: Jurassic Park* (1997) tie-ins were:

- Marks and Spencer – in the form of clothes and food, for example, dinosaur products such as chocolate, crisps and cakes, steaks and gums.
- Burger King carried the logo of the film on their trays and bags.
- Kellogs, KP and Tetley also produced related pack promotions.
- Toys were produced by Hasbro.
- The novel of the film by Michael Crichton had already been published by Random House and a movie tie-in version was published by Arrow Books Ltd.
- Music soundtrack by John Williams was also sold on CD.
- The making of the movie books.
- Junior versions in the form of board games, comic books, or video games.

Cross media links

Films today, especially those from Hollywood, attract a great deal of attention because they are extremely well publicised through trailers and posters. The marketing and promotion departments of film companies produce a plentiful supply of images and extracts of the films, before they are released, so that they can be endlessly seen and talked about across television, newspapers, radio, videos and magazines. This type of promotion also includes trailers and posters in the cinema itself. Films are often linked to other media, for example, when *Titanic* was first released in 1997, the music soundtrack single by Celine Dion went straight to the top of the UK music industry charts.

Teasers

The teaser campaign is usually a poster or a trailer which comes out before the film is released and which states: 'Coming soon' or 'at your local cinema' on a particular date. The information is very basic and tells you little about the film itself. It is designed to whet your appetite and tease you into thinking, 'I wonder what this film is about?' The teaser for *Independence Day* (1996) involved using the initials ID4, which created a sense of mystery. Independence Day itself falls on 4 July, when America celebrates its anniversary of political independence. Hence the date was used in much of the teaser campaign to convey the desired message.

The teaser campaign for the independently produced *Trainspotting* (1996) involved pictures of the main characters on posters placed around the London underground and bus shelters, with only their name and a little orange block of colour – the plot of the film was never given away but the word of mouth campaign which went with the film made it into a cult movie upon release. The soundtrack of contemporary Brit-Pop music was another selling point.

Press release

A press release is a news summary about an event or a new launch. In the film industry, a press release is often included as part of the Electronic Press Kit (EPK). This pack includes photographs (stills) of the film as it was being made, stills from the final film, trailer clips of the film, cast and credit lists and a press release.

Press releases are aimed at film review journalists and cinema owners who need information in order to write about the films or to show them. A press release ideally comes with a video or CD of the film that gives the reviewer plenty of information with which to write about or to hire the film.

Marketing an independent film

Celia is an Australian film made in 1989, which is about the psychological development of a young girl (Rebecca Smart) who suffers a number of traumatic experiences that lead to a fatal killing. The UK film poster suggested it might be a horror film, using the shadow of a creature's claws cast on the background.

The film was shown in independent cinemas, often known as Art House cinemas, and was popular with those people who went to see it. However its poster publicity did not give a true sense of the psychological drama of the film; it certainly was not a horror film, even though the poster gave that impression. The marketing agent promoting *Celia* confessed to finding it difficult to market this complex though gripping film.

One main reason why independent films do not become box office successes so frequently is because they are not aiming to appeal to everyone. The second reason is that they are competing with the massive marketing and publicity machine of the Hollywood industry. They are competing with the 'blockbuster', the film that will fill all the seats in all the main cinemas in America in its first and second weekends of screening.

Compare the low impact of *Brassed Off* (1996) with the phenomenal success world wide of *The Full Monty* (1997). Although *The Full Monty* was not intended to be a blockbuster, it was supported by Twentieth Century Searchlight as its distributor, thus making its American release much more assured. Both films were about the effects of unemployment and the attempts to salvage some respect in the face of indignity.

Posters

There are three types of film poster:

1 The teaser poster – this poster contains basic information to whet the appetite of the film audience. It may not indicate much about the plot.
2 The main poster – this contains the main information about the production personnel and distributors.

Fig 7.5   *Men in Black* promotional poster
Source: © BFI

3 The poster with the short, one line reviews, often to accompany the video release.

ACTIVITY 4

Discuss
What are the typical elements of a film's main poster? How many elements can you can think of? Discuss information, images and layout.

Key elements of a poster:

▌ Images of the key settings and the main characters are usually incorporated into the film poster. They are literally blended without concern for real perspective or size relationships between people and setting.

▌ Most posters are horizontal or landscape in shape, however, if they go onto a bus shelter or magazine page they are vertical or portrait in shape.

▌ The catch or tag line indicates the action,

genre or attitude within the film. For example, 'Protecting the earth from the scum of the universe' was the tag line for *Men in Black*. 'A chilling, bold, mesmerising, futuristic detective thriller' was the tag line for *Blade Runner* (1982)

■ The title – typeface and graphics indicate the style.

■ The billing block includes credits and information. The credit block gives details of the main people in the cast, making and distribution of the film.

■ Certificate – for example, PG, 12, 15 18.

Poster analysis

Compare posters from two films *Chorni* and *Romeo and Juliet*.

Fig 7.6   William Shakespeare's Romeo and Juliet *poster*

Source: © BFI

TASK 1

a   Denotate and connotate the two posters in Figures 7.6 and 7.7 (see Chapter Two).

(10 marks)

b   Which poster do you think is more effective and interestingly designed? Explain your answers.

(5 marks)

c   What *mise-en-scènes* are suggested in these posters?

(10 marks)

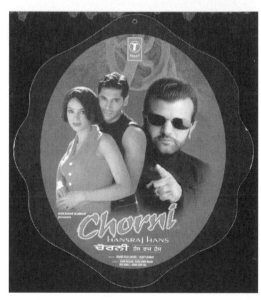

Fig 7.7   Chorni *poster*

TASK 2

What type of personalities are illustrated by the images of the characters in each poster?

(5 marks)

TASK 3

What would you say the posters' makers wanted to emphasise as the unique selling point (USP) in each poster? For example, is it the plot, the themes, the setting or the characters?

(10 marks)

TASK 4

Why do you think the posters might make audiences want to go and see these films?

(10 marks)

Film people

Stars

Actors and actresses are turned into celebrities; their faces and fame are often used to sell a film. Will Smith, Leonardo DiCaprio, Kate Winslet, Julia Roberts and Cameron Diaz are some good examples. Films often command massive budgets and films like *Titanic* can recoup enormous profits when helped by big stars' names and images.

Fig 7.8   *Will Smith: stars can make a movie a success*
Source: Associated Press

Budgeting for stars

There is also the issue of how many stars, if any, will feature in a movie, and who will be selected, according to the budget. Hollywood actors and actresses are given 'star ratings' by film magazines such as *Variety, Entertainment Weekly, Hollywood Reporter* and *Premiere*. These ratings can help film makers assess which stars they can afford to hire, and are divided into 'A*', 'A' and 'B' lists according to:

- Current salary
- Previous film successes
- Loyal audience following
- Behaviour on set
- Oscar winning capability

The lists which follow have been compiled from a number of sources (for example, *Variety, Hollywood Reporter* and *Premiere*) and are rated by audience popular choice. It should be noted that the composite list is the work of the author's and is not intended as a definitive or an objective statement of status or bankability.

'A*' list

Guaranteed foreign sale, regardless of the other elements the film contains. Examples include:

Tom Cruise	Harrison Ford
Mel Gibson	Tom Hanks
Brad Pitt	Jim Carrey
John Travolta	Julia Roberts
Russell Crowe	George Clooney

'A' list

Could be hired if the director and budget are right:

Michael Douglas	Drew Barrymore
Samuel L. Jackson	Jack Nicholson
Cameron Diaz	Jodie Foster
Tim Robbins	Gwyneth Paltrow

'B' list

Other factors in the production may prove to be more important.

Matt Damon	Gene Hackman
Kim Basinger	Michael Keaton
Liam Neeson	Wesley Snipes
Sigourney Weaver	

Fig 7.10   Gwyneth Paltrow

Fig 7.10   Tom Cruise

Fig 7.11   Samuel L. Jackson

Money matters

Average A* actors receive around $15 to 20 million for their roles in films. Therefore, it is possible that a quarter of a $100 million film budget could be spent on one star. A report in 1998 stated that 'A'-list actresses finally seem to be catching up with their male counterparts. Julia Roberts' salary for her role opposite Richard Gere in Paramount's *The Runaway Bride* (1999) was reported to have been more than $20 million. Jodie Foster reportedly received more than $15 million for Twentieth Century Fox 2000's *Anna and the King* (1999).

Directors

Even director's names can sell genres, such as John Carpenter and horror, Steven Spielberg and fantasy and historical drama, Quentin Tarantino and crime. Once a film has become successful, like Spielberg's *ET* (1982), then a studio can use its success and name to aid the promotion of another film. Of course, if a studio becomes as successful as Steven Spielberg, it can then afford to form its own production company. However, even Spielberg's production company has worked with a major studio, Paramount, to ensure greater distribution of films. The $80 million cost of *Deep Impact* (1998) was shared by the two companies and had to make $140 million to produce profits.

Biggest audience

The successful promotion of a Hollywood film depends on making it attractive for the audience to want to go and see it. It is important for the film to be easily categorised to reach the widest potential and global markets. If an audience can easily identify a film's genre, stars or its directors, then it will be more assured about what it is going to watch. The audience will be then more likely to risk spending money to go and see it.

Distributors

Distributors have to produce many copies of films to reach the widest possible audience, and they must reach the audience very quickly in first run theatres, usually in urban centres. The first weekend is crucial in gaining public interest and allowing word of mouth to promote the film.

How do distributors and audiences identify a film genre?

Posters, trailers on television or video hire copies, and cinemas are the main places where films are promoted. Labelling posters with words 'the ultimate horror spoof' is one way of telling the audience what genre they can expect to see. Films with easily recognisable genre categories such as science fiction, crime, westerns and musicals make it easier for the public to define what they are watching and whether or not to go to the cinema.

ACTIVITY 5

Study the list of distributors below. How many do you recognise? Can you name any four films that they have distributed? Where would you find out information on the distributors of a film?

1. Universal International Pictures (UIP)
2. Buena Vista
3. Twentieth Century Fox
4. Warner Bros.
5. Columbia Tri-Star
6. Entertainment
7. Polygram
8. Guild
9 Film Four
10 Rank
11. First Independent
12. Artificial Eye
13. Electric

Unique selling point

The unique selling point (USP) is the key element of the film which the promotions department want to push. It could be the stars, the special effects, the unusual storyline, or any combination of these elements. The USP is often fairly obvious, as it is stated in the slogan, the tag line or the voice-over commentary on a trailer.

ACTIVITY 6

Discuss
What is the USP of a film promotion you have seen recently?

Cinema

In the early period of cinema between the late 1890s and early 1900s, the idea of setting up a special building as a cinema didn't catch on for a while, until it became profitable. When it did, the Americans were the fastest and most effective at making money from it. Although the French had perhaps done the most to take the leading role in developing technical inventions (the travelling shows of the Lumière Brothers toured and amazed citizens of the major cities of the world), the Americans were the first to really turn the whole process into a business.

The early days

Cinema as a real presence on high streets began when the first new buildings made for screening were erected. In Britain there were cinemas around in the early 1900s and by the 1920s, lavish and grand theme-based cinemas were constructed in America, often adding to the glamour and attention paid to the moving pictures, their stars and studios.

By the 1930s Hollywood had managed to establish itself as the major global economic force in the film industry. It had the advantage of great financial support from East Coast American bankers, and plentiful sunlight on the west coast of America to film all day in any season. Hollywood also attracted a high number of creative artists, actors and actresses, writers and production crew who were interested in making a serious living from films. Film was not only the new twentieth century art form, but was now big business.

In the 1890s and early twentieth century, films were very short and several films of different kinds might be shown in the same viewing. There were two reasons for this. Previously, in Europe, music hall entertainment consisted of several performers, such as comedians, trapeze artists and dancers each of whom would do a short act before the next performer. The second reason was that initially films only held a novelty value and simple dramas or scenes from real life were shown to introduce the newcomer to moving pictures.

The rise of the multiplex

By the sixties, cinema going fell into decline due to factors such as the advent of television. However, by the 1980s numbers visiting cinemas began to rise, as people sought new places to spend their leisure time.

Today, cinema goers can see mainstream films at multiplexes, where several films are shown in different cinemas throughout the building. The costs of keeping the building running are paid for by showing several of the most well publicised films for as long as they remain popular. As many as 500 prints are produced for the first screenings in the USA; as opposed to perhaps only 250 for the most popular films in the UK.

Where and how you view films is today more varied. Video hire and sale are both relatively new formats and can be watched at home. Films are shown on television, cable and satellite; it is possible to see films on aeroplanes, in pubs and private clubs films. New technology such as Digital Versatile Disc (DVD) also extend the range of domestic formats now available.

Certification

Films have to be submitted to the British Board of Film Certification (BBFC). This is a service that the film industry has created for its own members, for classification into U, PG, 12, 15 and 18 categories. This means that audiences can be assured of the type of material they can expect to see. Certification can also give street credibility to a film, and if the film gains an 18 certificate the distributors can entice the older teenager to watch it, in the knowledge that violence, sex or bad language may be included. Distributors' main target audience is the age group of 15 to 18 years, and if this audience can be reached then the chances of a box office success will be more likely. The widest possible audience is for a PG rated film.

Case Study 1: Comedy Fiction

Fig 7.12   Police Academy

ACTIVITY 7

Discuss and write notes on the following questions

1. What films do you think are funny?
2. What can you remember that was funny about the films you saw?
3. In comedy films, outline the ingredients of a typical:
   a plot
   b central comic character or set of characters
   c setting
4. Which film comedians do you find the most funny?

As with all genres there are different types of comedy films: ranging from **slapstick,** to **farce** to **screwball** to **satire** and **parody**. Sometimes these different types are created because we, as audiences, have different tastes, often age-related. Whereas a situation drama like *American Pie 1* (1999) and *2* (2001) might be more popular with teenage audiences, a sci-fi, spoof crime thriller film like *Men in Black* (1997) might also appeal to an older audience.

Before film was invented people went to the local theatre or musical hall to hear comedians stand up and tell jokes, or to mimic other people, or, in pantomimes, chase each other round the stage and bump into each other, fall over or hide where the audience could see them but the other person on stage could not. Television today has replaced the theatre as the main place where we can hear stand up comedians or watch variety acts performing mime or even conjuring tricks.

Slapstick

A **slap stick** was a goat's bladder on a stick which one entertainer would use to hit another one – this would make a slapping sound, and the hit person would then fall over, clown-like, in mock surprise.

When films started in the 1890s it was not possible to record sound onto film, so initially, comedy films were primarily visual with no speaking, puns or rude jokes or silly noises. Many of the early filmmakers enjoyed capturing simple shots of people making silly faces contorting the nose, eyes and mouth and even wriggling ears to show off the versality and eccentricities of the human face. Many of these films were very short, often less than a minute long and not usually longer than 10 minutes.

Special effects

Special effects were basic but essential part of the fun. For example in *The House that Jack Built* (1900) a pile of bricks is made to fall down and then, in rewind, build itself up again. It is still true today that comedy films use special effects to fetch a laugh from the audience. Modern films like *The Mask* (1994) or *The Nutty Professor* (1996) depend on special effects to distort the body shape. In cartoons like *Shrek* (2001) or *Antz* (1998), for example, bodies can stretched and put back together to comic effect, without worrying the audience. *Who Killed Roger Rabbit?* (1988) is one of the best examples of mixing animated characters with real dramatised action.

ACTIVITY 8

Research
Select two or three films you think are funny.
Identify and write notes about them under three headings:

a the characters – what makes them funny? why are they funny? Are they ridiculous or silly, clever or idiotic, e.g. Austin Powers' over exaggerated sense of his own sexual prowess?

b the situations – what is it about the situation which makes it funny? Are there typical situations e.g. the cover up, the wrong clothes or words for the occasion, the mix up, the mad caper or scramble to get to the church on time?

c comic acting skills – what is it about the comedy actors that makes you laugh e.g. ability to mime, imitate accents, dress in quirky clothes, make funny faces, flout conventions, get away with outrageous behaviour, tap dance, act the idiot, sing, sense of timing etc?

Situation comedy – farce

As soon as films became longer than a minute and actors such as Charlie Chaplin started making 10 and 20 minute long films, then the need to create a **situation** and a **narrative structure** became apparent. From resembling a stand up act on a stage, comedy films now began to include embarrassing situations, cases of mistaken identity and often exaggerated the friction or silliness between two characters as they clowned around or funny things happened to them, for example, the hose going off accidentally in the face etc.

ACTIVITY 9

Watch one or two Charlie Chaplin, Buster Keaton, Laurel and Hardy, or Mr Bean films. Find a piece of music like Scott Joplin's *Ragtime* to play over the visuals.
Act or work with one or two people and video a mimed piece of acting to the following directions. It helps to read aloud the instructions to help the actors change movement.
Find suitable props: scarf, hat, stick, newspaper, long coats etc.
Play the music while recording the voiceless mime in Chaplinesque style.

Ext:

Asleep lying along the whole of the park bench.
Someone comes to sit down and can't find any space.
They try to wake up the snoring sleeper, by shaking them, then by tickling their nose with a feather/paper, then finally by pushing them along the bench opens a newspaper to read.
The sleeper wakes up somewhat alarmed but still drunk.
The drunkard offers a drink to the newspaper reading sitter who declines.
The drunkard shouts at people going past to join him.
He is then bothered by a wasp and tries to swat it on his neck, his leg and his nose.
Of course, the wasp eventually goes onto the newspaper and the drunk crumples the paper in his eagerness to get rid of it, to the annoyance of the reader.
A police officer comes along and asks the drunk to walk in a straight line. After three goes this is clearly not possible so the police officer finally takes pity on the drunk and offers to take him home. At the house the drunk thanks the police officer profusely and the police officer tells off the drunk. The drunk cannot find his key and then cannot put it in the key hole. He sits down in the doorway and proceeds to sleep.

This has many variations including a romantic theme, more slapstick elements etc.

Edit the music onto the videotrack to erase any spoken elements and play back for assessment of what is required for:

a) the comedy of the situation to be clear
b) the comedian who relies on the body and face for expression.

Speaking pictures

As film making progressed and synchronised, sound was introduced in 1927, then comedy genre introduced dialogue – this changed the possibilities immensely – now the actors could be heard to make jokes, putting on funny voices and speaking with different accents, making word puns, using 'one liner' quips, as well as singing, tap-dancing and playing instruments. Filmed comedy became mixed with musical romances and situation comedy like the Marx Brothers zany farces of improbable antics *Duck Soup* (1933) and *Horse Feathers* (1932). There was still room for classic double acts with highly distinctive visual characters – who were amusingly little and large, for example, Laurel and Hardy. They could still make a whole sequence without speech, although with musical accompaniment, for example, about carrying a piano up hundreds of steps, only to have it slide back down to the bottom again.

Fig 7.13   Laurel and Hardy

Screwball comedy

Screwball comedy was invented as a typically Hollywood sub genre of comedy. *Bringing Up Baby* (1938) involves a self-absorbed professor, Cary Grant, linking up with a wilful millionairess, Kathryn Hepburn, who has a cheetah for a pet. Today, screwball comedy is more associated with an actor like Eddie Murphy, in *The Nutty Professor*, or Jim Carrey, in *Ace Ventura* (1995) – where they do outrageous tricks to get their own way and make the audience laugh in the meantime.

Television personalities

Today, the comedy film is often built around the well known comic, the eccentric comedian, a television star performer who can 'do' funny faces, silly walks, falling over, especially on banana skins, and accidental collisions that continue the stage traditions of all the basic elements of **slapstick comedy**. This formed the basis of what made Charlie Chaplin famous with his distinctive moustache, bowler hat and walking stick.

Fig 7.14   Charlie Chaplin

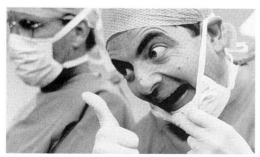

Fig 7.15   Rowan Atkinson as Mr Bean

Mime

Rowan Atkinson, *Mr Bean*, from the UK and Jacques Tati in the fifties and sixties in France would be considered masters of the contorted face and body using **mime** as their main vehicle of humour. Their near speechless dramas revolve around their inability to see or fit in with the reality of the everyday world. Their disregard for conventions is never intentional and they seem lonely and separate from common sense norms.

Parody – spoofs

Today, we have **spoofs** and **parodies** of other films. Films produced by Mel Brooks, like *Blazing Saddles* (1974) send up the Western genre. The white folk in the chain gang sing what is usually a black spiritual, to what is usually a white but is now a black sheriff. *Young Frankenstein* (1974) featuring a wild-eyed Marty Feldman is a spoof of the horror genre. Mike Myers plays the excitable *Austin Powers* in the films with the same title that are a **parody** of the James Bond films and 1960s culture.

Fig 7.16   Mike Myers as Austin Powers

Steve Martin, Whoopi Goldberg and Eddie Murphy, *The Nutty Professor,* are professional comics who also play full feature length comedies with witty one-liners, socially embarassing situations and slapstick knockabout humour. Some comedians like Eddie Murphy and Peter Sellers play many different characters in virtuoso performances so the audience can take pleasure in seeing them in different guises.

Forrest Gump, starring Tom Hanks, is a film about a simple-minded character whose fame precedes his fortune and the success of the film seems to indicate an American audience's sympathy for the underdog – a theme Charlie Chaplin explored endlessly.

Satire

More recently, social satirical films such as *American Beauty* (1999) and serious genre films with comedy elements such as the horror film *Scream* (1996) show that comedy appears in other genres as irony or light relief.

British comedy

British comedy films have ranged from the 1940s and 50s Ealing comedy caper farces set in all girl school, St Trinians, to the robbers who, pretending to be a group of musicians, hide in a small rented accommodation with Alec Guinness in the *Ladykillers* (1955). In more recent British comedy the violence is likely to be more graphic as in the crime comedy *Lock, Stock and Two Smoking Barrels* (1998) where the robbers steal from each other and the police have little role in their comeuppance.

More recently actors have moved from comedy series on television to the world of film like Lenny Henry, Robbie Coltrane and Kathy Burke, Meera Syal, Dawn French and Alison Saunders. Asian directed films such as *Bhaji on the Beach* (1993) and *East is East* (1999) are examples of attempts to make comedy about contemporary multi-ethnic Britain.

Fig 7.17   East is East

Comic animation

There has been an increase in feature length comedy animation films after the success of the Aardman brothers with *The Wrong Trousers* (1993), *Close Shave* (1995) and *Chicken Run* (2000). Popular TV serials, such as *South Park* (1999), have also become cult films. Recent Hollywood animation fairy tale epics have also focused on comedy. The tale of the battle between large and small insects in *Antz* is both comic and epic, and *Shrek* is an upside down fairy tale with an ogre as its hero charged with rescuing the fairy tale characters from the baddie.

Fig 7.18   South Park

Hybrids

Other examples of combinations of comedy with another genre, **hybrids**, are:

Naked Gun (1998) – crime-comedy and *There's Something About Mary* (1998) – horror-comedy

---

ACTIVITY 10

Situation comedy
Select three films which are parodies of other films for example: *Austin Powers* (James Bond), *Scary Movie* (Horror), *Blazing Saddles* (Westerns).
Identify what is funny about them.
Explain which three scenes were the main moments of comedy and why.

1. Outline in less than 200 words a spoof plot and setting of a) a science fiction film or b) a murder mystery film.
2. Identify:
   a) Main characters,
   b) Key comedy situations,
3. Cast the characters using real people, drawn from your knowledge of suitable actors/actresses.

Example of textual analysis (OCR style) of Shrek's opening sequence

For the following activity you will need to obtain a video/DVD of *Shrek* as you will be studying the opening sequence shot by shot.

Fig 7.19   Still from Shrek

Fig 7.20   Still from Shrek

Narrative Image	Narrative Sound	Music lyrics
1. **Close up** of book with final page of story Connotation – the classic cartoon often starts with a shot of the literary source of the story (e.g. *Jungle Book*) to give the opening a sense of being based on a real story, with a storyteller voice to make it like a children's bedtime occasion, albeit it is a fantasy. The music and the images convey a typical fairy tale plot line with princesses in the tower and fire-breathing dragons guarding her from the brave knights. However, this film tries to undermine the cosiness of these cliches by introducing an element of cynicism with the unlikely hero who is not physically attractive but the ultimately endearing Shrek. Shrek's scoffing at the storyline is part of the attempt to be more down to earth and accepting of misfits and imperfect types of character and physical attractiveness.	Mike Myers' (Shrek) voice reading the fairytale book "'… for her true love's first kiss'… Like that's never going to happen [Rustling paper, toilet flushing] What a load of …" Connotation: the idyll of the fairytale storytelling is broken by the sound of a toilet flushing and the abrasiveness of Shrek whose dismissive tone adds a spirit of mischief and down to earthness. Initially, the pastoral music suggests an idyllic peacefulness of harmony and contentment. When the rhythm of the reggae-rap music starts the style and tone turns to contemporary pop and creates a light urban gritty but hopeful mood.	**Pastoral – stringed instruments.**
2. Low angled **medium long shot** of Shrek's outside toilet door + Shrek opening it. Connotation: the film has a number of jokes about passing wind and excrement that is intended to appeal to audiences who like 'toilet humour'.	Door crashes open. Connotation: Shrek's loud and brash character is demonstrated.	**Reggae-rap upbeat rhythm** 'Somebody once told me the world is going to roll me. I ain't the sharpest tool in the shed. She was looking kind of dumb With a finger and thumb, A shape of an 'L' on her forehead,
3. **Long shot** of Shrek's house in the swamp Connotation: the sunlit oasis that is Shrek's swamp is meant to appear desolate and unappealing. It is an important establishing shot to locate where the character lives and it is a point of view shot of an outsider, one adopted by the many fairytale characters who camp on his land later.		The years start comin' And they don't stop comin' Fed to the rules And I hit the ground runnin' Don't make sense not to live for fun, So your brain gets smart, But your head gets dumb, So much to do so much to see You'll never know if you don't go,

Narrative Image	Narrative Sound	Music lyrics
4. Crabbing and rising crane driven **medium shot**, framed by tree branches, of Shrek cleaning himself in swamp. Connotation: The hiding of the naked Shrek bathing in the water by carefully placed branches is a reference to **Austin Powers** where the same actor playing Shrek i.e. Mike Myers is naked but his private parts are always obscured by a strategically placed object between the camera and his body.		So what's wrong with takin' to the backstreets You'll never shine if you don't glow, Hey now, you are an all-star Get your game on, go play.
5. **Close up** over the shoulder shot of Shrek in mirror as it cracks. Connotation: Shrek's smile cracks the mirror suggests the unattractiveness of the character in a comical visual gag.		Hey now, you are a rock star, Get the show on, get paid. All that glitters is not gold –

6. **Close up** of Eddy Murphy's name as a credit.
 	
Connotation: The four main stars have equal status in terms of size of lettering and prominence in the opening credit titles – Mike Myers, Cameron Diaz, and Jonathan Lithgow are also featured prominently at this stage.
		Only shooting stars break the mould....'
		    All Star written by Greg Camp
		    performed by Smack Mouth
		    Copyright Universal Music
		    Enterprises
		
		Connotation: the inference is that if you get up and go you can do what you want ... anything is possible if you want to do it that badly.

Specimen Examination Question: AQA

These tasks are not actual examination questions. The questions are the sole work of the author and are devised to match the style, mark allocation and format of the relevant question papers from AQA. They are designed for examination practice. It is essential candidates check the specified topics for the year of their examination, with the examination board.

Controlled Test (Higher Tier)

In three hours you will need to attempt all four questions.

You are recommended to read the whole paper before starting to answer the questions.

You are recommended to answer the questions in the order they are given.

Study the material before answering the tasks set.

TASK 1

1. Explain, from your own study of one or more films, what the typical ingredients of a comedy film are?
   a) Characters **(10 marks)**
   b) Situations **(9 marks)**
   c) Comic acting skills **(6 marks)**
   [Total: 25 marks]

TASK 2

Study the Resource Sheet, and the cover of **DVD Monthly** in the colour section.

1. Having read the advantages of DVDs, explain **the unique** advantages in terms of film promotion of each of the following media.
   a) **Radio** – give two advantages **(2 marks)**
   b) **Bus shelter** – give two advantages **(2 marks)**
   c) **Television** – give three advantages **(3 marks)**
2. What **age of audiences** do you think you are *more likely* to reach by using each medium? Give your reasons and examples, using the following demographic age ranges: **8-15, 16-24, 25-40, 41-60, 60 years old plus. Note: it is not necessary to use all of them.**
   a) **Radio** **(6 marks)**
   b) **Bus shelter** **(6 marks)**
   c) **Television** **(6 marks)**
   [Total: 25 marks]

Resource Sheet

Advantages of DVD as a medium over video tapes.
- DVDs can fit in more additional interviews with director, cast and crew, film clips and out take material etc because they can compress more information than video.
- It is faster to jump forwards and backwards with the remote control using a DVD player.
- The sound and visual quality is much better than videotape.
- It is possible to play interactive games with the film's characters.
- There is usually more information about the film company, cast, and crew.

Disadvantages
- Unless you have an expensive portable DVD player it is harder to play DVDs when you are travelling.
- Unless you have a DVD recorder you cannot record programmes off air.

Glossary
DVD is a digital versatile disc
Film clips are short extracts of the film
Out takes are extracts that were not included in the final version of the film, often with humorous mistakes
Off air is the recording of programmes from the television by satellite, cable or aerial.

TASK 3

Either
a) Design and produce a (rough) sketch for a **poster advertisement** to fit into a bus shelter space i.e. a vertical rectangle – a door shape, promoting a DVD release for the 'U' rated film of *Shrek*. Use a plain A4 sheet for this purpose.
   Audience: the promotion is designed to reach the 8–15 year old market.
   (10 marks)

TASK 3

b) Explain the content, style, colours and design and layout ideas and the effect you want for your audience. Note: this task does not depend on knowledge of any real promotion for *Shrek*. **(10 marks)**

c) Write an explanation of how the poster will appeal to both ends of the 8-15 audience age group. **(5 marks)**

OR

a) Create a radio advertisement promoting the soon-to-be-released DVD of *Shrek*.
Include the music, jingle, words and catchphrases, using the form provided (see page 254). **(10 marks)**

b) Explain the content, style, sounds and meaning of the advertisement and the effect you want to create for your listeners. **(10 marks)**

c) Write an explanation of how the advertisement will appeal to both ends of the 8–15 audience age group. **(5 marks)**
[Total 25 marks]

TASK 4

Write a letter to the executive producer of your client, Dreamworks, Steven Spielberg.
Explain a) where b) when and c) how the poster OR radio campaign is going to be launched.
[Total 25 marks]
Overall total 100 marks

Case Study 2: Science Fiction

In Chapter two, the word 'genre' was introduced. The important art of selling films to the public depends on explaining the genre

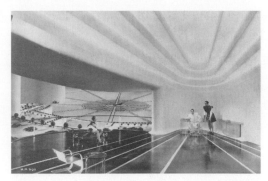

Fig 7.21   Things to Come
Source: © BFI

of the films simply and clearly. One theory is that the public need to be told what to expect, although this can annoy many people who enjoy sophisticated mixes of genres.

Many science fiction films originally come from novels. Jules Verne's *2000 Leagues under the Sea* (1954), H.G. Wells's *Things to Come* (1936) are examples of filmed versions of novels.

When we read a science fiction novel we experience emotions and ideas differently than when we sit down to watch a science fiction film.

Fig 7.22   The Invisible Man (1933)
(see colour section)

Fig 7.23 Hollow Man *(see colour section)*

We might think more about the special effects in a film. We might think about when and how the monster will jump out and scare the victim in a thriller film. In a crime thriller, we might try to work out which of the suspects in the police line-up committed the crime.

In a novel we are left to our imaginations, through the written descriptions of the creature from outer space. In the film we are shown the actual shape and figure of the evil alien, through music, sound effects, various shots, special effects, props and creative make-up and costumes. If the make-up or special modelling is shown to be superficial, audiences will feel let down by the lack of ingenuity and sophistication. Such is the demand for realistic and specialised effects, or so many people in Hollywood think.

ACTIVITY 11

Science fiction films have a distinctive set of elements. Write down, on your own and then discuss in pairs, what these elements are under the following headings:

1. *Mise-en-scène*
2. Situations
3. Characters: good and bad
4. Plot lines
5. Narrative structure
6. Iconography (for example, typical icons of a western are cowboy hats, saloon bars and tumble-weed strewn deserts)

Mise-en-scène

Examples of setting in science fiction include:

▌ Space
▌ Another planet
▌ Earth
▌ Time travel
▌ Spaceship
▌ A futuristic place that exists only as a concept in the mind (for example hell or paradise)

Mise-en-scène also includes costumes, camera movement and framing, lighting and acting.

Situations

These could include:

▌ Earth is threatened by an alien force.
▌ A space mission goes wrong.
▌ Earth has already been destroyed or taken over – only a few heroes or heroines survive.
▌ Machines rule a future world – what role is there here for humans?
▌ A futuristic world of a mix of planets and space travellers co-existing in space. Who or what is the dominant force?
▌ Everyday life is turned upside down by a freak of nature, such as an excess of ants or spiders.

Characters

These tend to follow the types and stereotypes of any dramas. The qualities of reasoning versus intuition are explored best in *Star Trek*, between the logical alien Dr Spock and the emotional, intuitive Captain Kirk. Evil characters are usually physically repellent and often given reptilian features to make them appear sinister, for example in *Alien*. In many films, such as *Invasion of the Body Snatchers* (1956) and *Men in Black* (1997), the aliens inhabit the bodies of human beings to disguise themselves.

Plot and narrative structure

The science fiction writer Ray Bradbury once said:

'The thing about science fiction is that it is not about tomorrow, it is about today.' The setting may be technologically beyond us (although often it is not) but the stories we, science fiction writers, are telling are the issues of today.'

In Michael Crichton's *Jurassic Park* (1992) we are taken into the world of biological science: of genetics and the control of DNA. The science fiction film is often based on ideas deriving from real scientific discovery: to extend the natural life span, cloning birth outside the womb, perfect genetic planning, biological warfare and robotic intelligence.

Much of a plot is based on the 'what if?' factor. The narrative structure tends to fit the normality, to displacement, to normality pattern. A tranquil setting is attacked by an unidentified force, chaos ensues – the antidote for which the defenders must find if they are to survive – and finally order is restored.

Themes are often contemporary, for example, the role of the action women or computer guided robotic intelligence. Sigourney Weaver in the *Aliens* film series plays a female heroine who is the supreme fighter, and she is more capable than any man of handling the monster. Is it possible for a robot to have a memory or even be more human than humans, for example in the films *2001: A Space Odyssey* (1968) and *Blade Runner* (1982)?

Themes

Broadly speaking Science Fiction films can be split into two main themes:

Marvellous – the spectacular, the wonderful and the futuristic visions of new technology, new worlds and the unknown e.g. *2001: A Space Odyssey*

Disastrous – the spectacular but calamitous effect of meeting with a more powerful superior force, the science experiment that gets out of control: *Alien, Frankenstein* etc.

Iconography

This can include:

- Alien creature
- Paranormal evidence (flying objects, invisible movement)
- Spaceship (complex control panels)
- Space (galaxies)
- Sophisticated weaponry (lasers)
- Technology (scanners and computers)

Where do ideas for science fiction films come from?

Books

Science fiction films are often based on novels. *Jurassic Park* (1992) and *The Lost World* (1997) are based on novels by Michael Crichton. *The War of the Worlds* (1953), *The Invisible Man* (1933), *Things to Come* (1936), and *The Invisible Thief* (1909, based on *The Invisible Man*) were first written as novels by H.G. Wells. *2001: A Space Odyssey* (1968) was based on a short story by Arthur C. Clarke.

Previous films, radio or comics

Star Wars (1977) was originally going to be a remake of the 1930s *Flash Gordon* serials, but was stopped due to copyright problems. In this case there were references to the Holy Grail, the Bible, *The Adventures of Robin Hood* (1938), *The Wizard of Oz* (1939) and the western genre. *Judge Dredd* (1995) was based on the comic of the same name by 2000 AD comics.

Television

Some science fiction films began as TV series, such as the cult series *The X-Files* and *Star Trek*, the latter of which has had numerous film versions made of it. Interestingly, the popularity of the science genre in television serials has continued with *Babylon 5*, *Space Precinct* and the satirical comedy sci-fi series *Red Dwarf*. Comics are also a source for films such as *Judge Dredd* (1995).

ACTIVITY 12

Science fiction saw a revival in 1977 with the massive success of Star Wars. In the 90s, a whole series of Aliens and Star Trek films were successful.

Discuss:
1. Why is science fiction so popular?
2. Why do you think TV programmes like the X-Files hold so much interest?

ACTIVITY 13

1. Read the short descriptions of the following films and make notes under two headings: theme and *mise-en-scène*. What are the main themes and *mises-en-scène*?

a *Things To Come* (1936) – the creation of a one world state after a devastating world war.

b *The War of the Worlds* (1953) – alien invasion from Mars. How does Earth respond?

c *I Married An Alien From Outer Space* (1958) – aliens take over human beings' bodies. Expectant fathers at a maternity hospital save the day. Comedy.

d *2001: A Space Odyssey* (1968) – the evolution of man has been subject to strange forces which have waited until mankind has the reached the point at which space flight is possible – a serious space journey.

e *Star Wars* (1977) – the intergalactic wars are raging and Princess Leia Organa is being pursued by an Imperial Star Destroyer. Will Darth Vader wipe out the last of the good Jedi Knights who

have kept the world a safe place as warrior-guardians? Good does triumph over evil, but only until the sequels.

f *Blade Runner* (1984) – space cop Harrison Ford has been sent back to earth to track down a group of killer robots who have hidden themselves in the bodies of earthlings.

g *Independence Day* (1996) – the world watches as spaceships hover over the earth's major cities. These extra-terrestrials have only one aim, which is to destroy the world as we know it, on the fourth of July – America's independence celebration day.

h *Star Trek – First Contact* (1998) – the crew of the Starship Enterprise fight to prevent a time-travelling plot that will change the world forever.

2. Imagine, you are to select six films from 1936–1984 and they are to be released today as a new classic sci-fi video six pack box collection. What would be the box set's unique selling point: what catch lines could you write for each film's mini poster?

Film costs

How much do films cost?

Typical costs include the following:

- Development of script and contracts for rights
- Producer's unit
- Direction
- Cast
- Travel and living costs
- Production staff
- Set and staff
- Wardrobe, make-up and hairdressing
- Special effects
- Camera department

- Second unit
- Transport and locations
- Film editing
- Music and sound
- Main and end titles

Above the line and below the line costs include: fees for the producer, director, or actors and technicians. These costs are generally known before the production.

Below the line costs include: film stock expenditure, equipment hire, hotel and catering costs, scenery, costumes and location hire. These costs can vary. The cost of feeding and accommodating a crew can rise if the weather is bad and rain stops filming. If this requires more filming to be done these costs can become very expensive.

Star Wars (1977)

Star Wars (1977) was one of the most expensive films ever made. Star Wars cost $11 million to make, which was $1 million more than the original agreed budget. It then took a further $16 million to release and promote it. A breakdown of the film's costs follows:

Cost	$
Development money	10,000
Final script	50,000
Cast including the director	750,000
Other salaries	2,100,000
Music	100,000
Film and processing	200,000
Costumes	300,000
Stage rents (studios)	300,000
Insurance	200,000
Set construction/lighting	1,600,000
Special effects/models	3,900,000
Transport and location costs	700,000
Interest on loans, etc.	800,000
TOTAL	**11,000,000**

Fig 7.24   Breakdown of costs for Star Wars
Source: Adapted from Screen International, January 1978

Today, an average large scale film costs $100 million to make. Waterworld (1995) and Titanic (1997) cost over $200 million. Although Waterworld was considered one of the most expensive box office flops, after five years it made profits through video sales. It is important, therefore, to look at films' expenditure and profits over a period of time. Citizen Kane (1941) was given poor reviews because it appeared to criticise the real life newspaper tycoon Randolph Hearst, but over the years it has been voted the top of the viewers', critics' and film makers' polls.

In May 1998 a record $50 million (£31 million) was taken in US cinemas. These days Hollywood films need to receive over $100 million each to become hits. The $80 million production costs of Deep Impact (1998) were shared by Steven Spielberg's DreamWorks and Paramount. The film had to clear $140 million in order to produce profits. Deep Impact grossed $40 million in its first weekend, which shows that it is possible to make substantial profits if the marketing is successful. In order to make Lethal Weapon 4, with Mel Gibson in 1998, Warner Bros. spent $180 million. They had to spend 40% of the budget on the stars alone.

Men in Black (1997)

Men in Black was a comedy that sent up some of the conventions used in traditional science fiction films.

Synopsis

New York Police Department cop Will Smith is recruited to join Tommy Lee Jones on the super secret team that monitors thousands of aliens who already populate the earth, without most people knowing it. One violent alien turns up and it is then a race against time to find the prize the alien is looking for, before the earth is blown up. Based on a comic by Lowell Cunningham.

Fig 7.25   Men in Black

Production notes

Men in Black took two years to make from the time the pre-production was started to the film's release. The second year was spent in post-production, where special effects were produced by the company Industrial Light and Magic.

Film Industry Simulation Game

Working in a team, form a film production company and give it a name.

Your production company would like to make a science fiction film but you need finance to make it. You will need to approach a sponsor or studio to gain backing for your amazing idea for a film. Note that you will also need to decide on the breakdown of the estimated budget expenditure according to the information you have been given in this chapter.

TASK 1

Decide on the following:

a The genre.   **(2 marks)**

b The narrative (200 words max).
                                             (8 marks)

c The characters (brief outline of main cast) and the settings (consider budget).   **(10 marks)**

d The stars (give reasons for casting) and the director (explain your choice).   **(10 marks)**

e Merchandise and spin-offs (specify potential consumers and audiences).
                                             (5 marks)

f The promotional campaign (what, where and when).   **(10 marks)**

g Budget (consider what proportions will be for casting, promotions and special effects).   **(5 marks)**

TASK 2

The sponsoring distribution company you have approached also owns: a whisky and fizzy drinks company, a clothes store and fashion design house, a major rock band they want to play on the soundtrack and a publishing company that publishes newspapers, magazines and books.

a Discuss whether your production company will co-operate with the sponsoring distribution company's wishes. The sponsoring company has its own stars, locations, tie-ins and product placement (i.e. their clearly branded whisky and fizzy drinks must appear in the opening sequence of the film). You may or may not want to co-operate with their demands for content and casting, however you must remember that you will need their money to back your film. There is talk of the sponsoring company wanting to

TASK 2

make a sequel called *Women in Black*, however this may only be a rumour.
Explain the reasons for your decision.

b Choose a suitable director from those you know to be established or new directors who show promise. Some examples of established directors of science fiction are: Steven Spielberg (*ET*, *Close Encounters*), George Lucas (*Star Wars*), Paul Verhoeven (*Robocop*, *Total Recall*, *The Starship Troopers*) and Barry Sonnenfield (*Men in Black*).
Explain the reasons for making your choice.

(5 marks)

c You may wish to opt for co-production, and work with another more experienced production company to gain respectability. This will of course mean sharing the profits of the film. Discuss this in your group and make notes on your choice. Examples of experienced production companies include: Amblin Entertainments which produced *Men in Black*, Lucas Films which produced *Star Wars* and Columbia Tristar which produced *Starship Troopers*.

(5 marks)

TASK 3

Present your pitch to the sponsoring company in order to persuade them that your film will be a huge box office hit. Present all the items in the checklist, including the general budget predictions. The sponsoring company will then need to ask questions and make a judgement based on what they hear, and what they discuss as a team panel.

Examination format

The format of the sample question paper which follows relates specifically to the OCR syllabus Section A: Film and Section B: Film Promotion and also fits the Welsh syllabus. Please refer to AQA's previous examination papers for precise layout and format. The Film Simulation Game which precedes this section could be used as a preparation for the board's simulation style of question.

Specimen examination Question: OCR

These tasks are not actual examination questions. The questions are the sole work of the author and are devised to match the style, mark allocation and format of the relevant question papers from AQA and OCR. They are designed for examination practice. The tasks are designed to follow the examination paper timings and mark allocations. It is essential that candidates check the specified topics set for the year of their examination, by the examination board. For previous examination papers contact the examination board direct.

Paper 1: Section A (Textual Analysis)

Select an extract from a popular mainstream film. The beginning or the end of a film are suitable extracts because they compress narrative, themes and characterisation.

Textual analysis   **(Total 50 marks)**

Spend one hour on this section, viewing the video and taking notes, and 30 minutes answering the questions.

1 **Unseen audio-visual text: viewing the extract.**

You will have 30 minutes viewing time of the video extract. First you will be able to read the questions. Then the extract will be replayed. You will then have the opportunity to view it again before answering the questions. Notes may be made during the second viewing.

Watch the six minute closing sequence of *Men in Black* including the end credits and answer a) to e):

a i Describe the elements which identify it as a science fiction film.

(6 marks)

ii Give two examples of how **excitement** and **suspense** is created by each of these:

■ the use of the camera **(6 marks)**
■ the soundtrack **(6 marks)**
■ special effects **(4 marks)**

b What kind of audiences would you expect this film to appeal to?

Give brief reasons for your answer.

(4 marks)

c Create a storyboard of at least 10 frames for the opening sequence sequel to *Men in Black*, entitled *Women in Black*. Use the blank storyboard sheets provided in the Appendix.

(14 marks)

d Explain your storyboard and discuss *mise-en-scène*, lighting, music and soundtrack, casting and director.

(10 marks)

Section B

Essay: Film promotion

(Total 25 marks)

Choose one or more films that you have studied. Describe and analyse the effectiveness of how it was promoted, including the following information: audience, type of film, promotional strategies, and where and when the film was seen.

 Extension Tasks

1 **Choose** a new film that is about to be released. Collect the teaser and the main trailers to this film. Local newspapers often have press packs left over when they have finished with them so this may be worth exploring. Write a case study of the campaign, detailing whether or not you think it was successful. If you think it was unsuccessful, explain why.

2 Which UK film had the most successful world box office sales figures last year? **Write notes** to account for its success. Did this film also have the top UK sales figures? Use the *Guardian Media Guide* or the *BFI Film and Television Annual Yearly Report* to help your research.

3 **Identify** two images from the opening sequence of another film that you think would be suitable to use as publicity stills for the film. **Describe** the images and **explain** briefly why you have chosen them. Where would you place them and what written text (for example tag lines) would you add to them?

4 **Research** one month's figures for UK cinema attendance and profit from box office returns. What percentage of films are from the USA, compared to UK productions? What percentage of films were non-UK and non-USA?

5 **Research** the latest film festival that attracted a world film screening, for example Cannes, Moscow, Hong Kong, Berlin, Burkino Faso, New York, Sundance or London. Find out which films were given awards and which countries produced them. Find out what categories of films were awarded prizes or accolades. Do you consider it likely that you would want to watch them? Do you think these films are likely to be seen in the UK and if so where (for example, at the major cinemas or at Art House cinemas)?

6 **Research** a current breakdown of costs and receipts for a multi-million dollar film in the

USA. Compare figures to those of a multi-million pound film in the UK. *Screen International* and *Moving Pictures* are useful magazines to use for this research. What genres of films tend to be the biggest sellers?

 Examination Skills

Knowledge and Understanding

Explain, supporting with examples, key terms such as: *mise-en-scène*, genre, camera shot, camera movement, size, angle and framing, lighting, editing, soundtrack, special effect, direction and acting. Students who can demonstrate an understanding of the conceptual aspects of the course – languages and categories, audience, agency, messages and values (ideology) and signifiers – will score highest marks; the clearer the answer the better. Successful completion of an essay question demands an awareness of targeted audiences (gender, age, race national), and all the elements described in the section on promoting a film (see pages 92–104) – tie-ins, teasers, posters, tag lines and merchandise.

Textual Analysis

For coursework and the OCR and AQA Examination simulation questions textual analysis skills are required. The ability to denotate and connotate the sounds and moving images is essential.

Suspense is created by short, sharp edits, which cut between the action and the reaction shots of the main characters. The action is mixed with special effects, which are designed to show the massiveness of the menacing alien overshadowing the diminutive special agents. The effects soundtrack consists of loud and violent crashing sounds to convey the drama of the fight.

Practical Work

Write a review of a film you have seen for your local paper. Explain why it is or is not suitable for the classification given.

8 Television and radio news

What's the story?

What you will learn

What is newsworthy? In this chapter you will find out about the how, why, who and what of news broadcasting. Studying news involves considering where news comes from, and the way news is processed and presented. There are questions to be asked, concerning who makes news, for whom it is made and why certain items are selected. The reasons why some items are not selected for broadcasting or printing should also be investigated.

KEY WORDS

- selection
- construction
- format
- news values
- gatekeepers
- sources
- agencies
- broadcast
- network
- mode of address

TECHNICAL WORDS

- bulletin
- human interest story
- lead story
- running order
- scheduling
- teasers
- title sequence
- voice over commentary

Features of news

To create and maintain an audience, TV and radio news must be broadcast at regular intervals or at fixed times each day, such as 'on the hour every hour'. Some TV channels have 24 hour news channels only, however other channels have just a small amount of time allocated for news, often in the form of bulletins. If broadcast news is to be believed, then it has to prove to its audience that it is accurate and reliable.

The news also has to be presented in a shape that is recognisably typical of the forms and conventions of news programmes that the listener or viewer are familiar with. For example, the music that is heard at the start of a news bulletin on the radio or the television tends to have a rhythm and beat that conveys a sense of urgency and immediacy. It is a style of music that audiences associate with news programmes.

Even the names of the programmes should give an indication of their content. Examples of television news programmes are:

- The News at Ten
- The Nine o'clock News
- Channel 5 News
- GMTV
- Newsround

Fig 8.1 ITN News at Ten, *2002, with two presenters, one male, one female*

Agenda setting

News television and radio news stations select and produce news. They cannot report on absolutely everything that happens. They must select what they consider to be the most interesting and relevant news items for their audiences. This is called agenda setting. An agenda is a list of items drawn up for a committee to discuss. Only items on the agenda are discussed, therefore if there is something happening which is not on this list then it is not discussed. In the section on news values agenda criteria are detailed.

Print or broadcast media?

The majority of audiences today prefer to watch the news on television.

(Discuss

Discuss why you think that television is the favourite medium for watching news?

What is media news?

ACTIVITY 1

Discuss the question in this heading. Make notes on your definition.

Discuss the following definitions of news. Which definition do you think is nearest to your own definition discussed previously. Which definition from the list below seems to you to be the most accurate?

1. News is about information and updating events.
                              (Student)
2. News by itself is not entertainment; it is information about current events, but it does have to be made into interesting stories for the viewer.
                   (News programme director)
3. Good news stories are based on other peoples' misery. Media news depends mainly on negative happenings – otherwise we wouldn't have anything to talk about.
                        (Trainee journalist)
4. Media news leaves out stories about political issues, womens' sports and third world countries, unless they can be reported in a bad light.
                    (Oxfam charity worker)

5. News is about people; people stories interest viewers most.
                           (TV presenter)
6. Television news needs visuals and interviews with eye witness accounts to make it seem real.
                     (News programme editor)
7. All news is pre-packaged by publicity managers and spin doctors*.
                              (TV critic)
8. News is just becoming like a goldfish gossip bowl: the lives and wrong-doings

of celebrities and the famous are what people want to ogle at.

(TV news executive producer)

Your news versus *the* news

Personal news is what you tell to a friend or someone in the family. When you tell friends about your news, what type of event do you discuss? For example, do you discuss what happened to you at the weekend and how do you tell them what you have done? Is it a momentous, strange or funny happening? Is it simply plain chit-chat about the usual activities? What would you have to do to get into the TV or radio news?

Sources

ACTIVITY 2

How do you usually find out about the news? Where do you find out about world, national or local news stories? Select from the list of sources below:

▌ television
▌ newspaper headlines
▌ radio
▌ a friend or someone at home
▌ schoolteacher
▌ any other ways?

*Spin doctors are people paid to feed journalists with press releases and carefully presented briefings. They present the ideas that the organisation they work for would like the public to hear.

TASK 1

1 Conduct a survey of your group, or four people of your own age group. Ask each member to describe the main way they find out about what is in the news, by giving them a choice of the sources listed previously. What is the most common answer and what is the least used source?

2 Now ask four people over the age of twenty years the same question. Then compare the responses of each age group. Are they the same or different? Write down why you think they are the same or different.

Which medium?

In the last 30 years more people use the television as their main source of news than any other medium.

TASK 2

Discuss the following:
1 Why do you think TV news is less appealing to young people, as research has shown?

2 How does watching television differ from reading the newspaper? List two ideas.

3 What is the difference between the television news and the radio news? Aside from the fact that one medium is visual and the other is sound based, list another difference.

News programming

Technology

Broadcast news, in television and radio, is what an organisation like the BBC transmits to a mass audience. Consider how the transmission of broadcast news to the mass audience has changed over the last hundred years.

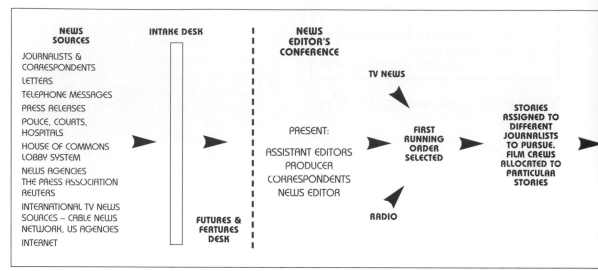

Fig 8.2   Diagram of bi-media news flow and processors (continued on page 127)

Fig 8.3   Travelling caravan, showing news reels in the early twentieth century pre-television

Source: BFI

Pre-production

Where do news organisations find their stories and how do they process the information? Although we may feel TV news programmes are immediate and recent, a considerable amount is achieved in the pre-production preparation before the broadcast.

Newsrooms are constantly sent press releases and letters telling them when events are going to happen. Court cases are often scheduled weeks in advance and anniversaries, for example, are always known and planned out well in advance. Hospitals and police stations provide a steady supply of stories and the journalist has simply to check the day books of either of these places to gain information. Many journalists will scour local newspapers for stories and they will also have contacts who will supply them with potential stories.

The Lobby System

At national level there is the Lobby System in the House of Commons, which allows MPs and government officials to talk to a select group of journalists, often called political correspondents. All this information goes into the forward diary and this is looked at each day to see if it can be used or if it is too old to pursue.

Some items become features because they do not depend on being immediate and can take two or three days to research and produce. They can then be included into the latter part of a news programme.

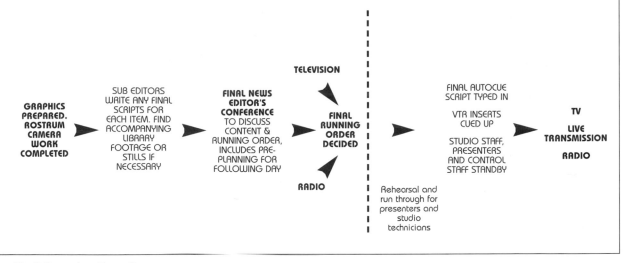

Fig 8.2   (continued)

Sources and intake

There is a constant flow of information into the newsroom and some of it comes from commercial stations such as Euronews and The Press Association via their Newswire. There are also international news agencies that provide news information and ready-made moving images, plus stories packages, Cable News, Reuters, US News and World Transatlantic News. Satellite and the Internet provide fast link-ups 24 hours a day.

New developments

Locating and producing TV and radio news in big organisations such as the BBC is linked together in what is called a bi-media process. This saves on staff and cuts down on costs in terms of space and technology.

Gatekeeping

The people who decide what news is selected to go into production are the editors. The editor, the producer and journalists who decide are called 'gatekeepers' in Media Studies terms. They define what is newsworthy and what is important for the public to hear. The criteria they use for deciding what is newsworthy depends on news values. These are discussed a little later in this book.

On the morning of an evening programme the most senior staff meet and they create a provisional running order. The running order is the sequence of items in the order in which they will be presented on the programme. Stories that need to be developed are assigned to different people and these are produced during the day. In the afternoon, another meeting takes place and the final running order is decided. If a story of a fire the previous night is no longer as important as a new story that has broken about a man dying in a police cell, then the fire story may be relegated to further down the running order. If a story cannot be produced for lack of material, then a pre-

prepared feature can be shown to fill the space.

Production
Subeditors

Subeditors write most of the stories, process the information and write links between stories to make it all join together smoothly. They are usually given a precise amount of time to work with. They may have to find library film or photographs if the item requires additional visual footage.

Presenters

Presenters practice their lines and links between items and prepare themselves for the live programme at the appointed hour.

Tell me a story

Storytelling is at the heart of news – it is not simply the information, but the way in which the story is told that interests the listener.

ACTIVITY 3

Decide from the list below which news items are type (a), (b) or (c):

a regional TV stories
b national TV news stories
c stories that could be either national or regional

1. Prime minister's helicopter lands on school playing fields.
2. Five MPs lock themselves in cages outside Westminster buildings in demonstration about animal rights.
3. Route for town bypass agreed.
4. International conference for tall people (over 6' 4") held today in London.
5. The Queen visits South Africa.

Select one of the above stories. Invent and write an interesting script for a radio presenter to read out. You must use no more than 60 words.

Scheduling
When is news on?

The news is available on the television or radio at regular times each day. Programme planners try to ensure that their news feels fresh and up-to-date throughout the hours of their schedule. Some channels simply have short bulletins and other channels devote whole programmes to serious news analysis. For example, on Channel 4's early morning programme, *RI:SE*, there are regular bulletins, however at 7.00 pm Channel 4 also has 50 minutes of reports and analysis.

ACTIVITY 4

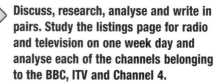

Discuss, research, analyse and write in pairs. Study the listings page for radio and television on one week day and analyse each of the channels belonging to the BBC, ITV and Channel 4.

1. What are the published times of the radio news? On which channel are they broadcast? Is the news on at times that are not written in the listings?
2. Which TV channel broadcasts the most number of hours of news? What does this tell us about the type of channel it is? What types of people do you think watch it?
3. Is it possible to watch news on some television channels 24 hours a day (BBC and CNN, for example)?
a Why do some news programme makers think it is necessary to have continuous news?
b Do you think you would be interested in a 24 hours a day news channel? Explain your reasons.
c Are all TV news programmes the same? How do they look different? Remember, it's not what you say but the way that you say it!

ACTIVITY 5

Watch and compare three or four breakfast news programmes, for example, *RI:SE*, GMTV, Channel 5 News or BBC News.
Make notes on at least two of these programmes describing and analysing the following:

1. Programme title and time of day (and minutes).
2. Mode of address.
3. Presenters: number, age, gender, race and accent.
4. Sets and furniture.
5. Pace and tone of delivery.
6. Music and colours.
7. Type of content.
8. Title sequence and graphics.

Format

'Our local television news is part of what we call a magazine show. Like a magazine it has serious stuff at the front, some more personal items in the middle and sport and lighter entertainment at the end.'
                                        TV News Editor

There are five types of news programmes:

1 bulletins
2 news updates
3 magazines (e.g. *GMTV*)
4 serious news programmes with analysis
5 newsflashes

The format, or shape, of the regional evening news or evening news programme tends to follow a pattern that has become conventional in many news programmes:

▌ hard news

▌ brief round up of serious news (shorts)
▌ heart-tugger story
▌ lighter features
▌ sport
▌ funny (known as 'skateboarding duck') story
▌ 'bye bye and 'see you tomorrow' link

This format tends to make news programmes more like magazine programmes, with some information but with the emphasis on entertainment and relaxing the audience at the end of the day.

ACTIVITY 6

From the list below identify which stories fit into the categories listed above:

1. Man arrested for stealing pillow cases oversleeps and misses his court case.
2. Bomb goes off in Manchester town centre.
3. Little girl learns to walk again.
4. President of USA drinks a pint in Birmingham at World Summit Talks.
5. New England manager of women's cricket team appointed.

ACTIVITY 7

Compare a non-contemporary news broadcast (over two years ago) with a contemporary one. Write notes comparing: a) Format b) Presenters c) Balance of serious, light items d) How the programme ends e) Theme music and titles f) set design, desk etc.

Selection and newsworthiness

Consider what types of stories are selected for broadcast – how do any of them become news suitable to print or broadcast? Millions of events happen every day all over the world and a fraction of these end up being printed in newspapers or broadcast on television and radio.

News values

There are several theories about why events turn into news stories. These theories are sometimes referred to as 'news values'.

Is the event important or big enough to be 'newsworthy'?

The greater the size of the event, the more likely it is that it will find itself in the media. A story about a man growing the largest tomato in London is less newsworthy than one about a freak tornado sweeping the south east of England. A bomb going off in Number Ten Downing Street is likely to be far more newsworthy.

Is the news negative?

Generally 'bad news is good news' for television, radio and print. If someone dies in a car accident it is more likely to appear in the news than someone passing away in their sleep. Bad news is arguably more obvious and complete than positive events. Positive events are less easy to dramatise, whereas with bad news stories it is easier to make a story out of human conflict or misery.

Has it happened recently?

Is the news fresh enough by the time the story is broadcast? Yesterday's fire at the swimming pool is not as recent as today's unexplained death of a man in the police cell. If the story is also an 'exclusive', that is, one which no other news station has managed to obtain, then the story will be unique.

Is the meaning clear?

The simpler the meaning of the event, the more likely it is to be reported. The headline 'Man dies in police cell' makes more immediate and direct sense than 'Report into proposed road bypass recommends three possible options'.

Is the news relevant to us?

There are many events that happen in the world that we might think we should know about. In reality, we do not want to know or we simply cannot find out about all the events in the world for the following reasons:

- Not every event is reported to the media.
- Not every event is selected by the editors and journalists.
- Most national news channels tend to focus on their own country's stories, sometimes almost exclusively.
- It is unlikely that we, the audience, would be able to find the time to find out about every country's news.
- Most people do not have access to all types of media technology, such as satellite, Internet and radio, required to find out about global news.
- Whatever is selected to be 'in the news' depends on several people: the editors, the journalists and the news agencies. These people decide, on our behalf, what the news should be. They may have a limited set of ideas they think we ought to know about.

Headlines such as 'Briton dies in plane crash over Turkey' tend to be favoured by news editors over '500 killed in Afghanistan earthquake'. Much as we may disagree in principle, the relevance to news nearer to home is often favoured above the scale of the event.

Is news expected?

When an election is announced, we can predict that there will be pre-election and election news coverage. This is also true if there is a fixed calendar date for a sporting event such as Wimbledon. We can expect that there will be interviews, debates, information and news accounts leading up to the event. In the case of the O.J. Simpson trial, for example, where the court case lasted a year, it was known that each day there would be some drama, therefore the courtroom scenes were televised. Simpson was already a national US celebrity and sportsman when it was alleged he killed his wife – this story attracted national and international interest. The proceedings could be likened to a daily soap opera.

Is news unexpected?

If an event is out of the ordinary, then news editors may want to emphasise this fact. They can focus on certain aspects of a story in order to make the story appear more dramatic. A fire is an unexpected event and the story may be dramatised to draw attention to the firefighters' heroism and to make the dangers they faced appear more perilous: 'Family rescued in towering flats inferno'. The more bizarre aspects of a case can also be emphasised: 'Dog bites man' may not be news, but 'Man bites dog' is a classic example. In recent years, tabloid newspapers have competed to see who could create the most outrageous headlines, based on the flimsiest of evidence. 'Freddy Starr ate my hamster!' is another classic example.

Is it already in the news?

News such as a murder trial or a royal family scandal tends to carry on over several days, even for weeks. A news item might even be introduced as, for example, 'the latest in the continuing storm over the political scandal'.

Does the news item fit into the overall balance of the programme?

Most television news tends to contain a mix of what is known as 'hard' and 'soft' news. News programmes often sequence their items, starting with serious news at the top of the running order and moving on to lighter items, finally ending on a more humorous or cheery note. Television news generally follows the following sequence: hard news items, bulletins, heart tuggers, soft news (including sport), light and witty shorts, weather '... and finally' a happy story to end.

If there are no light items, then the programme's customary tone and balance can seem inappropriate. This means that the programme will not be filled with too many of the same type of stories, otherwise there will be no variety of topic or change of mood. News editors believe the news programme should not only be about informing people; it should also entertain and relax them.

Is it possible to personalise the news and make it a story about individuals?

News editors believe audiences find it is easier to identify with a person than the company or the institution they work for. It is easier to video people who represent the human face of an institution than to have a reporter explain abstract ideas such as monetary union or European Common Agricultural Policy.

News tends to use individual names rather than groups, for example, 'the Prime Minister announced a new deal for jobs' rather than 'the Government announced a new deal for jobs'. News in which there are clearly defined 'goodies' and 'baddies' makes the topic more easy to convey. News that does not have a human face is more difficult to convey. In this situation, radio may have the advantage over television in that ideas are more easy to focus on in a listening-only medium.

Is the news about top powerful world nations?

American and European news often dominates our screens, radio airwaves and papers. If the US, European, Chinese or the Russian Governments are involved in a global dispute, it raises the possibility of world conflicts. If there is a conflict in a small country, it is often not reported until a major powerful nation becomes involved. In contrast, we tend not to hear about successful stories from African or Indian nations – we more often hear about natural disasters in these countries, and the image conveyed is inclined to make them victims.

Is the news about famous or powerful people?

Much of the news is focused on celebrities from the public world of sport, television, film and music industries. There is also a great deal of attention paid to royalty, politicians, gentry and foreign statespeople. There has been much debate as to whether the media focus on the lives of public people has been unhealthy, especially in prying into the private aspects of their relationships.

Is it simply that news editors are satisfying the public's basic instinct to gossip about the lives of the rich and famous? Should there be rules governing press intrusion and harassment of individuals going about their private business? What rights should we allow to people who make their money and status from being famous, to restrict journalists from reporting their activities, especially in public spaces such as restaurants and beaches?

Questioning the news

Another fundamental question we might ask news editors and the public alike is: is news entertainment or information?

Some critics of modern news claim that the news focuses more on violence, sex and celebrities than the serious issues and stories of the day. News of rising unemployment figures can be ignored while soap and music stars' love lives are given prominent positions. On the other hand, some people argue that there is far too much serious talk of politics and parliamentary activity and that they would prefer a lighter approach to news programmes. Other people say they do not watch television news because they prefer newspapers or radio. Some are not interested in the news at all, in particular the 15 to 25 year old age group.

Further factors that television news editors in particular are concerned with before starting production:

- Is there any visual footage?
- Are there eyewitnesses to interview?
- Are there any experts to interview?
- Is there any live material to show that the news is happening right now? For example, an explosion or an election result being announced.
- Is the information exclusive to the television channel, i.e. before other television channels and newspapers can reach it?

Who decides on the news?

Several people are involved in the production of news, but only a few make the important decisions about what is actually selected. Can you name the different production jobs involved in the production of the news?

Mode of address

This concerns how a programme addresses its audience. It is usually visible in the style of the presenter's clothes, the way they look at or away from the camera, the tone, pitch and speed of delivery of the words, the sets and background colours and the music etc. For example, the *BBC News* is more serious, measured and formal, whereas the news on *RI:SE* and the news on *Newsround* is fast and friendly.

GMTV News

Presenters: male and female hosts, with news presenter.
Setting: studio, sofas, coffee tables, venetian blinds, cityscape in the background.
News presenter at desk, neutral background.
Dress code: smart but informal.
Format: magazine with bulletins.
Audience: 30 years of age upwards, home managers, C2D.
Camera: medium shot, straight on.

BBC Breakfast News

Presenters: male and female.
Dress code: smart and formal.
Format: bulletins and in-depth reports.
Audience: business, ABC1.
Camera: long shot to medium shots.

ACTIVITY 8

Compare two breakfast time programmes. Write down what you find out about: presenters, dress code, format, audience and cameras.

News simulation

You are a member of **FutureWorld**, which has produced various news programmes for cable channels in Europe. You specialise in the 15 to 25 year age group. You have a publicity and promotions department, in addition to a programme making section. Channel 6 is a new channel and is looking to produce a news programme that broadcasts at 7.00–8.00 am. Below is the letter containing the brief given to all companies tendering to produce this new programme.

CHANNEL 6

FutureWorld
Surrenden Road
Birmingham
BST 600

Channel 6
Box 6
London
W6T TL

20 April 2002

Dear Colleague,

Channel 6 is looking for a news programme that suits and promotes our company's wonderful approach to our audience. You must come up with ideas and a design for a new programme and outline its unique features in response to the tasks that follow this letter.

Our audience is 15 to 30 years of age and are male and female, fun-loving, style conscious Cosmopolitan, Minx, Mojo and NME readers and clubbers who read books, watch movies and party. They like music, fashion, food and culture but are bored with programmes like The Big Breakfast. They find all the other news programmes too middle-of-the-road and just a little too resigned to over 50s suburbia.

We want ideas for a news programme that is:

- issues based
- controversial
- consumer based
- informative, fun and not patronising

Our channel is committed to equal opportunities and we are definitely not interested in sexist or racist approaches. A good understanding of forms and conventions in presentation and programme construction and programme composition is required.

We look forward to hearing about your interesting and innovative ideas.

Yours sincerely,
Jean Bateman

TASK 1

a Describe and analyse what you think are the key features of television news programmes.

(20 marks)

b Provide a title for your new breakfast television news programme and explain the thinking behind it.

(5 marks)

c Describe your breakfast television presenters and how will they will appeal to the audience. Comment on style, dress, voice and accent.

(10 marks)

d Describe what your breakfast studio sets will look like and explain how the effect will appeal to the audience.

(5 marks)

TASK 2

Note: use the storyboard sheets for part **a** and the plain paper for part **b** (see Appendix).

Either

a Draw, design or describe a ten-shot title sequence for the news programme that will suggest the style and identity of the channel and its treatment of the news.

(15 marks)

or

b Design a set for the news programme (floor plan, channel and news logo).

(15 marks)

TASK 3

Note: use plain sheets for part **a**. Your news programme will need an advertising, and promotion campaign to grab the interest of its target audience. Use notes, scripts, sketches, diagrams and graphic designs to provide ideas for a campaign advertising the new news programme in each of the three activities following:

a **Either** i) Design a full page advertisement for a television listings magazine.
or ii) Write a 30 second radio advertisement for local commercial radio.

(15 marks)

b Describe a range of products that could be advertised during the breaks of the programme, which will appeal to the target audience.

(10 marks)

c Suggest other ways in which you might promote your new news programme.

(5 marks)

TASK 4

Produce a covering letter to accompany your proposal, explaining how the key features of your TV news programme successfully meets the requirements outlined in the letter from Channel 6.

(15 marks)

Specimen Examination Question: OCR
Cross Media Topics (1918/6)

To answer this question it is also advisable to study the next chapter on Newspaper Tabloids and Broadsheets,

Answer Questions 1 and 2 **(Total: 60 marks)**

1 With detailed reference to two examples you have studied, from more than one medium, identify and describe the processes of:
   i) newsgathering
   ii) presentation

(30 marks)

2 With reference to at least one medium discuss how the reporting of news has changed in terms of content and values.

(30 marks)

 *Extension Tasks*

1 **Select** a story from any television news programme that you think has a chance of being continued in bulletins throughout a day or for several days (for example, sanctions against Iraq or pigs go missing from farm in Oxfordshire). Monitor how long it stays in the news over a day/week/month. From the description of news values explained earlier in this chapter identify how many values the story covers. Why does it remain in the television news for the period it lasts? Why does it finally lose its place in the news programmes?

2 **Study and compare** the national and regional evening news over a period of two or three days. Look to see if there are any stories in your regional news programmes that also appear in the national news. Compare how

they differ in the way that they are presented or treated (for example, a royal visit, accident or a criminal incident). Write notes on how the stories are shaped according to the interests of the national or regional point of view. For example, '6 year old Jamie Bean met the Queen today . . .' (regional) or 'the Queen spoke to spectators of all ages . . .' (national).

3 **Adapt** a recording of a news bulletin of about two minutes length, taped off air. Change the script by rewriting the voice overs to suit a different audience. For example, voice overs on ITN's *Evening News* could be re-scripted for a youth comedy programme entitled *Not the ten o'clock news*. Play the news bulletin with the sound turned down in the right places and read out your new script to accompany the images. How does the new script change the meaning of the images and how does it differ from the original script?

4 **Research** the ITC (Independent Television Commission) through your local library or your teacher. Find out what the role of the ITC is. Find out what the ITC says about the way broadcast news should be reported. Why do you think that radio and television have more restrictions on being politically unbiased than newspapers?

5 **Research** the news agencies Reuters, Agence Press and Visnews on the Internet. Find out which TV channels they supply news to.

6 'And finally . . .' **write and video** a script for a 1 minute 50 second bulletin, to be broadcast at the end of the evening news. The proposed content includes an interview with a local person who has just invented a new device for detecting which lottery cards have winning numbers on them, under the silver scratch panels. Create three sections: the presenter and the introduction, the interview and the footage, and the link back to the studio. The length of time has to be no more or less than 1 minute 50 seconds. Alternatively, invent your own 'and finally . . .' bulletin that is upbeat, amusing or is an animal-related story.

Examination Skills

Knowledge and Understanding

Examiners setting questions on TV news are looking for a broad knowledge of the typical forms and conventions (media languages) used to present news. You will need to be able identify, compare and explain the different ways the news is presented. You need to show an understanding that producers have different ideas about their audiences in terms of their interests, age, gender, race and nationalities. You will therefore need the skills of memory recall, detailed explanation of common features of news presentation, and a strong understanding and knowledge of recent examples of news values.

Textual Analysis

To produce fully detailed and knowledgeable answers you will have to be able to analyse the presentational aspects of news programmes. For example, what are the differences in style between *GMTV* and ITV's *Evening News*? If you are asked to explain the effects of music, title sequences, colours and studio sets and design you must use language which indicates a strong ability to interpret the producers' intentions and imagine the likely variety of responses from the audiences. For example, a piece of writing might compare two styles of presentation:

The blue sets of the BBC are much colder in their effect than the warm, sunny and domestic colours of the sofa-filled GMTV studio. The suits and skirts of the BBC man and woman are a typical convention of the BBC's more formal approach to broadcasting. They have to appear authoritative and serious, so that they are perceived as credible sources of information.

The GMTV presenters, on the other hand, sit on sofas throughout the programme wearing smart casual dress.

Practical Work

In the examination, practical activities include: creating storyboards, writing bulletins, designing posters or submitting a treatment or outline for a new programme or title sequence. The kind of skills required here demand an ability to think of ideas visually, and in terms of sequences of images and sounds that create interesting television. A series of shots consisting of only a presenter in a studio would not be considered very interesting. A set of shots that had a variety of location, reporter, archive footage and studio presenters would be considered to follow usual conventions of variety.

Clearly, the language of news presenters can be sensational, for example, 'alarm at rural increase in drugs' or it can be more factual, for example, 'a government report today suggested that drug use was more evident in non-urban areas'. The skill of the candidate is to use the appropriate tone and language for their type of channel and audience.

Storyboards – these should include the variety of locations that news presentation tends to cover, the news studio, the reporter and the location footage. The storyboard should be clearly and fully detailed, explaining the type of shots and sounds that are on screen at any given moment. There should be a clear sense of how the words of the report add to the pictures, not simply describing pictures but letting them speak for themselve.

9 Newspaper tabloids and broadsheets

What's the story worth?

What you will learn

This chapter covers the forms and conventions, style and content, values and legal aspects of broadsheet and tabloid newspapers.

KEY WORDS

- forms and conventions
- denotation and connotation
- news values
- agenda
- selection
- construction
- gatekeeper
- processors
- mode of address
- privacy
- intrusion

TECHNICAL WORDS

- format
- tabloid
- broadsheet
- editorial
- advertorial
- house style
- libel
- readership and circulation

Format

The format is the shape and layout of a newspaper. There are two main formats of newspapers: tabloid and broadsheet. Daily national newspapers such as *The Times*, *Financial Times*, *Telegraph*, the *Independent* and the *Guardian* are broadsheets. They are large format, A1 in size. The smaller A3 size papers are described as tabloids, such as the *Sun*, the *Mirror* and the *Star*. As a group, these tabloids are otherwise known as the 'red tops', as they have a wide band of red print at the top of the front page.

Newspapers such as the *Daily Mail* and the *Express* are also tabloid in shape but their content is considered to be 'middle brow'. The broadsheets are also sometimes refered to as 'high-brows', 'qualities' or 'heavies'. 'Middle brow' means that the content is mostly serious but is also mixed with lighter items, such as you would find in a magazine. In 2002, the *Daily Mail* has the highest circulation figures (number of papers sold) of the middle brow tabloids and broadsheets, as a result of successfully attracting the bulk of readers in the middle of the market. 'High brow' means that the content is serious and contains a higher proportion of political and economic news.

Masthead

Puff

Pug

Headline

Splash

Strap

Standfirst

Byline

THE Mirror

Thursday April 4 2002

NEWSPAPER OF THE YEAR X2   32p

KOP GUNS

LIVERPOOL....1   B LEVERKUSEN....0

Oh little town of Bethlehem

How still we see thee cry

A PALESTINIAN mother weeps for her dead son yesterday as battles rage in Bethlehem.

This grieving woman's 22-year-old boy was killed by Israeli troops.

Palestinian casualties lay in the streets of Bethlehem where gunmen remained holed up in the Church of the Nativity – traditional site of Christ's birth.

Without food and water, the plight of the scores taking refuge in the church was

ALEXANDRA WILLIAMS REPORTS AS THE ISRAELI CONFLICT RAGES AT JESUS CHRIST'S BIRTHPLACE

increasingly desperate. Wounded gunmen were being tended to by priests and nuns.

Outside, Israeli paratroopers moved street by street after 48 hours of fierce fighting.

Bethlehem lawyer Tony Salman said in a phone interview: "We are afraid that we

are facing a disaster. No water, no food – we must do something."

Ambulances took the bodies of three civilians, and two wounded men, to hospital from near Manger Square in Bethlehem.

Seven Britons trapped in the holy town

were allowed to leave last night. Hundreds of Israeli tanks moved into three more West Bank towns, and Palestinian leader Yasser Arafat spent a sixth day imprisoned in his headquarters at Ramallah.

But the focus of the crisis was the fight for Bethlehem, where the most sacred areas have become a battleground.

Israel said gunfire from the church had not been returned. An army spokesman said: "It's a sacred place and we don't want to use live fire against it."

FULL STORY: PAGES 4 AND 5

Picture: REUTERS

Fig 9.1   *The* Mirror: *main features of a newspaper front page*

Source: The *Mirror*, 4 April 2002/Mirrorpix.com

Parts of a newspaper
Layout, typical features and technical terms – featured also on Figure 9.1

Masthead

The masthead is the title block or logo identifying the paper at the top of the front page. Sometimes an emblem or motto is also placed within the masthead. The masthead is often set into a block of black or red print or boxed with a border. The *Independent* has an eagle (standing for fearless independence), the *Daily Mail* has an emblem consisting of the words 'Dieu et Mon Droit' (God and My King) underneath the royal crest of a lion, a unicorn and the imperial crown on a shield with St. George's cross. The latter suggests English patriotism. For the *Mirror*, the 'x2', known as a puff, is a self-promotion about its sucess as newspaper of the year.

Pugs

These are at the top left and right-hand corners of the paper and are known as the 'ears' of the page. The price of the paper, the logo or a promotion are often positioned there. Pugs are well placed, to catch the reader's eye. They can promote the new price of the paper. On the right-hand side of the *Mirror* the pug includes the image of a Liverpool football player, the words 'kop guns' (a pun on *Top Gun* the film) and the football score. In the *Voice*, the line is '20 years of campaigning excellence'.

Kicker

This is a story designed to stand out from the rest of the page by the use of a different typeface and layout. In the *Voice*, 1 April 2002, an interview with Alicia Keys is promised on pages 23 and 24. A small head shot is used with led lettens 'R 'n' B's golden girl'.

Exclusive

This means that the story is solely covered by that paper and no-one else. The paper will pay their interviewees to buy an 'exclusive' so that no other paper can get it. The idea is that people will buy the paper because it is the only place to find out about the 'real' story. In the *Voice*, they obtained an exclusive interview with Naomi Campbell's mother.

Other features of a newspaper include:

Splash – the 'splash' is the main story on the front of the paper. The largest headline indicates which this is. In this case, the Palestinian/Israeli conflict story, the splash reads: 'O little town of Bethlehem'.

Headline – this is the main statement, usually with the largest font size, describing the main story. A banner headline is when the headline spans the full width of the page.

Strapline – this introductory headline is usually just below the main headline. In the edition of the *Mirror* shown in Figure 9.1 the strapline is below the headline: 'How still we see thee cry'.

Standfirst – the 'standfirst' is the introductory paragraph before the start of the feature. This is in bold print in the edition of the *Mirror*. 'A Palestinian weeps for her dead son yesterday . . . Bethlehem'.

Cross-head – subheadings that appear in the text and are centred above the column of text. If they are set to one side then they are called 'sideheads'.

Byline – the name of the reporter, if they are important, is often included in the beginning of the feature, rather than at the end, or not at all. Here the byline reads 'Alexandra Williams'.

Caption – typed text under photographs explaining the image.

Sidebar – when a main feature has an additional box or tinted panel placed in or

Fig 9.2   *The* Guardian: *Broadsheets are twice the size in shape of the tabloids*

Source: The *Guardian*, 4 April 2002

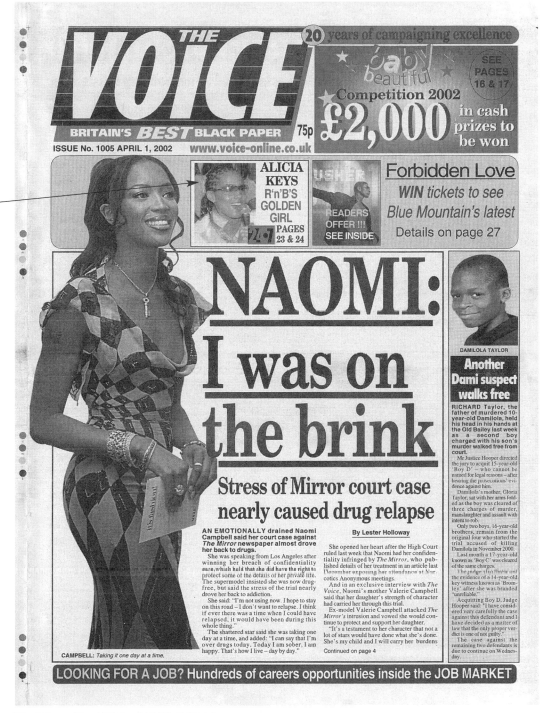

cker —

Fig 9.3   The Voice: a black tabloid newspaper

Source: The Voice, 1 April 2002

alongside it, this is called a 'sidebar'. Examples can be seen in Figures 9.2 and 9.3 (Damilola Taylor).

Credits – the author of the feature may be given credit in the form of a byline. Photographs may have the name of the person or agency who took the photograph alongside them – this is known as a credit.

The Voice

The *Voice* (see Figure 9.3) uses white lettering, a sans serif typeface, set on a black block, with a pinstripe effect. The font size is very large and the word slopes to one side, giving the impression of looking forward and being up-to-date.

Newspaper language

Study the headlines from the *Mirror* and the *Guardian* shown previously in Figures 9.1 and 9.2. Note that these headlines did not appear on the same day.

Both headlines relate to the occupation of Palestinian towns as a result of an escalation of the conflict between Israel and the Palestinians.

Discuss

Discuss the approach and tone of each of the headlines and the message they each convey. How do they reflect the papers that they belong to?

Approach and tone

The approach of the *Mirror*, for example, is to make use of a well known Christmas carol. It uses a very large point size for the lettering. The tone of the words is critical, expressing tragic concern for the Palestinians.

Similarly, the *Guardian* uses a critical but more neutral approach in highlighting the

'trail of destruction'. The headline is a long sentence, as the paper is a broadsheet, therefore there is plenty of room for text. The use of upper and lower case makes it more like a strapline.

The *Guardian* uses a mix of factual and emotional languages as it charts the history of the recent escalation.

Typeface and type size

The choice of typeface is very important in creating an image of a newspaper. Broadly speaking, tabloids like the *Sun*, the *Star* and the *Mirror* use simple, and large fonts. This typeface, as used in the *Mirror*'s headline, is called 'sans serif'. All the letters are in bold and are in upper case format.

The broadsheets tend to use a typeface that is more ornate. This typeface style is described as 'serif', such as can be seen in the *Independent* and the *Daily Mail*. In the *Independent*, both upper and lower case headlines are used.

The typeface of the masthead also differs in each paper, to convey individual styles. The *Mirror* has a simple sans serif typeface, with the 'M' as the largest letter dropped below the rest of the word 'Mirror'. The *Daily Mail* uses what is known as Old English typeface, which suggests a more old-fashioned and traditional image. The *Independent* uses a serif typeface, which resembles the ordinary typeface used throughout the rest of the text.

ACTIVITY 1

1. Research other newspapers such as the *Daily Telegraph*, *The Times* or the *Sun*. Analyse and write notes on each of the following:
 ▌ style of typeface
 ▌ font size
 ▌ use of upper and lower case
 ▌ layout.

2. Are any of the following typeface or font settings used:
- ordinary
- bold
- italic
- roman
- Arial or Universe
- Serif
- Sans serif

3. What image of the newspaper does the typeface and size convey about itself?

Photographs

If you study the photographs in the *Mirror* shown on page 153 you will see that the images have been:

- snatched
- cropped
- captioned

The photo snatch

Many sensational photographs are taken without the consent of the people pictured. Even if they do not mind, there is sometimes no time to ask the subjects to stand still and pose. The photographer then has to 'snatch' a photograph as best they can in the time given. Often this means using a telephoto lens, which allows images to be taken from a long distance.

The effect of snatching a photograph often means that the front page contains slightly out of focus or blurry images. This effect is now associated with sensational news images and is sometimes deliberate. The image can be enlarged, to make it look grainy and blurred. The group of photographers who are said to track down celebrities are called paparazzis.

The constructed photograph

The *Mirror*'s photograph of the mother of Mohammed Saleh is not posed (see page 138). Though she seems to be looking straight at the camera, her expression is not one that has been staged purely for the purpose of the newspaper article. She appears to be vulnerable and distressed. The shadows around her eyes are created by natural light.

The photograph has been cut so that just a close up is used on the page. Her image is positioned next to the headline and strapline. This has the effect of making her face appear larger than life, so it stands out from the page. It also draws the eye up to and down from the football snapshot (pug) and the price in the masthead.

Cropped photos

The *Guardian* has used the same Reuters (Press Agency) photograph by Ahmed Jadollah.

Even if an image is in focus, it is sometimes not large enough to make out the detail. In the image of Mohammed Saleh's mother, for example, the picture editor has cut out the rest of the face. This technique of cutting out unwanted material is called cropping (see Chapter Two: Languages and Categories, for more examples of this). The cropping of this photograph makes the crying and tears more dramatic.

Captions

Captions will be written by a subeditor, whose job it is to bring together the visual layout and the copy (copy is the written text) from the journalists. The purpose of using captions is to fix the meaning (see Chapter Two on anchorage) and add some explanation of what is happening in the picture.

Newspaper Photo analysis

Study the image shown previously in the *Mirror*.

a How does the caption focus on the meaning of the picture? **(3 marks)**

b Cover up the caption and devise two other captions. These should be different, but no less serious, than the original. **(4 marks)**

c i. Compare the *Guardian's* cropping of the photograph to the *Mirror's*. How does focusing close change the effect of the photograph's meaning?

ii. Which photograph do you think is more effective? **(5 marks)**

Collect two or three tabloids, broadsheets and regional or local newspapers. Study the photographs in these papers, including those inside. Write down the title of the paper and answer the following questions:

a How many photos have been 'snatched'? **(2 marks)**

b How many photographs have been posed and constructed with the co-operation of the subjects? Give evidence to support your judgements. **(3 marks)**

c What percentage of photographs are posed, compared to those which are 'snatched'? **(2 marks)**

d What is the difference between local and national newspapers in the way photographs are constructed? **(4 marks)**

What does your answer to Task 2, question (c) tell you about:

a the types of news that the papers tend to present? **(4 marks)**

b the age, gender, race, class, physical abilities or income of the readers? **(3 marks)**

Total = 30 marks

Newspapers: past to present

Since the 1980s newspapers have had to compete with television, teletext and radio for their audiences. However, print media still has an advantage over electronic news, as it is portable and can be read in different places and stored more quickly for reference. Instead of competing with other media formats for speed, newspapers have become more like magazines, offering a range of sections and services for different target audiences. The reader usually turns to the page that interests them, therefore it is important that the front page and the inside page tell them exactly where to find what they want. Readers are enticed by the following:

▌ special offers
▌ in-depth features
▌ supplements
▌ pages of letters
▌ gossip columns
▌ sports
▌ television and radio listings
▌ crosswords, horoscopes and cartoons

The decline in newspaper sales

Study the circulation figures for January 2002 for newspapers, published by the Audit Bureau of Circulation, on page 146.

The *Sun* is the highest selling newspaper with a circulation figure of 3.47 million.

The *Daily Mail* is the highest selling 'middlebrow' paper with a circulation figure of 2.47 million. The overall picture is one of a decline in circulation among the national titles. In January 1997, the daily papers together sold 14,064,089 copies. In January 1999, the total figure had reduced by 500,000. By June 2002, the figure was 13,648,792, nearly another 500,000 down from 1999. The Sunday titles have reduced by almost a million in two years.

ACTIVITY 2

1. Study three newspapers, for example, the *Mirror*, the *Guardian*, and the *Voice*.
2. Create a chart with the title down the left side and include the headings: 'Features' and 'Service/Special Offer' on the right. Use the following as a guide:

Title	Features	Service/Special Offer
The *Mirror*	'Kop Guns' Liverpool's football match.	cheap price (usually 30p) Newspaper of the year award ×2
The *Guardian*		
The *Voice*		

3. What type of feature or service/special offer does each front cover offer the reader? Discuss what is on the cover as well as what is promised inside.

The fight to retain readers

Newspapers tabloids and broadsheets have fought to retain and to win new readers over the years. The *Mirror* tried to win new audiences by changing its name from the *Daily Mirror*. Its old image was typically aimed at working class men over the age of 40. In 1995 however, the new image was targeted at trendy ABC1s (see Chapter Three on demographic profiles) who live in the cities. By introducing younger music world personalities, such as Tony Parson, and football stars to 'write' features, the *Mirror* hoped to fight back against the *Sun* who reduced the price of their paper to 10p, for long periods of time. It is generally accepted that this is what happened – in News Corp terms, it would be considered weak if such a strategy had not been undertaken. This proved unsuccessful however and so the *Mirror* has now returned to a more familiar approach of ensuring that show business features attract the over 20 year olds as well as those under the age of 30.

Sales boosting tactics

- Reduced price.
- Free gifts.
- Prize-winning competitions.
- Subscription offers.
- Increase in personalisation of stories, for example, the royal family or politicians' private lives.
- More show business stories.
- Changes in layout and format, for example, tabloid newspaper format.
- Supplements offering specialist sections, for example, women's page or financial guide.
- Changing editors more frequently.
- Slimming down the number of people employed.
- Using technology to download news feeds, information and images.

National Newspaper – 6 Monthly Report
National Newspaper Data for the six months of: September 2001 to February 2002

Title	Overall Total Average Net Circulation
National Morning Popular	
The Mirror	2,164,987
Daily Record	588,987
Daily Star	617,242
The Star – Republic of Ireland	104,966
The Sun	3,442,563
National Morning Mid Market	
Daily Express	955,256
The Daily Mail	2,476,559
National Morning Quality	
The Daily Telegraph	1,018,654
Financial Times	484,252
The Guardian	413,650
The Independent	231,221
The Scotsman	80,340
The Times	722,452
National Morning Sporting	
Racing Post	75,675
London Evening	
Evening Standard	432,026
National Morning Group	
The Mirror/Daily Record	2,753,974
Daily Star/The Star – Republic of Ireland	722,208
National Sunday Popular	
News of the World	4,022,807
Sunday Mail	4,694,216
Sunday Mirror	1,822,135
Sunday People	1,365,620
Sunday Sport	200,129
National Sunday Mid Market	
Sunday Express	847,111
The Mail on Sunday	2,374,527
National Sunday Quality	
Independent on Sunday	239,107
The Observer	465,580
Scotland on Sunday	90,230
The Business	65,467
The Sunday Telegraph	810,181
The Sunday Times	1,418,903
National Sunday Sporting	
Sport First	83,457

Fig 9.4   Circulation figures for national newspapers

Source: ABC

All newspapers have become more competitive about their audience. This has been described as 'dumbing down' if the paper is a broadsheet and 'dumbing up' if the paper is a tabloid. 'Dumbing down' means being less serious and including more sensational or leisure-related items.

Newspaper content

The content of newspapers differs for the following reasons:

▮ Cost.
▮ Expected literacy level of the reader.
▮ Each paper caters for what they think their particular readership is interested in, for example, sport, politics or culture.
▮ Readership varies according to social group (see Chapter Three: Producers and Audiences) class, age, gender and race. People make their choices according to their interests, politics, education and class and family tradition.
▮ Newspaper conventions about what is newsworthy – news values.

Cost

The cost of a newspaper is an important factor in the choice readers make. In 1999, tabloid papers can cost as little as 20p and the broad-sheet papers cost about 45p. With price wars dominated largely by NewsCorp, the owners of *The Times* and the *Sun*, the market has been tough for all newspapers.

Since electronic media have tended to take up to 70% of the market for news as a source (*Spectrum Magazine*, ITC, Winter 1996), papers have offered lower prices or occasional discounts to lure the reader to their paper. Free holidays, lottery tickets and free gifts are a few of the techniques used.

Readership

Every newpaper is thought to have some political leanings, some of which change according to the issue of the day. Following are some examples:

▮ the *Guardian* and the *Independent* – broadly left of centre and liberal politics.
▮ the *Mirror* and the *Daily Record* – traditionally old Labour but now said to be anti-Labour.
▮ the *Daily Mail*, the *Telegraph*, *The Times*, the *Sun*, the *Daily Star* and the *Express* – Conservative ranging from centre politics to far right.
▮ the *Voice* – black community politics.
▮ the *Daily East* – pro-Pakistan politics.

The politics of a paper is not a concern to everyone, and other factors such as age, specialist interests and price may be the overriding reasons for buying a paper.

Local papers tend to target the older demographic of over 25 year olds, though they can rely on the fact that events in schools, workplaces and the town generally involve everyone at some time. Classified adverts and 'what's on' sections are also important elements of local newspapers. Advertising revenue contributes more to local papers than the nationals, who earn more through sales. The massive increase since 1980 in free sheets (papers given away or posted through the letterbox) showed how advertising is an important part of financing local papers whilst also providing a service for bargain hunters and special interests needs. However, the recent decline in free sheets shows that even this tactic did not last.

News values

ACTIVITY 3

In Chapter Seven: Television and Radio News, the concept of news values was introduced. Review the following questions:

1. **a** Is the event big enough for people to find it interesting or 'newsworthy'?
   b Is the news negative? Has it happened recently?
   c Is the meaning clear? Is the news relevant to us?
   d Is it expected? Is it unexpected? Is it already in the news?
   e Does the news fit with other news in the paper?
   f Is it possible to introduce personalities into the story? For example is it Tony Blair's problem, rather than the Government's problem? Is the news about famous or powerful people?
   g Is the news about the UK, USA, Europe, Japan, or Russia?

2. Study the front covers of the papers pictured earlier in this chapter.
   a Draw up a list of types of news item for each paper using the questions above as a guide.
   b How many items are devoted to features that are about negative news or Westminster?
   c How many items are devoted to celebrity and leisure-related stories?

3. Write a summary of your investigations answering the question: is there any difference in the balance of types of stories between the different papers?

4. Study a selection of a day's newspapers and list the main items covered on that day by percentage of space column inches used. You could compare

coverage between a tabloid like the *Sun* to a broadsheet such as the *Telegraph*.

For example, from 9 September to 15 September 2001, the amount of column inches judged the most important by Britain's main 'highbrow' and 'middlebrow' papers (including the *Guardian*, *The Times*, the *Daily Telegraph*, the *Independent*, the *Sunday Times*, the *Observer* and the *Daily Mail*) were as follows:

Feature	Number of column inches
US terrorist attacks	6,612
TUC conference	570.5
Zimbabwe	562.5
Tory leadership	477.5
Northern Ireland	445
Middle East	300.5
UN conference on racism	176

Since September 11th 2001, when suicide aeroplane bombers destroyed New York's two World Trade Towers, the *Mirror*'s editor, Piers Morgan, has pledged to devote the *Mirror*'s front pages to serious news and not to celebrity-led gossip. The official reason given for this is to show an understanding of wide world affairs and how they affect the UK. Unofficially, the *Mirror* wants to attract more middle brow (male) readers who are interested in order of priority in: men's sport, politics and celebrity gossip.

Specimen Examination question: OCR
Print based textual analysis

Study the examples on page 153 (made into one page of small front pages) and page 138.

a) The *Mirror* April 22nd 2001(Ulrika! + Insurrection),

b) February 23rd 2002 (Beckham, Kylie +
   Blunkett – police)

c) March 28th and 29th 2002 (Campbell and
   Dud is Dead, Win a Naomi + The Slave
   Nurses) and

d) April 4th 2002 ('O little town of
   Bethlehem'), on page 138.

How far do you think the historical events of
September 11th 2001 have affected the
Mirror's front page coverage in its style and
content?   **(30 marks)**

Study last week's *Mirror* front pages on the
website: www.mirror.com to see how many
pages over a week are about serious world
affairs or about celebrities lives.

Format

What is interesting about *New Nation*'s and
the *Voice*'s 2002 layout is how similar they
are in relation to the *Mirror* a year previously.
Both run supplementary sections, like
magazines, and offer prizes and special
offers. The *Mirror* has simplified its cover – it
keeps an uncluttered masthead, one
subsidiary story and one main one – these
are given full space and design impact:
usually sport or celebrity supporting a world
or a social issue.

The Press
Freedom of the press

News stories are often written to tell the
public that someone is hiding something from
them. The media and journalism are one of
the four major forces in society, after the
state, the church and the family unit. The
national press is often the first to expose the
wrongdoings of politicians, personalities and
companies. The bigger the scandal; the
bigger the story. The paper involved can
claim a 'scoop', which is the term used to
describe the first paper to print the story
exclusively. 'Scoops' on allegedly corrupt
politicians and adultery in the royal family
have helped the newspaper industry to thrive
in the last fifteen years.

Journalists can also pay people to talk about
their neighbours or adulterous lovers. Some
journalists wait near school gates to catch
parents, to follow them into the house or
even to their sick beds in hospitals to snap
photographs. The resulting dilemma is not
easy to solve. On the one hand we want our
press to expose corruption and wrongdoing.
On the other hand we should have a right to
privacy and have no fear of harassment and
intrusion from greedy journalists.

Voluntary code of conduct

In the UK there has been no strict code of
conduct to prevent the press from intruding
on private lives, except if the subject is under
the age of sixteen. There is however, a code
of conduct that is voluntary.

This code is managed by the Press
Complaints Commission (PCC). The PCC self-
regulate the news industry. This means that
although there are no actual laws that can be
used, all papers agree to abide by this code.
An example of this was when the *Daily Mirror*
published pictures of Diana, Princess of
Wales training in the gym, and the paper was
fined and suspended from membership for a
short time.

Press control simulation

NEWSPAPER AND MAGAZINE PUBLISHING IN THE U.K.
CODE OF PRACTICE
(Ratified by the Press Complaints Commission 1st December 1999)

All members of the press have a duty to maintain the highest professional and ethical standards. This Code sets the benchmarks for those standards. It both protects the rights of the individual and upholds the public's right to know.

The Code is the cornerstone of the system of self-regulation to which the industry has made a binding commitment. Editors and publishers must ensure that the Code is observed rigorously not only by their staff but also by anyone who contributes to their publications.

It is essential to the workings of an agreed code that it be honoured not only to the letter but in the full spirit. The Code should not be interpreted so narrowly as to compromise its commitment to respect the rights of the individual, nor so broadly that it prevents publication in the public interest. It is the responsibility of editors to co-operate with the P.C.C. as swiftly as possible in the resolution of complaints.

Any publication which is criticised by the P.C.C. under one of the following clauses must print the adjudication which follows in full and with due prominence.

1. Accuracy
(i) Newspapers and periodicals must take care not to publish inaccurate, misleading or distorted material including pictures.

(ii) Whenever it is recognised that a significant inaccuracy, misleading statement or distorted report has been published, it must be corrected promptly and with due prominence.

(iii) An apology must be published whenever appropriate.

(iv) Newspapers, whilst free to be partisan, must distinguish clearly between comment, conjecture and fact.

(v) A newspaper or periodical must report fairly and accurately the outcome of an action for defamation to which it has been a party.

2. Opportunity to reply
A fair opportunity to reply to in-accuracies must be given to individuals or organisations when reasonably called for.

★3. Privacy
(i) Everyone is entitled to respect for his or her private and family life, home, health and correspondence. A publication will be expected to justify intrusions into any individual's private life without consent.

(ii) The use of longlens photography to take pictures of people in private places without their consent is unacceptable.

Note – Private places are public or private property where there is a reasonable expectation of privacy.

★4. Harassment
(i) Journalists and photographers must neither obtain nor seek to obtain information or pictures through intimidation, harassment or persistent pursuit.

(ii) They must not photograph individuals in private places (as defined in the note to Clause 3) without their consent; must not persist in telephoning, questioning, pursuing or photographing individuals after having been asked to desist; must not remain on their property after having been asked to leave and must not follow them.

(iii) Editors must ensure that those working for them comply with these requirements and must not publish material from other sources which does not meet these requirements.

5. Intrusion into grief or shock
In cases involving grief or shock, enquiries must be carried out and approaches made with sympathy and discretion. Publication must be handled sensitively at such times, but this should not be interpreted as restricting the right to report judicial proceedings.

★6. Children
(i) Young people should be free to complete their time at school without unnecessary intrusion.

(ii) Journalists must not interview or photograph children under the age of 16 on subjects involving the welfare of the child or of any other child, in the absence of or without the consent of a parent or other adult who is responsible for the children.

(iii) Pupils must not be approached or photographed while at school without the permission of the school authorities.

(iv) There must be no payment to minors for material involving the welfare of children nor payment to parents or guardians for material about their children or wards unless it is demonstrably in the child's interest.

(v) Where material about the private life of a child is published, there must be justification for publication other than the fame, notoriety or position of his or her parents or guardian.

★7. Children in sex cases
1. The press must not, even where the law does not prohibit it, identify children under the age of 16 who are involved in cases concerning sexual offences, whether as victims, or as witnesses.
2. In any press report of a case involving a sexual offence against a child –
(i) The child must not be identified.
(ii) The adult may be identified.
(iii) The word "incest" must not be used where a child victim might be identified.
(iv) Care must be taken that nothing in the report implies the relationship between the accused and the child.

★8. Listening devices
Journalists must not obtain or publish material obtained by using clandestine listening devices or by intercepting private telephone conversations.

★9. Hospitals
(i) Journalists or photographers making enquiries at hospitals or similar institutions must identify themselves to a responsible executive and obtain permission before entering non-public areas.

(ii) The restrictions on intruding into privacy are particularly relevant to enquiries about individuals in hospitals or similar institutions.

★10. Reporting of crime
The press must avoid identifying relatives or friends of persons convicted or accused of crime without their consent. Particular regard should be paid to the potentially vulnerable position of children who are witnesses to, or victims of, crime. This should not be interpreted as restricting the right to report judicial proceedings.

THE PUBLIC INTEREST
There may be exceptions to the clauses marked ★ where they can be demonstrated to be in the public interest.

1. The public interest includes:
(i) Detecting or exposing crime or a serious misdemeanour.
(ii) Protecting public health and safety.
(iii) Preventing the public from being misled by some statement or action of an individual or organisation.

2. In any case where the public interest is invoked, the Press Complaints Commission will require a full explanation by the editor demonstrating how the public interest was served.

3. There is a public interest in freedom of expression itself. The Commission will therefore have regard to the extent to which material has, or is about to, become available to the public.

4. In cases involving children editors must demonstrate an exceptional public interest to over-ride the normally paramount interests of the child.

★11. Misrepresentation
(i) Journalists must not generally obtain or seek to obtain information or pictures through misrepresentation or subterfuge.

(ii) Documents or photographs should be removed only with the consent of the owner.

(iii) Subterfuge can be justified only in the public interest and only when material cannot be obtained by any other means.

12. Victims of sexual assault
The press must not identify victims of sexual assault or publish material likely to contribute to such identification unless there is adequate justification and, by law, they are free to do so.

13. Discrimination
(i) The press must avoid prejudicial or pejorative reference to a person's race, colour, religion, sex or sexual orientation or to any physical or mental illness or disability.

(ii) It must avoid publishing details of a person's race, colour, religion, sexual orientation, physical or mental illness or disability unless these are directly relevant to the story.

14. Financial journalism
(i) Even where the law does not prohibit it, journalists must not use for their own profit financial information they receive in advance of its general publication, nor should they pass such information to others.

(ii) They must not write about shares or securities in whose performance they know that they or their close families have a significant financial interest, without disclosing the interest to the editor or financial editor.

(iii) They must not buy or sell, either directly or through nominees or agents, shares or securities about which they have written recently or about which they intend to write in the near future.

15. Confidential sources
Journalists have a moral obligation to protect confidential sources of information.

★16. Payment for articles
(i) Payment or offers of payment for stories or information must be made directly or through agents to witnesses or potential witnesses in current criminal proceedings except where the material concerned ought to be published in the public interest and there is an overriding need to make or promise to make a payment for this to be done. Journalists must take every possible step to ensure that no financial dealings have influence on the evidence that those witnesses may give. (An editor authorising such a payment must be prepared to demonstrate that there is a legitimate public interest at stake involving matters that the public has a right to know. The payment or, where accepted, the offer of payment to any witness who is actually cited to give evidence must be disclosed to the prosecution and the defence and the witness should be advised of this.)

(ii) Payment or offers of payment for stories, pictures or information, must not be made directly or through agents to convicted or confessed criminals or to their associates – who may include family, friends and colleagues – except where the material concerned ought to be published in the public interest and payment is necessary for this to be done.

Published by The Press Standards Board of Finance Ltd., 142 Queen Street, Glasgow G1 3BU. Registered in England & Wales No. 2554323.

Fig 9.5   Newspaper and magazine Code of Practice

Source: The Press Standards Board of Finance Ltd.

Read paragraphs 1 to 6 inclusive of the Code of Practice. You are the editor of the local newspaper and you also have children who attend school in the area. You are also a school governor and are keen to maintain the favourable reputation of the school in the community. You have a duty to inform the public of matters of 'public interest'.

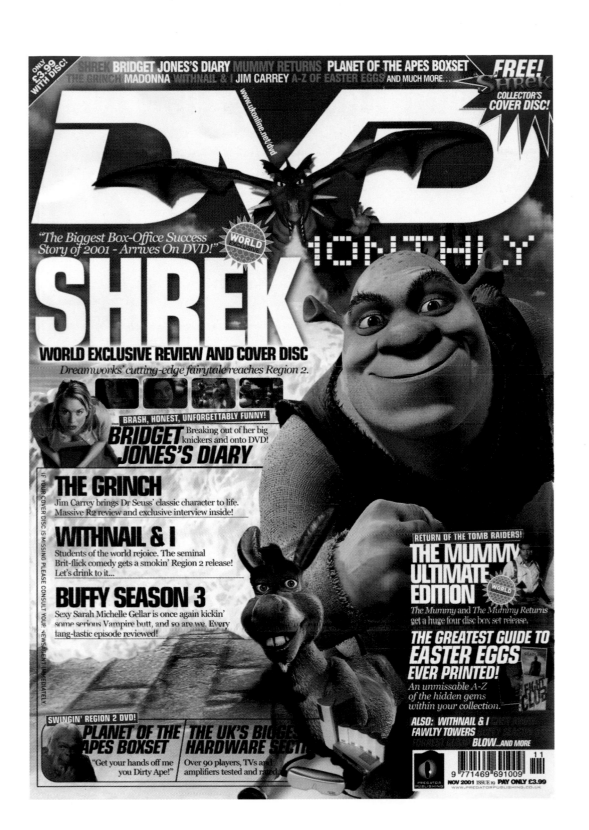

ONLY £3.99 WITH DISC!

SHREK BRIDGET JONES'S DIARY MUMMY RETURNS PLANET OF THE APES BOXSET FREE!
THE GRINCH MADONNA WITHNAIL & I JIM CARREY A-Z OF EASTER EGGS AND MUCH MORE... SHREK

COLLECTOR'S COVER DISC!

www.ukonline.net/dvd

DVD
MONTHLY

WORLD EXCLUSIVE

"The Biggest Box-Office Success Story of 2001 - Arrives On DVD!"

SHREK
WORLD EXCLUSIVE REVIEW AND COVER DISC
Dreamworks' cutting-edge fairytale reaches Region 2.

BRASH, HONEST, UNFORGETTABLY FUNNY!

BRIDGET JONES'S DIARY
Breaking out of her big knickers and onto DVD!

THE GRINCH
Jim Carrey brings Dr Seuss' classic character to life. Massive R2 review and exclusive interview inside!

WITHNAIL & I
Students of the world rejoice. The seminal Brit-flick comedy gets a smokin' Region 2 release! Let's drink to it...

BUFFY SEASON 3
Sexy Sarah Michelle Gellar is once again kickin' some serious Vampire butt, and so are we. Every fang-tastic episode reviewed!

IF YOUR COVER DISC IS MISSING PLEASE CONSULT YOUR NEWSAGENT IMMEDIATELY

RETURN OF THE TOMB RAIDERS!

THE MUMMY ULTIMATE EDITION
WORLD

The Mummy and The Mummy Returns get a huge four disc box set release.

THE GREATEST GUIDE TO EASTER EGGS EVER PRINTED!
An unmissable A-Z of the hidden gems within your collection.

FIGHT CLUB

ALSO: WITHNAIL & I FAWLTY TOWERS

BLOW...AND MORE

SWINGIN' REGION 2 DVD!

PLANET OF THE APES BOXSET
"Get your hands off me you Dirty Ape!"

THE UK'S BIGGEST HARDWARE SECTION
Over 90 players, TVs and amplifiers tested and rated.

PREDATOR PUBLISHING

9 771469 691009

1 1

NOV 2001 ISSUE 19 PAY ONLY £3.99
WWW.PREDATORPUBLISHING.CO.UK

NEW
BEST EVER FLAVOUR
Rival survival! No. 5/5
WALKERS®
Crisps
Cheese & Owen
Cheese & Onion flavour crisps

DAILY WALKERS®

CHEESE & ONION FLAVOUR 1999

RIVAL SURVIVAL!

Soccer hero Michael Owen and TV star Gary Lineker put their rivalry behind them today and publicly declared: 'We're the best of mates'. The pair decided to speak out in Britain's No.1 newspaper, The Daily Walkers, amid growing rumours of jealousy between the 19 year old superstar and the 38 year old former England golden boy. They toasted their friendship with a glass of champagne before going their separate ways and Michael even offered to drop his new pal off at his bus stop...

FOREIGN NEWS

CHEESE AND ONION FLAVOUR CRISPS. INGREDIENTS: potatoes, vegetable oil, cheese and onion flavour [flavouring, flavour enhancer (E621, E627), colour (annatto)], salt.
KARTOFFELCHIPS MIT KÄSE- UND ZWIEBELGESCHMACK. ZUTATEN: Kartoffeln, pflanzliches Öl, Käse- und Zwiebelaroma [Aromastoffe, Geschmacksverstärker (E621, E627) Farbstoff (Annatto)], Speisesalz.
PATATAS FRITAS CON SABOR QUESO Y CEBOLLA. INGREDIENTES: patatas, aceite vegetal, aroma de queso y cebolla, [aromatizante, potenciadores de sabor (E621, E627), colorante (annato)], sal.
CHIPS GOÛT FROMAGE ET OIGNONS. INGRÉDIENTS: pommes de terre, huile végétale, arôme fromage et oignon (aromatisant, exhausteur de goût (E621, E627), colorant (rocou), sel.
BATATAS FRITAS COM SABOR A QUEIJO E CEBOLA. INGREDIENTES: Batata, óleo vegetal, aroma de Queijo e Cebola [Aromatizante, intensificadores de Sabor (E621, E627), corante (anato)], Sal.
ΠΑΤΑΤΑΚΙΑ ΜΕ ΓΕΥΣΗ ΤΥΡΙΟΥ ΚΑΙ ΚΡΕΜΜΥΔΙΟΥ. ΣΥΣΤΑΤΙΚΑ: Πατάτες, φυτικά έλαια, άρωμα τυρί και κρεμμύδι [μπαχαρικό, βελτιωτικό γεύσης (E621, E627) χρωστική (αννάτο)], αλάτι.

EDITOR'S COMMENT..

✉ If you are not completely satisfied with this product, send the packet(s) and its contents, stating reason for return and when and where you bought it to:
CONSUMER SERVICES DEPARTMENT, WALKERS SNACK FOODS LTD., PO BOX 23, LEICESTER LE4 8ZU.
Applies to U.K. only.
Your statutory rights are not affected.
Packaged in a protective atmosphere.
Store in a cool, dry place.
WALKERS is a registered trademark.
The WALKERS Banner/Sun Logo is a registered trademark. ©1999.

TYPICAL NUTRITIONAL INFORMATION		
	Per 100g	Per 34.5g Pack
Energy	2257 kJ	779 kJ
	540 kcal	186 kcal
Protein	6 g	2.1 g
Carbohydrate	48 g	16.6 g
Fat	36 g	12.4 g

5 000328 748054 >

MINDESTENS HALTBAR BIS:
CONSUMIR PREFERENTEMENTE ANTES DE:
A CONSOMMER AVANT:
CONSUMIR DE PREFERENCIA ANTES DE:
ΚΑΤΑΝΑΛΩΣΗ ΠΡΙΝ ΑΠΟ:
BEST BEFORE

29 JAN 00 B316
08:58 0749 B13

CHEESE AND ONION FLAVOUR CRISPS
KARTOFFELCHIPS MIT KÄSE-UND ZWIEBELGESCHMACK
PATATAS FRITAS CON SABOR QUESO Y CEBOLLA
CHIPS GOÛT FROMAGE ET OIGNONS
BATATAS FRITAS COM SABOR A QUEIJO E CEBOLA
ΠΑΤΑΤΑΚΙΑ ΜΕ ΓΕΥΣΗ ΤΥΡΙΟΥ ΚΑΙ ΚΡΕΜΜΥΔΙΟΥ

34.5g ℮

LMP03099FKL2 .M

MARKS & SPENCER
Handcooked Crisp
175g℮
cooked in sunflower oil
SCHWARZER PFEFFER

FREE! SEXY R&B STICKERS INSIDE

COSMO *girl!*

FOR FUN, FEARLESS TEENS

BUMPER CHRISTMAS ISSUE AND STILL ONLY
£1.49
DECEMBER 2001

10 secret
love signs that say he's crazy for you!

World exclusive!
Destiny's Child
On Guys, Christmas Gifts and Growing Up in the Spotlight

Nail-biting real life story
"I survived a near-death ordeal on my school trip"

year-end special!
A Year Of YOU!
The teens who made 2001 rock

Channel Phwoar!
Single Sexy Snoggable
Which soap dish is right for you?

Ryan Kwanten, Andy McNair, Philip Olivier
PLUS! Jack Ryder and many, many more!

Party on!
Your 'eek'-est Xmas confessions ever!
Party-perfect hair special
Five-minute makeovers
65 sizzling looks (all under £30)

FREE! Xmas e-cards

www.cosmogirl.co.uk

Me, Lucy and Charlie

TASK 1

There is an anonymous phone call to the newspaper, stating that their son was beaten up by a group of girls at the school. Discuss.

(5 marks)

TASK 2

A teacher is suspected of having an affair with a student. Discuss.

(5 marks)

TASK 3

a How would you discover the truth behind one or both of the stories in Tasks 1 and 2? **(5 marks)**

b How would you avoid the charge of harassment or intrusion on the private lives of the suspects, victims, parents or the school? **(10 marks)**

c At what point do you think it is in the 'public interest' to publish the story? Would you publish all or any one of these stories? **(10 marks)**

Press controls

Other forms of press control are:

▮ No filming, photography or tape recording in law courts.

▮ The press can be excluded from the courts by the judge.

▮ The Official Secrets Act and The Prevention of Terrorism Act can be used to stop journalists revealing the whereabouts of army movements, for example.

▮ The police can confiscate journalists' material under the Criminal Evidence Act and the Criminal Justice Act.

▮ Libel is often the main weapon used by people to stop journalists from publishing material. Elton John sued the *Sun* successfully for accusing him of being an alcoholic, and Jason Donovan sued *The Face* magazine for suggesting he was a homosexual.

Policies   Page 1 of 2

Policy Positions

Press Wise

Where We Stand on Issues

Libel

We support the abolition of the current libel laws, which only serve to protect the rich and powerful, often from criticism and investigation in the public interest. We do not see the recent reforms as enhancing the rights of ordinary people. Our view is with the Human Rights Act, the Data Protection Acts, a more effective system of press regulation (see below) together with comprehensive Freedom of Information legislation should provide sufficient protection against abuse of media power for the libel laws to be repealed altogether.

The Press Complaints Commission

Experience has shown that even equipped with an improved Code of Practice following the death of Diana, Princess of Wales, the PCC remains a flawed and ineffective body. Flawed, because no commission funded by the newspapers upon which it adjudicates, and working to a code produced by the very editors liable to censure, can possibly inspire public confidence. Ineffective, because it is powerless to impose meaningful sanctions.

While opposed to statutory regulation of the press, we think that the PCC should be reconstituted as follows:

a. A membership comprised of the general public and working journalists (not editors), who would produce a revised code.

b. Funding via a levy on all daily and weekly newspapers proportional to their circulation.

c. The power to receive and consider complaints from third parties (following the pattern of broadcasting's regulatory bodies)

d. The power to require financial compensation for individual victims of media abuse (but not fines per se).

Privacy law

We are opposed to a Privacy Law specifically designed to limit the media, on similar grounds to our objection to the laws of libel. The protection of privacy, we believe, will be adequately dealt with by the Human Rights Act, which balances the right to privacy with the right

Site Navigation

Book Reviews

The PressWise view on new publications related to the media

Briefings

The PressWise view on topics of importance in the media arena

Bulletin Archives

15/11/99 – 16/5/00
23/5/00 – 10/5/01
27/6/01.....

Archives of PressWise activities, and information about media events since the establishment of this web site in November 1999

Data

The latest on the Data Protection Act

Ethics

A collection of journalistic codes of ethics from more than 60 countries around the world

Forum Reports

Full reports of forums staged by PressWise

Links

To lots of interesting sites (new listing for refugee/asylum seekers sites)

Fig 9.6   PressWise on the web

Source: © PressWise Trust

The Campaign for Press and Broadcasting Freedom and PressWise

The Campaign for Press and Broadcasting Freedom was set up to argue that the public should have a right to legal redress.

Campaigners for press freedom also feel that more controls over the press may lead to politicians getting away with actions they do not want the public to know about, for example, public money spent on overseas weapons supply or development.

There is a charity called PressWise which publishes material about the media. Their aim is to protect the vulnerable public, but also to allow investigative journalism into public life. As a body devoted to media ethics, they are not in a powerful position. However, in the light of the death of Diana, Princess of Wales in 1997, the debate about the rights of journalists and the public is still very strong.

Recent concerns about the roles of the Press Complaints Commission, the role of the press and the government and the law courts have lead to some sensational new developments. In the case of Naomi Campbell who the *Mirror* printed a photograph of, on the street, coming out of a drugs rehabilitation group session, the verdict of the court was to award Naomi Campbell damages for press intrusion into her privacy but to only award £3,500 in damages. Naomi Campbell saw the verdict as a moral victory and gave the money to charity – the symbolism of the success is noted by the *Voice* and *New Nation* – both papers representing mainly UK African Caribbean black communities. The *Mirror*'s response was to argue that the case was awarded only a nominal amount and that the judgement was technical not moral, and that she had lied in court.

ACTIVITY 4

Read the front pages of the *Mirror, New Nation* and the *Voice* (pages 141 and 153) What do you think is the right judgement in this case?

Should public figures accept that their success and moral conduct is dependent on public interest? Or should newspapers observe some areas of celebrities' lives as private?

(You can read further views on the case at www.guardian.co.uk/Archive if you select the period: March/April 2002)

ACTIVITY 5

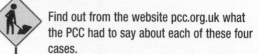

Find out from the website pcc.org.uk what the PCC had to say about each of these four cases.

- Sarah Cox, a radio and television presenter, had photographs taken of her naked on a private beach and successfully sued the *Sunday People*.
- Anna Ford, a newscaster, had photographs taken of her wearing a swimsuit on a beach she thought was private and part of the hotel she was staying in.
- The prime minister made a complaint to the PCC against the *Mail* and *Telegraph* about attempting to reveal the grades required for his son to get into University.
- JK Rowling (author of the Harry Potter novels) complained about photographs of her child that were taken and printed without her permission.

Write down whether you think these judgements were fair or not.

Press freedom to print or individual rights for privacy?

The European Human Rights Act was introduced into the UK in September 2000 and it stresses the rights of individuals for privacy and it also provides support for the freedom of the court.

Four recent cases show how the law is increasingly becoming involved in issues about rights for individual privacy and press freedom

- A married footballer unsuccessfully stopped the *Sunday People* from publishing his name in connection with two women he had affairs with.
- The film stars Michael Douglas and

Fig 9.7   The *Mirror*
Source: The *Mirror*, 28 March 2002/Mirrorpix. com

Fig 9.8   The *Mirror*
Source: The *Mirror*, 29 March 2002/Mirrorpix. com

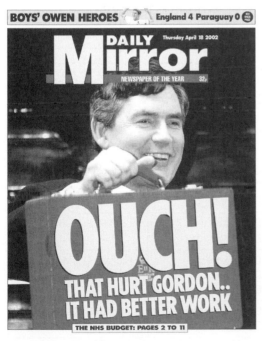

Fig 9.9   The *Mirror*
Source: The *Mirror*, 18 April 2002/Mirrorpix. com

Fig 9.10   *New Nation*
Source: *New Nation*, 1 April 2002

Catherine Zeta-Jones successfully sued *Hello!* magazine for undisclosed damages because they published wedding photographs without their permission.

∎ A headteacher won damages of £5000 after being falsely accused of harassing a member of staff.

∎ The *Sun* was successfully sued for falsely alleging Elton John had removed the voice boxes of nearby guard dogs that were making too much noise.

Payment for stories

Another area of moral debate is the question of whether people who are criminals or who might be criminals should gain money for publishing their stories.

Ownership

In Britain the print media are dominated by seven companies (as at June 2002). The following ownership statistics have been

ACTIVITY 6

Write an essay (maximum of 500 words) in answer to the following question.
Do you think there is a case for more laws or fewer to prevent harassment, intrusion or payment of money to the public?

adapted from *The Guardian Media Guide*, 2002. The percentage figures in Table 9.1 are of aggregated weekly sales according to ABC May 2001 figures.

Cheque book journalism

Cheque book journalism is where witnesses to an event are paid to tell their story. This raises the question of whether a witness will colour his/her story if they know it is for the money. Many witnesses of the murderer Rosemary West were paid by newspapers before they went into court to give evidence.

NATIONAL NEWSPAPER OWNERSHIP			
Group Name	**Market share**	**Title**	**Executive Control**
News International	34.5%	Sun The Times Sunday Times News of the World	Rupert Murdoch
Trinity Mirror	19%	Daily Mirror Sunday Mirror People	Victor Blank
Daily Mail and General Trust	19%	Daily Mail Mail on Sunday	Lord Ruthermore
Northern and Shell	12%	Daily Express Daily Star Sunday Express	Richard Desmond
Hollinger	7.5%	Daily Telegraph Sunday Telegraph	Conrad Black

Group Name	Market share	Title	Executive Control
Guardian Media Group	3.5%	Guardian Observer	The Scott Trust
Pearson	3%	Financial Times	The Pearson Board
Independent Newspapers	1.5%	Independent Independent on Sunday	Tony O'Reilly

Table 9.1

Source: Adapted from *The Guardian Media Guide,* 2002/Steve Peak and Paul Fisher © *The Guardian*

Regional and local ownership

This can be broken down as follows.

Group name (2000 position)	Titles	Weekly circulation
1 Trinity Mirror (1)	241	17,756,103
2 NewsQuest (Media Group) (2)	202	10,037,623
3 Northcliffe Newspapers Group (3)	95	9,239,058
4 Associated Newspapers (5)	7	6,043,475
5 Johnston Press (4)	190	5,509,417
6 Regional Independent Media	53	3,304,975
7 Guardian Media Group (8)	45	2,650,805
8 Eastern Counties Newspaper Group (9)	66	2,617,440
9 The Midland News Association (10)	19	2,216,118
10 Independent Newspapers (Regionals) (11)	26	1,590,675

Table 9.2

Source: Adapted from *The Guardian Media Guide, 2002*/Steve Peak and Paul Fisher © *The Guardian*

Most locals are owned by four big publishers and the top ten publish nearly four fifths of UK titles. There are more than 1,300 local newspapers in the UK, including 23 mornings, 74 evenings, 17 Sundays, around 530 weeklies and 700 free newspapers. 83% of all British adults read a regional newspaper (38 million people). 37% of people who read a regional paper do not read a national daily.

Locals are the largest advertising medium in the UK after television. Although by mid-July 2001 there was a big slow down in advertising revenue generally and as much as a 10% drop was recorded by Trinity Mirror for June alone.

Discuss

1. Who owns your local daily newspaper?
2. What are its current circulation figures?
3. Obtain a press pack from a local newspaper. Analyse how many people read it from different age groups. Which age group has the highest readership? How does the company gain its revenue?

Specimen Examination Question: OCR

Section One Question Two: Unseen Printed Text (this question should take approximately 1½ hours of the total 2 hours)

These Tasks are not actual examination questions. The questions are the sole work of the author and are devised to match the style, mark allocation and format of the relevant question papers from OCR. They are designed for examination practice. The Tasks are designed to follow the examination paper timings and mark allocations. It is essential that candidates check the specified topics set for the year of their examination, by the examination board. For previous examination papers contact the examination board direct. **The print extracts are from: the *Mirror*, 4 April 2002 and the *Voice*, 1 April 2002. Advice: study pages 138 and 141 in this textbook.**

You will have 30 minutes reading and note-making time.

▌ Before you study the pages read all of the questions first.

▌ Study both pages, including text, headlines, photographs and graphics carefully.

▌ You are to make notes on your answer paper and you should put a diagonal line through your notes at the end of the exam.

a i) What word or phrase would you use to identify this type of newspaper?
(2 marks)

ii) Give reasons for your answer.
(4 marks)

b How are the two front pages similar in the use of the following:

i) the type of language used **(4 marks)**

ii) layout, headline and headings
(4 marks)

iii) the use of pictures and captions
(4 marks)

c i) What kinds of audiences are each newspaper aimed at? **(6 marks)**

ii) Give reasons for your answers.
(6 marks)

d i) Compare the masthead blocks (where the title of the papers are) of the *Mirror* and the *Voice*. What do the words,

typeface and any other information tell you about each paper's image? **(8 marks)**

ii) In what ways is the story of Naomi Campbell presented differently by the two newspapers? Discuss both form and content. **(12 marks)**

Extension Tasks

1 **Research** one newspaper's history and how they have adapted to changing audiences.

2 **Track** a major story and see how long it stays in the news. **Assess** why it moves from the front page or out of the paper altogether.

3 **Take photographs** of a group of students, three of which are snatched and three of which are posed. Select the best image and crop or enlarge the result using a photocopier. **Select** the appropriate typeface font and point size. **Create captions** for each photo, for example, the snatched image could be used in a newspaper's negative story, and the posed picture could be used in a newspaper article about the school or college's excellent performance in exams, science, sport or drama.

4 **Research** press agencies such as Reuters and Agence Press France. These are accessible on the Internet. Find out what they do and who they supply news to.

5 **Draw up** a list of possible sources of news and how news comes to the attention of the editors of newspapers.

6 **Create** a press release to encourage the local press to come and take photographs of your event or item (see also Chapter Three).

Examination Skills

Knowledge and Understanding

There should be an understanding of the different audiences, both in terms of social group and how audiences are targeted as well as created by newspaper producers. Students should be able to use the technical terms as well as the key words listed at the beginning of this chapter. There should be knowledge of the processes, practices and technology involved in the production of newspapers. There should be a good understanding of the news values that each paper tends to use. Examinations will test the ability to categorise and distinguish the different types of paper through their ownership and by the editorial line taken.

Textual Analysis

Students must have the ability to analyse newspapers, and describe and interpret images, graphics, captions and headings, text and copy. Students should be able to explain the different forms and conventions across a range of tabloid and broadsheet formats.

Practical Work

Students should know how to manipulate finished photographs and crop or enlarge them to suit the paper's ownership, editorial style and audience. Students should be able to understand how typeface font, size and presentation effect the image of the newspaper. The selection of stories for front page mock-ups and production should demonstrate an understanding of the forms and conventions of the format chosen. The use of language and slogans should be appropriate to the type of newspaper.

10 TV hospital dramas and documentaries

Real Bedtime Stories?

What you will learn

In this chapter you will cover: fictional and documentary forms and conventions based on hospitals; types and stereotypes of characters; serials and series, messages and values; audiences; planning a treatment and a title sequence for a new drama.

KEY WORDS

- series
- serial
- realism
- narrative
- types
- stereotypes
- representations
- messages and values
- audiences

TECHNICAL WORDS

- settings
- *mise-en-scène*
- shot-reverse-shot
- tracking
- dolly
- trailer
- treatment
- episode
- voice over
- interior/exterior location shooting

Popularity

Hospital dramas have been very popular over the last few years. BBC1's *Casualty* has regularly exceeded 17 million viewers. The American drama *ER* is avidly followed in the UK as well as in the United States. There are also numerous documentaries about hospitals, including series about children's and animal hospitals.

Series and serials

A series is a sequence of programmes that has a finite length, for example 6 to 10 episodes for a drama. The serial is a continuous sequence of programmes, such as a regular two or three day weekly soap. For example, the serial *Casualty* has been running for over 13 years.

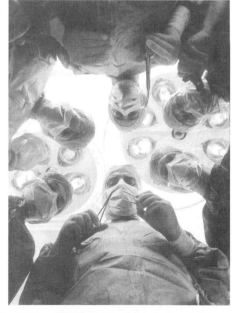

Fig 10.1   What is the appeal of watching doctors and nurses?

Source: © *Independent on Sunday*/John Ferrara, 1998

Why the fascination with hospitals?

Perhaps, as with crime films, we like to find out about behind the scenes of life and death situations – medicine also has a certain mysterious appeal. Or perhaps, we like to know that if we were ill and were taken to hospital we would be prepared for it? There are many and complex reasons for liking hospital dramas. There are also reasons for not liking hospital dramas, for example, the sight of blood is too much for some people. Others argue that hospital drama programmes are really another form of soap and that the entertainment factor lies in being able to identify with someone else's daily traumas and celebrations.

Workplace drama

In fact, hospital dramas are not simply about hospitals and the dramas surrounding the emergency care of patients. They are also about the workplace. One aspect of hospital dramas concerns the relationships between the nurses, staff nurses, doctors, porters and management. Other dramas, like the police serial *The Bill*, focus on the working relationships between the officers on the beat, the detectives and their bosses, in *The Bill*'s case in an inner city police station called Sun Hill.

Viewers identify with the workplace and see how other people react to typical work situations, feelings and actions. The audience can relate to rivalries, prejudice, competition for promotion, ambition, greed and petty teasing. How do colleagues stick together against their superiors? How is the new recruit treated by the more experienced officers? How do different officers handle the same job? What makes a good day's work or a 'bad day at the office'? These questions all have some basis in the viewer's own reality.

Why do men and women watch hospital dramas?

ACTIVITY 1

Read the following account of viewers watching *ER*, taken from an audio-taped transcript (*The Guardian Guide*, 1 March 1998).

ER

The notoriously gruelling episode in which Dr Greene fatally mishandles a problematic birth. Sensitive and self-effacing, Dr Greene is looking endearingly worried, having told the woman whom he eventually kills that all she has is a bladder infection. Transcript of **three women watching an ER episode**:

Jo: Where's George Clooney – he's not in this one at all?

Nicola: Probably off blow-drying his hair somewhere.

Jo: Yes, I notice he never has to wear those shower-cap things they all wear in the operating theatre, so he won't mess up his hair.

Nicola: Anyway, Dr Greene's the best.

Jo and Sarah: No way . . .

Nicola: No, he's vulnerable without being wimpy. He has a quiet authority; it's like he's sexy because he's good at what he does.

Sarah: Well, he's not very good here – he's the Mr Bean of the emergency theatre.

(This appears to be true. Dr Greene is busy bungling the birth, rushing frantically between mother and baby. With blood spurting everywhere, the patient finally departs. 'What did you use – a chainsaw?', asks Greene's waspish superior. The women watching are similarly aghast.)

Jo: I have to say I think George shows Dr Greene in a bad light. You look at him here and you think, what an idiot – he's just not

---

in control. But there are moments in the current series that show his vulnerability and yet are far more telling of his strength.

Jo: Yeah, right . . .

Nicola: No, like in the new series. Whether he's dealing with his relationship with Susan or deciding what to do about a patient, you get an insight into what he's thinking. Yet he's more confident and in control – here he is just like a med. student.

Sarah: But the whole show is a soap opera now – the operations are incidental, whereas in this one the medical drama is centre stage and there's virtually no interaction between the characters. I think it's definitely aimed at women. The men are more complex characters now, they've got no history, and that's why they seem sexy.

Three men talk about ER:

Alex: I never wanted *ER* to end once it started. I always fancied Dr Susan Lewis. She's the ultimate babe.

Paul: What are you talking about? She's completely ordinary.

(Meanwhile Paul and Jim revealed why they have no such obsession – the blood. It turns out that they can't even feel their own pulses without losing their lunch. As Dr Greene's patient seems to be bleeding profusely, this causes problems. Paul actually leaves the room.)

Paul (covering his eyes): I can't watch all that blood.

Alex (riveted): Shut up, I can't hear.

(Alex gets quite lost in the details, as the baby's blood pressure drops and he starts reminiscing about the birth of his own baby. At the tear-jerking finale, the men skilfully defuse the situation with hearty coughing and lame jokes.)

Jim: Men like seeing people being machine-gunned and all blown up, but not having strange blood-drenched things pulled out of them.

ACTIVITY 2

Discuss and write down your responses to the following questions.

1. In what ways are hospital dramas like soap operas? Consider:
   - characters
   - story line
   - dramatic interaction between characters
   - themes
   - workplace communities
   - the patients and the public

2. Do you agree that hospital dramas are aimed at women only?

3. What qualities do you think men and women find unattractive and attractive in *ER*?

4. How realistic do you think any hospital drama is that you have seen? What makes hospital dramas realistic or unrealistic?

5. What plots do hospital dramas tend to have?

Hospital dramas

Hospital dramas have developed from the 1960s merry japes of the *Doctor in The House* films, to the city-based realism of 1980s and 1990s in *Casualty* and *Holby City*. Over the years, a number of hospital types and stereotypes have emerged.

Types and stereotypes

Holby City was promoted in press releases and in TV listings magazines as a spin-off from *Casualty*. The cast contained some well-known faces, such as Michael French (played David Wicks in *EastEnders*), Angela Griffin (ex-*Coronation Street*), Phyllis Logan (ex-*Lovejoy*) and Nicola Stephenson (ex-*Brookside*).

The location is set in a cardiology unit in Holby, the unit where *Casualty* patients are sent when they need serious heart operations. The first series of this soap was in eight parts and deliberately set out to be linked with *Casualty*. Each episode was an hour long, and dealt with the relationships of the doctors and nurses. Unlike *Casualty*, the focus was on the professionals rather than on the patients, who play a more equal part in the drama of *Casualty*.

> 'We had to make *Holby City* different from *Casualty* or there was no point. That meant that the doctors had to drive the drama rather than work off the backs of the patients. There was no point in making it a homage to *ER*. This is Britain not America. What I noticed when I watched heart surgery during my research was the amazing calm.'
> Source: Tony McHale, in *Radio Times*, 9–15 January 1999

Doctors

- The father figure – offers advice and is decisive, calm and unruffled.
- The uncle figure – everyone can talk to him without strings attached.
- The aloof and stern figure – attractive to some women but obsessed with work and does not suffer fools gladly.
- The female doctor who is very professional and has high moral standards.

Nurses

- The women who are saints, unselfish and at the service of others.
- The women who are mother figures, and who listen to the problems of everyone, including the doctors.
- The nervous incompetent who suffers from stress.
- The severe matron who punishes the weak and rewards the strong.
- The flirt who gets her man.
- Male nurses who are caring and sensitive.
- Male nurses who are incompetent and cover up errors.
- Male nurses who are gay and male nurses who are from Afro-caribbean or Asian backgrounds have become more common. Doctors from these social groups and also lesbians are, however, still rarely represented.

How are hospital workers represented as a group?

To give an example, *Cardiac Arrest* was a hard-hitting six part series reflecting the cynical attitude staff adopted to cope with cutbacks and inhuman, incompetent management.

ACTIVITY 3

1. Study an episode of a hospital drama, such as *Casualty*, *Holby City*, *Peak Practice*, *ER*, or *Cardiac Arrest* (re-runs and earlier series can often be seen on satellite or cable TV). Identify the types of characters who are portrayed in these dramas.
2. Make a list of characters and write down their characteristics and attitudes.
3. Compare these types with another hospital drama. Are there any different types of characters? Consider the following:
   - managers
   - doctors
   - nurses
   - ancillary staff – porters or cleaners
   - ambulance crews

Cardiac Arrest

Character type	Characteristics and attitudes
Managers	1 New efficiency savings type. 2 Old fashioned fatherly type: 'It'll be alright on the night'.
Doctors	1 Female: realistic, not to be messed around and heart in the right place. 2 Brash and domineering male. 3 Lazy junior doctor, who plays pranks on everyone. 4 Young novice who starts trying to be nice to everyone but ends up being as cynical as the others.
Nurses	Vary in attitude to their job, doctors and patients. Some are very conscientious, others are plain lazy. Nurses and other staff are not the focus of drama.
Ancillary Staff: porters, cleaners, canteen staff, para-medics and ambulance staff	Unlike Casualty, the ancillary staff play a very minor role, as the focus is mainly on the nursing staff, doctors and management.
Patients	Patients are not the focus of the drama.

Table 10.1 *Cardiac Arrest: Character types and their characteristics*

Name: Chrissie Williams

Role: Ward Sister

Played by: Tina Hobley

Chrissie Williams swept into Holby City with the confidence of a woman who knows she's found her place in life. She runs an efficient ward and her staff all live in fear of incurring her wrath, especially poor Sandy. She's not a woman who suffers fools and that includes the patients!

Her personal life is just as hectic and she's not to be messed with once she's set her sights on what, or who, she wants. Chrissie can be far too direct and this doesn't always endear her to her fellow colleagues. Kath especially finds her hard to deal with. And when old flames come back to haunt her the sparks really begin to fly!

Name: Ric Griffin

Role: Consultant, Surgery

Played by: Hugh Quarshie

Ric appears every inch the consummate professional in the operating theatre. But the calm and controlled exterior he presents at work disguises the chaos of his personal life.

But Ric's optimistic nature never allows him to accept that everything will turn out other than perfectly. So the chaos never seems as bad as it really is ... He's a highly principled man and refuses to work privately, though his financial situation may force his hand on this.

Name: Danny Shaughnessy

Role: Student Nurse

Played by: Jeremy Edwards

When Danny first entered Holby hospital he worked as a Health Care Assistant. But it quickly became obvious that he wanted to be more involved with the patients and their care. So he realised he wanted to nurse and has gone to work on Otter Ward as a Student Nurse.

He's very well intentioned but sometimes messes up by getting too involved with the patients. Danny has yet to learn to distance himself from other people's problems. He's got a real eye for the ladies, but was devastated when he was dumped by Victoria. He two-timed Jasmine and Julie to get over her. But maybe now he's moved out of home he'll truly start to grow up.

Fig 10.2 *Holby City cast profiles. To see photographs and other cast profiles, look at www.bbc.co.uk/casualty/staff_room/holbycity_staff.shtml*

Source: BBCi/Holby City

Narrative and plot

Typical narratives in Casualty

Storyline method

Two or three incidents take place outside the hospital, in the city or the country. Emergency services do their best to contain the injuries and successfully treat them by the end of the episode in situ, or they are ferried back to the hospital for emergency treatment.

At the hospital two or three patients with minor injuries are seen by staff doctors and nurses. Some patients also have personal difficulties and relatives and relationships are put to the test. Nurses and doctors try not to act as social workers but usually end up offering some kind of advice, which is heeded.

During these scenes, the domestic relationships of the staff are also being tested. Issues such as love, hate, death, jealousy, children and work performance are explored, while the characters are under pressure at work. The main message of BBC1's *Casualty* is that they are dedicated public servants and that most of the staff, with a few notable exceptions, do their best to help people recover.

The final section of the programme ends with the struggle to save a life or the death of a seriously ill patient, and the doctors use life-saving equipment on the patient in the emergency theatre.

Locations

Exterior locations, such as quarries and caravans, and the emergency operating theatre provide the high suspense action sequences. Interior locations, such as the reception areas and the nurses' quarters provide the dramatic dialogues and the interactions between people.

ACTIVITY 4

Read the following sample script aloud and video it, as if for a hospital drama. Alternatively, read it as if for a radio play, creating sound effects when appropriate. Before you start recording, consider the following:

1. Who is this programme aimed at? Consider age, gender and class.
2. What are the types of people who are playing the doctor, nurse and patient? For example, is the doctor traditionally superior or are they equals in their approach? Is the nurse independent or obedient? Is the patient tough, meek or whining?
3. Plan how you will shoot the scenes to include a background, for example a bare wall or a curtain to resemble the hospital. Ensure that your background does look like a hospital, and not a school. See section following on video methods.

(Location is in a hospital cubicle, with a bed surrounded by a curtain or next to a blank wall.)

Doctor: So, how did you come to break your arm then, John isn't it?

Patient: Just walked into a door, stupid really.

Doctor: So, was there anyone with you then?

Patient: No, just my mother, that's all.

Nurse: Does she know you are here?

Patient: Yes, no, I mean, she's kind of . . . old . . . well, I didn't want to upset her. I just want to tell you what a good job you are . . . ouch! That hurts!

Doctor: Just sit up a little straighter

(taking the elbow and lifting it up a fraction and moving the forearm down a bit without any difficulty). How does that feel?

Patient: Feels OK, it's just down at the wrist it seems to be swollen or something.

Nurse: I'll get something for that, Jane?

Doctor: Yes ... I don't think that there's anything worse than a sprained wrist for the moment – just rest here and we'll be right back. That'll be all for now, nurse.

Nurse: Just sit there – do you want to ring your mother now?

Patient: No, but can I have my walkman – it's on the side there.

Nurse: Yes, of course – let's try to see if we can find it.

(It is found and passed over. Now doctor and nurse are walking out of earshot of patient and stop in the corridor.)

Nurse: Something fishy about his relationship with his mother, you don't think he wanted to get out of the house for a bit, do you?

Doctor: Yes, not so much a Psycho case but a sick case if you ask me. But Mary ... I wondered if ... I was going to ask you if you would like to come and meet my mother this weekend?

Patient: (loud crash and voice calls out) Doctor, Doctor I think I've broken my leg! (The doctor and nurse look at each other as though doubting the patient, laugh, and then walk fast back towards the patient.)

Filming techniques

The following methods of recording scenes on video can be used to film your background for the previous activity.

Shot-reverse-shot

Use the technique of shot-reverse-shot to film the sequence. This is where you film a head and shoulders shot of the doctor first,

recording the speech, then pause the camera and then film a head and shoulders shot of the patient. Next film the doctor, then back to the patient, and so on. You will need to stop and start the camera to record the scene as it would be presented in *Casualty*, or *Holby City*. One advantage of using this video method is that the actors only have to remember one line at a time.

Continuous

For an alternative method, video without stopping. Simply try to record as many shots of everyone's faces as possible, when they are talking, but let the camera move towards the subject of the conversations when appropriate, for example the patient's arm.

Evaluation of a video scene

ACTIVITY 5

Create a new hospital drama: write a 'treatment', an outline explanation or description of the following elements:

1. Setting and interior and exterior locations – settings for doctors, nurses, patients and managers.
2. Profiles of the main characters (minimum of five or six main characters).
3. Plots for the first episode.
4. A scene from your first episode.
5. Casting – are you going to use famous people from other dramas or have a completely new set of faces?

ACTIVITY 6

1. Play back the recording you made and evaluate the sequences.
   Discuss:
   - What worked and what did not.
   - How did you make the voices sound dramatic?
   - What types of shot did you use and did they vary at all in shot, size or angle?
   - Was the scene better using the shot-reverse-shot method rather than the continuous videoing?
   - What are the advantages and disadvantages of videoing without stopping?
   - What are the advantages and disadvantages of videoing one shot at a time?

2. Watch a hospital documentary and study how it is filmed. Are the sequences full of edits? To what extent is the camera left to wonder around freely without interruption? Do you think the camera crew make people perform for the camera? Does the way people appear on the screen feel natural, as though the camera was not there?

Hospital documentaries

Following are three typical documentary TV listings magazine previews, involving hospital related institutions.

1 **Animal ER**, Channel 5, 8.30 pm.
  The vets are called out to a pregnant horse entangled in barbed wire at the bottom of a field.

2 **The Coroner's Office**, Channel 4, 9 pm.
  A nine year old girl has been killed in a hit-and-run accident in front of her mother, and a 21 year old woman has died of a mystery illness after the local doctor refused to visit. Another day in the twilight world of Birmingham Coroner's office. The bodies are Muslim and according to Islamic tradition should be buried as soon as possible. Dr Richard Whittington is not in the business of rushing his autopsies and sensitive though he is to the need of families to bury their dead in their home country, rules are rules. As the jumbo jets taxi into position, the bodies are finally released and a sigh of relief can be heard from here to Pakistan.

3 **Cutting Edge**, Channel 4, 9 pm.
  The story of Friern Barnet hospital. The former mental institution was so large it had its own working farm – and gave birth to the term 'funny farm'. Now it has been transformed into a luxury housing estate. Former inmates of the hospital and present residents describe their feelings about the place.

Discuss

Discuss the types of drama that can be introduced to the documentaries to interest the viewers in each of Animal ER, The Coroner's Office and Cutting Edge. Study the language of their TV listings previews for clues.

Documentary style

Documentaries on television can be single programmes in slots, such as *Modern Times* or *Cutting Edge*. Alternatively, they can be long series such as *Animal Hospital* or *Children's Hospital*.
Documentaries:

- Tend to have a voice over.
- Tend to focus on the issues rather than on the character relationships, for example,

shocking working conditions rather than a manager's affair with a nurse.
- Tend to build up more of a sense of the setting.
- Do not have cliffhangers.
- Have a serious message.

Discuss

How many of those features do you think apply to documentaries that you have seen?

The fascination with documentaries set in hospitals is in part connected to the success of the hospital dramas, but is also due to the great interest in reality television. The low cost of not having to pay actors and create costly sets makes it an attractive option for television executives.

Camera work

Documentary camera work is not easy to perform without being noticed! The trick is to get close to the subject without them knowing or being aware that you are interviewing them. Trust has to be built up between the subject and the camera crew members. Filming in a hospital is a very intimate experience and the temptation to avoid the camera or play act is often very great.

There are at least four techniques for filming documentaries to make them look more 'real':

- 'Fly on the wall' camera work is designed to appear as though there were no film crew in the room at all; as though they were unseen on the wall, like a fly.
- Verite camera work is a continuous hand-held shot that simulates the experience of

the person looking and walking about the room. Many investigative journalists have to use this technique if they want to gain direct reponse to a question and record it.
- Secret microphones and cameras have become much more common. Hidden cameras in bags and jackets are used if it is known that the subject does not welcome the prospect of being exposed to the public at a later date.
- Video diary style is when the camera is given to a person in a particular situation, and they record the experience themselves, talking to the camera that is set up to record them in the corner of the room.

In the case of documenting hospital matters, the camera operator has to be prepared for emotional and stressful scenes. How the public feel about someone filming them depends on the sensitivity of the director and the camera operator.

Production

Dramas require a large number of staff and fixed sets and studios. Crew and staff use up a considerable part of the budget. In addition to the actors and actresses there are: the producer, director, production managers, camera operators, lighting electricians, sound recordist, make-up artists, wardrobe, set designers and props staff.

Documentaries involve a much smaller scale operation. With the arrival of new low light cameras there is often no need for a lighting electrician. A crew may consist of as few people as four in total: the camera operator, sound recordist, production assistant and the director.

Cost

The cost of a documentary, for example, £40,000 for a single hour long programme of *Cutting Edge*, is much cheaper than a wage bill for the staffing of a single episode of *Casualty*. This provides a great incentive for programme makers such as Channel 4 or BBC2 to make dramatic documentaries or docu-soaps, as they are cheaper. Real people can be paid much less than professional actors or actresses. Production costs are therefore much lower on location, as studios usually cost a great deal to maintain for a large cast and varied scene locations.

The docu-soap

The rise of the docu-soap, a highly personality-centred and conflict-ridden documentary set in the 1990s, has led to criticism that the art of documentary making as the representation of real life, has been lost. Makers of docu-soaps claim that real life is dramatic and that if there are real personalities 'out there', then they can only represent them as they are. Classic types are the sweaty, shouting and swearing chefs in documentaries on hotels and cooking. Another type is the endlessly patient and jovial passenger controller of an airport.

Specimen examination Question: AQA

Note: this question is one section from a 4 hour paper.

These tasks are not actual examination questions. The questions are the sole work of the author and are devised to match the style, mark allocation and format of the relevant question papers from AQA. They are designed for examination practice. The tasks are designed to follow the examination paper timings and mark allocations. It is essential that candidates check the specified topics set for the year of their examination, by the examination board. For previous examination papers contact the examination board direct.

Television hospital drama and documentary (you should spend an hour on this question).

Either

1 **Essay response** – Explain how television hospital dramas and/or documentaries set in hospitals use dramatic incidents and a variety of character types to interest their audiences. Discuss with reference to the programme, or programmes, you have studied. **(Total 25 marks)**

or

2 **Production response** – Read the following outline for a new television drama and then follow the instructions.

Airport hospital drama
Title: *Morby: a drama series*.
Location: Birmingham Airport.
Time slot: Thursday 8 pm, Channel 5.
Focus: Main focus is the work of the paramedics. Storylines for the first four episodes (two storylines for each programme, plus the staff domestic storyline each week):
Episode One:
Storyline One – animal smuggling and drugs smuggling. The passenger bitten by a 10 year old's escaped pet rat.
Storyline Two – the Nigerian carrier whose stomach contains drugs wrapped in balloons, which are now leaking and making the carrier suffer acute stomach pains.
Hospital staff domestic plotline – the chief nurse orderly who has to make a decision on whether to admit her own 17 year old son into the hospital due to a suspected drugs and drinks excess.
Episode Two:
Storyline One – the drunk (and ill) passengers who express their violence and abuse towards passengers and crew on Flight BA 3216 from New York.

Storyline Two – the check-in desk assistant whose medication makes him aggressive with customers. His short temper contributes to a violent attack on him by a customer who arrives too late to board the plane.

Hospital staff domestic plotline – the nurse whose promotion prospects seem to be undermined by a mysterious hoaxer. The hoaxer keeps ringing her boss claiming that she has a criminal record.

Episode Three:

Storyline One – illegal immigrants stowed on plane. Two Czechoslovakian romanies brought in with a broken arm and hypothermia, caused by holding on to the plane's undercarriage.

Storyline Two – the airline crew's strike and successful claim for more pay. This leads to massive congestion in the waiting areas, accidents and a premature birth.

Hospital staff domestic plotline – the female surgeon whose eyesight is not what it used to be, and her affair with two male staff who are her operating theatre assistants.

Episode Four:

Storyline One – the reunion of the 70 year old twins separated at birth, who both experience heart attack symptoms minutes before they meet at the exit point from immigration controls.

Storyline Two – the hospital administrator who is going to give up his job. He also has to call a beginning of shift meeting to announce cuts to the staff but cannot face it. He fakes illness at the crucial moment.

Hospital staff domestic plotline – the administrator's gay partner who has decided to force his partner to give up work, has a heart attack at the same time as the 70 year old twins. There are

not enough staff around to cope with all three of them.

The end of the series sees two interviews for a new recruit to the hospital management team and a new member of the nursing staff.

The hospital team includes: management, ambulance units, auxillary staff (porters, canteen, cleaners), nurses and doctors and reception staff. Airport staff include: administrators, cabin crew, reception staff, baggage handlers, mechanics and shops and services staff. The audience of the show ranges from 12 years of age upwards.

a **Devise** a title sequence for the series. The images should contain some idea of the different characters and settings of the drama. Draw at least ten frames (and no more than 20 frames) to show the key elements of the programme's title sequence. Include a title for your series. You should indicate key sounds to be heard on the title sequence, for example, music, special effects, voices.

(15 marks)

b **Write** a commentary (maximum of 300 words) explaining who the audience is for the programme. How will the title sequence attract the audience to the programme? **(10 marks)**

Extension Tasks

1 **Design** the front cover of a TV listings magazine and produce an appropriate image (drawn), heading and straplines for the new documentary series described previously. Alternatively, design a cover for the hospital drama you created earlier in this chapter. Produce an appropriate image (drawn), heading and straplines.

2 **Essay**: what are the typical representations of health professionals in hospital dramas? (write a maximum of 700 to 1000 words)

3 **Devise** a ten minute radio phone-in programme, where different members of the class discuss why they think their favourite hospital programme is more realistic than others, for example, *ER* and *Casualty* or *Holby City* and *Casualty*. As a presenter, construct a set of questions covering characters, story lines, settings and themes. Ensure that the speaker identifies him/herself and is not allowed to ramble. Record the discussion on tape and invite another group to comment on your recording. Listen to the tape and write up your comments and observations of the different perspectives. Write about the practical aspect and the decisions you had to make in organising the radio programme, before and during the phone-in.

4 **Compare** an American hospital drama with a British hospital drama, such as *Casualty*. Are there differences in the filming and editing styles? How does each of them attempt to be realistic? Discuss settings, characters and story lines.

Examination Skills

Knowledge and Understanding

Candidates will need to show an understanding of the typical forms and conventions of a hospital drama or a documentary. They should have knowledge of typical representations of hospitals and types and stereotypes of staff, and explore similarities and differences across dramas. The candidate should be able to refer to more than one type of documentary filming style. There should be an awareness of different audiences for different subject material.

Candidates should be prepared (if they choose not to write an essay) to invent a preparatory product such as a storyboard title sequence, a trailer or a scene (cliffhanger) from the programme. Alternatively, there may be a task of writing a treatment or a promotion of the programmes in the form of posters or advertisements.

Students should analyse the relationship between producers and audiences and how hospital dramas satisfy the audience or not. Schedules and target audiences are also areas that students should cover and analyse.

Textual Analysis

Students should be able to analyse the representations, and forms and conventions of hospital drama story lines, *mise-en-scène*, types of characters and their messages and values. They should be able to derive meaning from the messages and values that depict doctors as experts and nurses as carers.

Practical Work

The student should be able to demonstrate a good understanding of the formats for producing storyboards, treatments, scripted scenes, radio programmes and magazine covers. They should know how to annotate a storyboard soundtrack. Candidates will **not** have to be able to draw. The work will need to show good organisation and keen attention to appropriate shape, form and content. The products should show awareness of the institution (real or imagined) in which it was produced.

11 Reality television: game, talk and chat shows

'There's no such thing as a sanity clause.'
Groucho Marx

What you will learn

In this chapter you will learn about the category of television programme-making often labelled as 'Reality TV'. You will study how channels compete with each other to get people to watch their channel's programmes by mixing reality programmes with fiction material. You will also consider the issue of whether real people use or are used by television and whether audiences are inevitably voyeurs without a reality.

KEY WORDS

- ratings
- docu-soap
- realism
- celebrity
- entertainment and documentary
- scheduling
- pre-echo
- hammocking
- inheritance

TECHNICAL WORDS

- factual programming
- TV magazine format
- game show
- talk show
- lifestyle show
- circulation figures

'Fame, fortune, glamour … finally all Baltimore knows I am big, blonde and beautiful.' Rikki Lake in *Hairspray* 1988

'True stories, widening people participation.' BBC Producer

'Celebrity-fronted human cannon-fodder chasing the programme ratings.' TV critic

ACTIVITY 1

Study the categories of programmes as listed on the internet site for ITV.com: Soaps and Dramas, Entertainment, News and Current Affairs, Gameshows, Lifestyle, Kids.

1. Which categories of programme do you think include ordinary people as participants in them?

2. What titles of programmes can you think of that are made with real people in them?
3. What type of programmes do you call the ones you have chosen?
4. Find a TV listings of programmes for one day and identify how many programmes are dedicated to real people participating in the show.
5. Break these programmes into smaller labels e.g. cooking, gardening, house makeovers, game shows etc.

Real or not?

A great deal of programme making is given over to real people, their responses and the dramas which can be constructed 'for real'. As we saw in the last chapter, traditional documentaries use the voiceover and this voice/presenter has seriously persuaded the audience of their point. Modern audiences are now very familiar with the presenter-led studio show or the interactive and open ended video diary style of 'real people' programme.

For example, a member of the public could be on programmes as:

∎ a contestant on the game show with the celebrity presenter Barrymore;
∎ an aspiring star like Will Young in *Pop Idol*, or a singer in *Stars in Their Eyes*;
∎ romantic match hopefuls in *Blind Date*;
∎ victims, wrongdoers or confessionalists in *Trisha;*
∎ speaking members of an audience with the topical *Kilroy* or the more risqué *So Graham Norton*;
∎ willing recipients, having a house or garden makeover in *Groundforce*;
∎ guests in a chat show or a topical chat and magazine programme such as *Richard and Judy*?
∎ The subject of a documentary for example, about teenage drinking.

From ordinary to notorious

In the last ten years television has pushed forward the idea of introducing 'real people' as we, the audience, agree to slowly build them into minor celebrities. This can occur even with the person who is subject to mishaps and scrapes, such as Maureen the woman who failed her driving test over 80 times. Or the airport customer agent who became a presenter after television producers liked their natural television ability in a documentary series about airports (*Airport*, ITV1). Public hate figures such as harassing traffic wardens also become famous, for a short time.

Games to watch and games to be seen to play

Although we might watch celebrity-filled quiz shows such as *They Think It's All Over* and *A Question of Sport*, there are now also elaborate participatory game shows for the public, in specially constructed environments. For example, the BBC's *It's a Knock Out* was a series of obstacle courses with mainly members of the public participating and Channel 4's *Crystal Maze* was a series of timed physical and mental 'tests' set in and around a maze of obstacles, tunnels and houses. *Countdown* is probably the simplest and cheapest form of game where Maths problems and word building are the main tasks.

More recently negative game playing has been introduced in games like ITV's *Dog Eat Dog* that involves the rest of the contestants ganging up on one person to drive them out of the competition. *The Weakest Link* is a general knowledge game in which you must vote after each round to make sure your nearest competitor doesn't overtake you.

Physical endurance

We are now watching the ultimate in games as simulations of extreme conditions where people have to live out and simulate stressful conditions, often cooped up together under the surveillance of closed circuit television. ITV's *Survivor* is a TV concept trialled in America, where people share the experience of an island without basic facilities and tests are introduced to weed out the weaker participants, week after week. *Castaway* was a BBC version of this with a large group of volunteers from all walks of life who spent a year in a remote part of the Scottish Isles – it was less of a game than an experiment in seeing how different people could cope with the artificial social-mixing.

Fig 11.1   Big Brother contestants from the first series

Big Brother

The most popular of people-based shows have been ITV's *Big Brother* and *Who Wants to Be A Millionaire?* In *Big Brother* CCTV video cameras and numerous microphones were rigged up in a house where the carefully selected participants had to live in specially created living accommodation under the watchful eye of 'Big Brother' – the Endemol television company organising the proceedings. Every week the participants had to vote on who they would like to leave and their votes would be secretly cast so that one person left each week. *Big Brother* had several tie-ins, for example, with scratch cards in *The Mirror* and *The Sun* to boost interest in the programme. At its height in 2001 the number of viewers was nearly 5 million. The term sometimes given to the several week long programmes is docu-soap.

There is also the reward of the cash prize or a holiday. All of these programmes depend on having losers and winners and a big audience to watch how the participants react under pressure. The programmes are dependent on strong presenters, and audience curiosity is also whipped up by newspaper articles about all the characters' real lives, digging up gossip or scandal and treating their real lives in the manner of a soap.

When real mini-celebrities agreed to go into the Big Brother house there were some bizarre moments.

Variations of the 'big winner cash prize' contestant game have been in television as far as back as the 1950s. The Saturday version of the National Lottery provides a spotlight on two competitors who have to answer general quiz questions to win the next stage of world travel opportunity at the end of each Saturday's Lottery programme. The lottery draw itself has become a small part of the programme as now the focus at the end of the programme is a battle of wits between two people to win a quiz game for the next stage of a holiday abroad.

Cash for questions

The *Who Wants to Be A Millionaire?* quiz show is considered by its producers to be a novel format in its use of audience participation – if you can't guess the right answer from four given options you phone a friend to help with answering the quiz, or ask the audience to vote to give an idea of which answer to select. The finance from the programme comes largely via the cost of the phone calls charged to people ringing up to get on the show.

The newest US game import is *Murder in a Small Room* (BBC) which involves participants acting out and guessing who has committed the murder in the manner of a Cluedo board game.

Documentary

Not all reality-based television is based on sensational docu-soap or prize-winning – many documentaries have been made about serious topics. In the BBC's *Real Lives* project, video cameras were given to individuals to record their everyday life. People from every part of the UK have been involved in telling their stories about what they do and how they feel on camera recordings made by themselves and then edited at the BBC. One extraordinary do it yourself documentary, 'The man who loved Gary Lineker', was made in Romania by a doctor who learnt all his English from BBC World Service and was fanatical about Gary Lineker.

Channel 4's *Cutting Edge* and the BBC's *Panorama* slots both aim to investigate real people as well as serious political issues about national concerns. But there have been concerns that the BBC has 'dumbed down' to appeal less to the serious-minded citizen: interested in social issues such as obesity (body size), abuse or bullying, for example. The popular documentary tends to focus more on the soap values of conflict within a family. Critics of the serious documentary have argued that more people now watch real people and that the majority of the licence-paying population are watching BBC now the emphasis has changed to lighter items.

Talk shows

Talk shows presented by well known celebrities such as Trisha, Oprah Winfrey or Kilroy involve a mix of intimate personal experience and confessional television. The television presenter brings out the person's 'problem' partly to focus on the individual's problem for an audience to engage with it personally. The presenter may act as an agony aunt or uncle or bring in the experts to offer advice. The process of confessing or making a revelation also allows for difficult issues such as physical abuse, bullying, or drugs and alcohol related obsessive and addictive behaviours to be aired and shared. Whether people are 'healed' or further confused by televised 'airing' is open to question.

ACTIVITY 2

Study the following talk shows.
Michael Parkinson Show
Dress code: wears tie and suit – quite formal
Presenter: his own show plus guests and a singer/band backed by a studio orchestra/band.
Format: guests are interviewed about new films/books as well as their upbringing and personal history.
Furniture and set: simple chairs and plain set
Audience: over 40s, middle age.
Channel: BBC1
Time: Late evening – Saturday

Priory TV
Dress code: casual, trainers etc
Presenters: Jamie Theakston and Zoë Ball
Format: chat, gossip, lively interaction with the in-house crowd, music and video reviews.
Furniture and set: comfortable sofas and various areas for dancing or doing interviews with large milling studio audience of 15–20 year olds.
Audience: 8–20
Channel: Channel 4
Time: early evening 5.30.

Trisha
Dress code: smart
Presenter: Trisha
Format: personal and domestic problems/issues are aired by people who are invited to talk about problems and invited to challenge Confessional mode.
Furniture: stage, seating, large studio audience.
Audience: female 16+
Channel: ITV1/Anglia
Time: morning 9.30

Using the list above: dress, presenters, format, furniture and set, audience, channel and time:

1 **compare** BBC1's *Kilroy* broadcast at 9.00 a.m. with *Trisha*.
2 **compare** Channel 4's afternoon talk show *Richard and Judy* with *GMTV's* breakfast show, 7.00–9.00 am.

Technology

One reason for having more reality TV is that camcorders and digital cameras have allowed more mobility and access to places bigger cameras and older light sensitive cameras couldn't reach.

Ratings

The other pressure is to make popular programmes which people will watch and to boost ratings. Prime time television i.e. 5.30 to 10.00 tends not to have the old serious documentaries like BBC1's *Panorama* – this is late on Sunday night now. The docu-soap is likely to compete with the real soaps for two or three evenings in the week. *Big Brother* ran over Thursday, Friday and Saturday deliberately competing with the other channels for a share of the audience ratings.

Survivor (ITV1) had a terrible time trying to compete with *Big Brother* in 2001 so it started its second series of screening earlier, in the Spring of 2002.

Even shows like *Who Wants To Be A Millionaire?* have limited lifespans as the American version of the show lost interest in 2001.

Survivor goes once a week

ITV's is to cut back its reality TV show *Survivor* to one show a week.

The decision appears to confirm criticisms that the reality TV show has been a ratings disappointment to the channel.

From 11 June *Survivor* will be scheduled just once a week on Mondays at 9pm.

Thursday's programme will be dropped and, from 18 June, the interview-based *Survivor Unseen* will be shown after Tuesday's News at Ten.

"we are changing the scheduling to give

Survivor the best possible chance to grow"

David Liddiment

Fig 11.2   Survivor
Source: BBC News Online (article)/PA Photos/Sean Dempsey (photo)

Scheduling

A **schedule** is a plan for the day. In television a schedule marks out the timing and the length of each programme and is carefully organised by schedulers. Each channel has a person dedicated to organising the schedule. The BBC needs to justify its licence fee and commercial channels need to prove to advertisers that they have a steady audience who will watch programmes and the advertisements at predictable times of the day. The key moment in a TV channel's programme schedule comes with their sure-fire high ratings programmes. For example, *EastEnders* (BBC) and *Coronation Street* (ITV) can guarantee upwards of 12 million people and sometimes over 17 million at a dramatic high spot. A football event like an England World Cup semi-final fixture can sometimes reach over 25 million people.

In order to plan an evening to keep an audience the scheduler's trick is to catch the audience when they come in from school or work and keep them hooked. At the very least it is hoped that audiences are making a preference for that channel the next week. It is important that at around the 6.00 to 6.30 slot the news is there for the adults and for the younger audience programmes like *The Simpsons*. *The Simpsons* programmes are considered worth paying enormous amounts of money for from the Americans to ensure audience loyalty – Channel 4 and BBC 2 have competed fiercely to purchase them exclusively from Twentieth Century Fox/Sky. The hope is that the audience will feel lazy and stay with that channel especially if there

is more than one episode of *The Simpsons*. This is called **inheritance**. Equally the audience may sit down to wait for their favourite programme so they don't miss it. This means that programme schedulers can put weaker programmes on beforehand because they know the audience is preparing for their main choice – this is called **pre-echo** scheduling. If there is another strong programme on later then a sandwich is arranged so that a strong programme is followed by a weaker one and then another strong one comes after. This is called **hammocking**. (Refer to page 37.)

BBC1	BBC2	ITV1	Channel 4	Channel 5
3:45 pm Rugrats Cartoon about toddlers who find high adventure in the world around them. In 'The Jungle', the babies imagine themselves on a wild jungle adventure at the local gardening store. And in 'The Old Country', the Pickles family prepare for a weekend at Grandpa Boris and Grandma Minka's cabin. *Repeat. Ceefax*	**3:30 pm Esther** Esther Rantzen meets people with unique stories to tell and debates their ideas and feelings with a studio audience. *Ceefax*	**3:50 pm Cardcaptors** Children's animation about Sakura, a schoolgirl who has to capture the legendary Clow Cards with the help of her best friend Tomoyo and Kero, the guardian of the cards. Starring: Voices of Sam Vincent, Brian Drummond *Subtitles*	**3:45 pm Fifteen to One** (Quiz Show) William G Stewart asks the questions in the fast-moving quiz. *(Subtitles, 3 Star)*	**3.35 pm 'Noises Off'** (Peter Bogdonavich, 1992) Film based on theatre farce by Michael Frayn.
4:10 pm The Cramp Twins *Walk Like A Man* Animation about ten-year-old twins Wayne and Lucien Cramp – brothers who are complete opposites of one another. Lucien paints stubble on a sleeping Wayne and glues tufts of hair under his arms in an effort to make him behave more responsibly. However, thinking that he is now a man, Wayne enthusiastically adopts a macho stance – much to the delight of Wendy Winkle, and the horror of Lucien. *Repeat. Ceefax*	**4:30 pm Ready, Steady, Cook** Ainsley Harriott presents the culinary challenge in which talented chefs battle against the clock to create delicious dishes in twenty minutes. *Ceefax* **5:15 pm Weakest Link** Anne Robinson presents the quick-fire general knowledge quiz in which contestants must decide at the end of each round which of their number should be eliminated. *Ceefax*	**4:15 pm How 2** Weird, wacky and factual information about the world **4:35 pm My parents are aliens** The Valentine. Children's drama series about extraterrestrial visitors. Josh makes the foolish mistake of taking Brian's advice on matters of the heart. While Sophie enjoys discovering romance, Mel struggles to fight off her admirers. Starring: Tony Gardner, Carla Mendonca, Danielle McCormack, Alex Kew, Charlotte	**4.15 pm Countdown** A game show testing mathematical and word building skills. **5.00 pm Richard and Judy** Chat Show Celebrity and topical chat.	**5.30 pm 5 News**

BBC1	BBC2	ITV1	Channel 4	Channel 5
4:25 pm The Make Shift Michael Underwood and Sophie McDonnell present a programme crammed with ideas for things to make and do. With ideas for a noisy microphone, and jokes to play on your friends. *Ceefax* **4:35 pm The Ghost Hunter** *Ghost Children* Ghoulish drama series based on Ivan Jones's novel. Eric and the Chillwood ghosts have been captured – who is going to protect the young trainee spirits from Mrs Corker? *Repeat. Ceefax* **5:00 pm Blue Peter** Children's magazine with Konnie Huq, Simon Thomas, Matt Baker and Liz Barker. In this programme, the boys don skirts in an effort to remain at the cutting edge of men's fashion, and musical theatre comes courtesy of Stomp. *Ceefax* **5:25 pm Newsround** Topical news magazine for children. *Ceefax* **5:35 pm Neighbours** Libby's magazine arrives, but the excitement is short-lived. Mitch lets Joe off the hook – or does he? Steph makes a move on Mitch. *Shown earlier. Ceefax*		Francis, Patrick Niknejad. *Repeat, Subtitles* **5:05 pm Airline** Documentary series following the passengers and staff of budget **airline** easyJet. In Liverpool, Kevin Reardon has been put on night shifts, to the dismay of his wife. But two girls from Preston are looking forward to working nights – they are flying to Majorca to become night club dancers. In Luton, an angry Australian cannot understand why Jane won't let him board his flight. *(Repeat, Subtitles)* **5:30 pm Crossroads** Soap set in a Birmingham Hotel.		
6:00 pm BBC News *Ceefax* **6:30 pm Regional news programmes; Weather**	**6:00 pm The Simpsons** *Homer versus the 18th Amendment* Cartoon comedy. When prohibition is revived in Springfield, Homer becomes a beer baron. With the guest voice of Joe Mantegna. *Repeat. Ceefax* **6:20 pm The Fresh Prince of Bel Air** *I, Done* In the final episode, with the Banks mansion up for sale, Will reflects on his lack of personal achievement. *Second of two parts, Repeat. Ceefax*	**6:00 pm Tonight** Local news	**6.00 pm Friends** American twenty-somethings sitcom.	**6.00 pm Home and Away** Australian teen soap.

ACTIVITY 3

Schedule Simulation

You are in the role of scheduler for either BBC 1 or ITV1. For one day in the summer you will be allowed to programme the afternoon's programmes (nearly) as you would like in the ideal world. You will need to consider what your age group would like and be aware that both male and female audiences are watching the channel. Race and physical disability are also considerations to bear in mind.

Study the TV programme schedules for March 11th 2002 as shown in the table and follow these instructions.

1. **a)** Make a list/chart of what programmes were shown between 4.00 and 6.00 on BBC 2, Channel 4 and Channel 5.

   b) Study the list of every channel's programmes that began at 6.00 – and mark whether they are fiction or factual programmes, e.g. *The Simpsons* is fiction.

   c) Identify from every channel which programmes were:

   i) fiction programmes e.g. cartoon and drama;

   ii) reality-based programmes e.g. *Blue Peter*;

   iii) Audience: judging from the content of these programme schedules decide what age and type of audience you would expect to be watching.

   a) BBC1

   b) BBC2

   c) ITV1

   d) Channel 4

   e) Channel 5   **(10 marks)**

2. Work out roughly what percentage of programmes were reality based and which were fictional?   **(4 marks)**

3. Plan your ideal Monday 4.00–7.00 viewing for either BBC 1 or ITV1 for a summer holiday special. Note, however, you must have the national and regional news and the channel's soap in their usual time slots. What restrictions do you notice about what you can programme: lengthwise and time-wise?

   Write a letter of proposal for a new channel **Coolyouchoose** which allows you more choice to suit your age group. You can buy in programmes from other channels.

   Include:

   ▮ Your list of programmes, 4.00–7.00.

   ▮ What you think your main programmes are.

   ▮ Say why you have chosen each of these programmes.

   ▮ Why you think they are in the best order.

   ▮ Support any new programme ideas for news or presenters with an explanation.

   ▮ What you think this channel can offer the age group 12–20 that they haven't had before, at this time.

   Address it to Head of Programmes at **Coolyouchoose**, BTV, CCTV Way, Endgame, East Ender. E16 ETL

   (16 Marks)
   [Total 30]

Examination Skills

Knowledge and Understanding

You will have understood how the content of TV programmes depends on what comes before and after each programme. The schedule simulation should give you skills to consider why certain programmes are on when they are and what potential audiences are watching.

12 Magazines

Who is the prettiest of them all?

What you will learn

In this chapter you will study the forms and conventions of magazines, who owns them and who is involved in their production and distribution. What type of audience buys the magazine and how is an image of the target audience created? You will compare and contrast mass and niche market magazines including: fanzines and zines, women's and teenage girls' magazines, TV listings, men's magazines, a 'society stars and their homes' magazine.

KEY WORDS

- mass
- niche
- magazines
- fanzines
- demographic
- target and constructed audience
- mode of address

TECHNICAL WORDS

- circulation
- readership
- glossy
- style
- weekly
- periodical
- headlines
- puffs
- straplines
- cover lines

Magazines – What are they?

A magazine is generally recognised by its colour cover and its stapled or stitched pages. Most newsagents' wall displays are covered in magazines of one type or another. Generally speaking, magazines are published at regular intervals and contain articles by more than one person. Magazines publish weekly, monthly and sometimes daily. A periodical magazine refers to a magazine that comes out monthly or only a few times a year.

Magazines can be divided into fiction and non-fiction, with the bulk of magazines falling into the non-fiction category.

Differences between magazines, newspapers and books

Many newspapers have supplements for almost every day of the week. The *Daily Mail* has *FeMail*, *The Guardian* has the *Saturday Weekend Review*, *The Voice* has *Woman2Woman*, and Sunday newspapers also produce glossy magazines that appear similar to weekly magazines.

One type of early magazine was started to introduce gossip and intellectual discussion pages for high society, such as *The Gentleman's Journal* in 1692, which covered news, philosophy, music and poetry. *The Ladies Mercury*, which started in 1693, provided advice about love, dress and marriage. Other early magazines, like the *Athenian Gazette*, covered scientific questions such as where fire goes when it is extinguished.

The New Scientist is a modern equivalent of a serious periodical covering scientific matters. Today's *Fortean Times* is a more populist magazine that deals with the irrational areas of human experience, including cult and supernatural matters. *Fortean Times* is a sci-fi cult magazine that has grown out of an interest in the supernatural and science fiction. This has been witnessed in the following of the TV programme *The X-Files*.

A literary magazine, *The Spectator*, which started in the early 1700s, included famous writers such as Addison, Swift and Congreve, who wrote witty observations on everyday life, poetry and also articles. The magazine carried a good deal of advertising on wine, books, medicines, perfumes, boot polish and theatres, amongst other things, and still exists today.

Lifestyle

Magazines provide a chance for consumers to relate to their lifestyle interests; hence the term 'lifestyle' consumer magazines. In theory, newspapers' main purpose is to provide news and the front covers of newspapers tend to relate to a current topic. It has been questioned whether newspapers have become more like magazines. During budget week, March 1999, several newspapers gave greater front page space to stories about behind-the-scenes on a television programme, rather than reporting serious news stories. For example, the *Daily Star*, *The Sun*, *The Mirror* and the *Daily Mail* all printed scandals about the quiz show *Who Wants to be a Millionaire?*

Magazines tend to take at least a week to prepare, and the front covers present a range of features and services. Magazine covers are used to promote its contents. In contrast, a newspaper's headlines, photograph and front page story sells the topic of the day, for example, the budget or the scandal of a politician's private affairs. As 70% of magazine purchases are impulse buys over the counter in newsagents, it is essential that they have eye-catching covers. The other 30% of purchases consist of subscriptions.

Magazines differ from newspapers as they feature:

▌ Specific interests, hobbies, services.
▌ Different forms and conventions of layout and presentation, and selective approach to content.
▌ Tighter focus on a specific target audience.
▌ Parent company's sources of finance, method of working and organisational structure.

Types of magazines

Mass and niche markets

There are currently over 7500 magazines on the market and these are divided into two broad areas: business and consumer.

The business area includes over 5000 titles and the consumer area covers around 2500 titles. The business area is less publicly distributed. For example, the shopkeeper's title, *The Grocer*, is not seen in WH Smiths, John Menzies or your local paper shop. This type of professional magazine is bought by subscription and is delivered regularly through the post direct to the subscriber. 66% of business area magazines are sent for free, the cost of which is covered by advertising revenue.

The market is broken into mass and specialist interest groups. Specialist interest groups are known as niche markets.

Publications range from specialist comics such as *Judge Dredd* to *Flight International* and *Golf Monthly*.

Broad interest magazines made for the mass market, such as TV listings magazines, satisfy a very common need. Mass audiences draw in the widest group of audiences in every demographic group, economically and geographically (see also Chapter 3: Producers and Audiences):

▪ professional class (for example, ABC1)
▪ age
▪ gender
▪ region

┌ ACTIVITY 1 ─────

Study the two tables for magazine circulation figures.
Which magazines suffered the greatest drop in circulation between 1998 and 2001?

Title	Average circulation figures per issue
1 *What's On TV*	1,765,369
2 *Radio Times*	1,400,331
3 *Reader's Digest*	1,302,659
4 *Take a Break*	1,273,820
5 *T.V. Times*	850,282
6 *FHM*	751,493
7 *TV Quick*	740,800
8 *Woman*	711,133

Table 12.1   *Top Eight Magazines July–Dec 1998*
Source: Audit Bureau of Circulations, 1998

Title	Average circulation figures per issue
1 *What's On TV*	1,652,138
2 *Radio Times*	1,197,927
3 *Saga Magazine*	1,168,236
4 *Take a Break*	1,135,905
5 *Reader's Digest*	998,016
6 *TV Choice*	783,240
7 *Woman*	629,216
8 *T.V. Times*	627,028

Table 12.2   *Top Eight Magazines July–Dec 2001*
Source: ABC's Top 100 by Total UK/RoI Actively Purchased Circulation

The titles in Tables 12.1 and 12.2 can be purchased from shops. They are not free for club members or for favoured retail customers as, for example, with *Sky TV Guide*, *Safeway Magazine* or *Cable Guide* etc. These are given away as part of the membership service, so they are not in the table.

From the titles listed, we can see that the types of magazines that were the most popular in 1998 were TV listings and adult women's mainstream magazines. Following on from these were the teenage women's magazines. Since the 1980s there has also been a rise in the popularity of men's magazines. *FHM* is now one of the best selling UK magazines and has even overtaken *Woman* and *Woman's Own*, though the 'male' magazine market has dropped off as the novelty has worn off. There is, however, still an absence of any general lifestyle magazine targeted at 11 to 19 year old males.

Interest in men's, computer and general interest magazines has fallen since 1999 and during 2001 three men's magazines folded: *Sky, Mondo* and *Later*. Three women's magazines also folded: *PS, Nova* and *Women's Realm*.

┌ ACTIVITY 2 ─────

Read the two summaries of ROAR's research from March 2001 and August 2001.

1. Keep a score of how many Yeses and how many Nos of these findings apply to you, in any way.
2. To what extent do you think these findings are truthful?

R.O.A.R's Survey of Youth: March 2001

1. **Parents** may be good for handing out dosh but they are unlikely to be **role models** for today's youth, who look to **celebrities** for this purpose – a fact reflected in their media consumption. Nearly a quarter read *Hello!* regularly, 16 percent read *OK!* and 15 percent, *Heat*. Favourite TV shows are *Friends*, *Big Brother*, *CD:UK* and *Sex and the City*.

2. Influenced by these role models, **looking good** is more important than ever, with many teenage girls expressing **a willingness to have plastic surgery.**

3. The **desire to travel** is increasing, with 59 percent of 15 to 21-year-olds saying they have, or want to, backpack around the world. But, more conscious than ever of the importance of a good career, they don't want to take too much time out, and will happily consider pre-packaged travel.

Youth Research R.O.A.R's Again: Mediatel, August 15th 2001

The latest wave of Right Of Admission Reserved (R.O.A.R) research into the media habits, lifestyles, attitudes and brand preferences of 15–24 year olds is under way.

Running from August to October the research will look closely at the role of media in the lives of 15–24 year olds, and will examine their attitudes towards TV advertising, SMS and Email advertising, sponsorship and ambient media.

The last instalment of R.O.A.R research, for Spring 2001, was carried out by 2CV and assessed a panel of 600 15–24 year olds via a variety of methods including; group discussion, online surveying and SMS polling. The topics covered included brand ratings, values and aspirations, as well as the consumption of, and attitudes towards TV, press, radio, cinema and new technology.

Some of the key findings were as follows:

4. When choosing brands, purchasing is driven by **brand names** and **friends' recommendations** instead of **choosing ethical brands**, although ethics are slightly more important to older respondents.

5. Sony and Nokia are the **highest rating brands**, but this is mainly driven by the younger males. Heinz and Kelloggs rate higher for older respondents.

6. When asked their **favourite TV channel**, Channel 4 comes out top for 15–24 year olds, but E4 is highest for 15–17s.

7. *FHM* and *Q* are the **top two magazines** for 15–24s, although men exhibit narrower magazine repertoires than women.

8. When asked their **favourite radio station**, Radio 1 comes out on top, but Kiss and Virgin perform well as second favourites.

9. Respondents strive for the rock n roll lifestyle – **alcohol, drug culture, pubs/clubs – and the need to pull is paramount.**

10. There are very high levels of **technology adoption** amongst 15–24s – 78% own a PC at home and 42% have digital TV.

11. Over half of the respondents go to the **cinema once a month or more**. Almost half of 15–24s saw *Gladiator* and *Snatch* at the cinema and these were the most popular films among the sample.

12. 69% of respondents turn to **national newspapers to catch up on the latest news**.

ACTIVITY 2 (Cont.)

What's your score?

If you have scored over 9 Yeses ...You fit the ideal marketing type of R.O.A.R's Youth profile.

If you have scored over 6 Yeses….You are going in the main direction of R.O.A.R's Youth profile.

If you have scored over 6 Nos…….You are going against the trend of R.O.A.R's Youth profile.

If you have scored over 9 Nos…….You are strongly acting against the trends of R.O.A.R's Youth profile.

Whatever your score, these research findings greatly influence the way advertisers and magazines think about what, how, and where they communicate their messages.

In February 2002, R.O.A.R's research showed that it is now becoming almost impossible to define a separate male or female audience since:

1. both sexes are listening, reading and watching the same material.
2. youth is more committed to certain TV programmes, not TV channels. This is why the BBC outbid Channel 4 for *The Simpsons*.

Messages and values
Female magazines

The messages of mainstream women's magazines are dedicated to the ideal image of a woman who is independent, sexy and looks after her appearance in order to catch a man. Fashion and cosmetics, and advice on relationships tend to dominate teenage female magazines. The ideal woman is often depicted as thin and tall. However, a famous Body Shop advertisement stated, there are only eight women in the world who look like this, and they are top fashion models.

Male magazines

The messages of mainstream men's magazines are focused on the man who enjoys being a lad without a conscience, ogles at women's bodies, drinks large amounts of alcohol, watches football and plays loud music. If he is at all sensitive, he does not want to show it. Men's magazines such as *Loaded* tend to include scantily clad women and articles on sex, football, drinking, fashion and music. The aim is to be wild, witty and to include interviews with the stars. This attitude has softened a little as laddishness has lost its appeal (as shown by the decline in sales of *Loaded*) but *FHM* (684,548 copies sold per week) is still doing better than the top female specific title *Women* (602,842/week) in circulation figures.

Alternative magazines

Alternative magazines try to present a different perspective on the world, such as the magazine *Sibyl*. The magazine was not sold in the main distributors such as WH Smiths, but by subscription. *Sibyl* was dedicated to women who care about women's issues and politics. *Red Pepper* is a political discussion journal that covers issues which the writers think the current Labour Government does not deal with in terms of socialist politics. These magazines all differ from mainstream magazines, as they express alternative viewpoints and ideas about how men and women should live.

Children's and teenagers' magazines

The children's end of the market includes comics ranging from *Beano*, to teenage comic strip *Dick Tracy*, to graphic comics like *Judge Dredd*, *Love and Rockets*, *Electra* and *Toast*. Some comics cross over into the world of film. The Japanese comic *Akira* became an animated movie, featuring cyber-punk motorcycle gangs doing battle on the streets of post World War 3 Tokyo.

Young people's interest in futuristic stories has now transferred over to Nintendo and Sega games. This has led to a growth in PC games magazines such as *Segapower*, *Bad Influence* and *PC Zone*. Many of these magazines offer free software samples on CD.

Fanzines

Fanzines are an alternative to mainstream publishing. Fanzines are written by the fans. Many fanzines are about music, football and skateboarding and they tend to be sold in the street. For example, football fanzines are often sold near the grounds. Music fanzines are sold at clubs and at venues where bands play. Shops with skateboarding and surfing equipment also have fanzines on the counter. *Blockade* is a fanzine for *Prisoner Cell Block H* fans. It once included a feature on the character of prison officer Joan 'the freak' Ferguson. Copies were available from a PO Box address.

As fanzines do not have the benefit of large team of writers and are often written by one or two people, there is very little or no advertising. There is therefore very little incentive for businesses to invest in such a magazine, when only between 50 and 200 copies are likely to be sold.

Format and content

Fanzines are usually the size of an exercise book and are a series of photocopies stapled together. Sometimes they have photographs, however these are only roughly reproduced. There are line drawings and also images recycled from other magazines.

Fanzines do not usually feature articles with famous pop stars. They do however, often express strong opinions about the topics they cover. They are often written without fear of censorship or complaint, as they tend to

Fig 12.1   *Maximum Rock and Roll Drum and Bass: a mock-up for a worldwide fanzine by Alex Hill*

circulate only in the group of fans who read the 'zine. *Stay Free* is a fanzine produced by one woman from New York, and is dedicated to mocking the advertising industry.

New technology publishing is now thriving on the Internet and major print-based companies have websites. Interactive CD-Roms may replace printed materials, but the companies who produce the print versions may be reluctant to lose revenue from advertising. New technology could change the face of newspaper magazine shelves. If not, then it could be that people access their magazines and ask questions and gain advice more interactively using their home computer screens. People may only want to download the pages required, for storage in print form.

masthead

white lettering

bright orange

pug

FREE! SEXY R&B STICKERS INSIDE

COSMO girl!

BUMPER CHRISTMAS ISSUE AND STILL ONLY
£1.49
DECEMBER 2001

FOR FUN, FEARLESS TEENS

"usive" view

bright pink background

10 secret love signs that say he's crazy for you!

World exclusive!
Destiny's Child
On Guys, Christmas Gifts and Growing Up in the Spotlight

Nail-biting real life story
"I survived a near-death ordeal on my school trip"

feature article photograph

year-end special!
A Year Of YOU!
The teens who made 2001 rock

Party on!

headline

Your 'eek'-est Xmas confessions ever!
Party-perfect hair special
Five-minute makeovers
65 sizzling looks (all under £30)

cover lines

Channel flavour!

Single Sexy Snoggable
Which soap dish is right for you?

Ryan Kwanten, Andy McNair, Philip Olivier
PLUS! Jack Ryder and many, many more!

FREE! Xmas e-cards

www.cosmogirl.co.uk

Fig 12.2   A typical magazine cover layout: Cosmo girl!
Source: Courtesy of Cosmo Girl! Magazine © National Magazine Company

Forms and conventions

Layout and design

A typical cover of a glossy mainstream lifestyle magazine shows what is inside, but does not tend to include any articles (see Figure 12.2).

ACTIVITY 3

Compare the following covers and content of the teenage magazines *J-17* and *Empire* (see colour plate):

1. What are the main elements of the cover headlines?
2. How do they define the age of their audience?
3. Denotate and connotate (see also Chapter 2) the images and printed text on the front cover.
4. What are the differences between the two magazines?

Forms and conventions: typical elements

All magazines have some elements in common, be it a TV listings magazine or a simple advertising vehicle. Common elements include:

Advertising	In our next issue
Advice columns	Letters page
Book adaptations	Lists
Campaigns	Make-overs
Competitions	Merchandising
Contents page	Opinion columns
Covers	Quizzes
Diaries	Reviews
Do-it-yourself features	Strips (comic)
	Supplements
Fiction	Surveys
Horoscopes	

ACTIVITY 4

1. Which of the magazines in Figure 12.3 would you read?
2. Which of these magazines would you say are for:

a. teenage boys
b. teenage girls
c. both

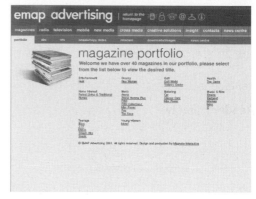

Fig 12.3   Emap Advertising

The audience profile (demographic) for *Empire* shows a greater number of boys and young men reading the magazine:

Empire

Brand values: glamorous, celebratory, in-the-know

Editorial: *Empire* celebrates film and has unrivalled access to the film industry, giving compulsive, behind-the-scenes coverage of the stars and their movies.

Reader's lifestyle: *Empire* readers are 16–30 year olds interested in reading about film, with more male than female readers. They are early adopters who want to be in-the-know about film, so they can impress their friends. They go to the cinema around twice a month but also consume films on video, television and DVD. They are interested in latest technology – internet, DVDs etc but are not obsessed about it. They enjoy socialising and particularly like sitting in pubs discussing film with friends.

Readership: (15–30): 26
15–19 Readership: 519,000
Male readership: 372,000
(EMAPadvertising.com/magazines)

Compare *Empire* with *J-17*'s advertising profile:

Brand values: Cool, sassy, real

Editorial: In a bubblegum teen world, every month *J-17* is exciting and original. Like a cool older sister, it gives emotional advice, lots of laughs and is in the inside track on what's in right now. The *J-17* brand has heritage, so readers trust it.

Reader's lifestyle: The average *J-17* reader is 15. She thinks boy bands are manufactured but fancies Lee from Blue. She wants to know how to make a boy laugh as well as how to snog him. A bit of a tomboy, she'd only wear a sparkly top if she could dress it down with some baggy jeans. She's thinking of getting her eyebrows pierced (but won't actually do it). The *J-17* reader's typical weekend is watching *CD:UK* while text messaging her mate, a shopping trip in town then hanging out in the park (because there's nowhere else to go).

Readership: (11–19) 15
11–19 Readership: 754,000
Source: Youth TGI

Magazine content

Textual analysis: J-17

The magazine *J-17* is a teenage magazine for women, specifically targeted at 13 to 14 year old girls. The straplines on the cover (see Figure 12.4) are that of typical teenage magazine content, with articles on how to get a boyfriend and features such as 'Get Flirting'. The model is dressed in simple clothes and her expression is bright and full

Fig 12.4   *J-17, November 2001. Further information on Emap publications is available at www.emapadvertising.com*
Source: Emap Élan

of bounce and clean fun just like the image of the magazine. The artificial lights create a glossary effect.

Much of a typical issue of *J-17* is taken up with music, film and television celebrity features such as Britney Spears and, in particular, young men. There is a strapline on make-up, suggesting that that will be an advice feature. There is also the offer of a free Fortune Kit splashed across the centre in a major strapline. Below the masthead is a line that states that *J-17* is 'the world's spookiest mag … definitely'. This is a running 'puff' line with variations on the idea of the 'coolest'. The idea of Halloween runs throughout the strapline: coffins, dead people, spooky, etc.

J-17 had a face-lift four years ago when it wanted to increase the numbers in the lower end of its age range (11 to 13 years), so it lost the word 'seventeen' and substituted the numeral '17'.

Images of young women

It is usual for the image of a woman on a magazine such as *J-17* to be looking directly out at the reader. If you study women's magazines' front covers, you will find that almost all will have a head and shoulders shot, and the woman will be looking directly out, as though looking straight at the reader. The effect of this positioning of the front cover model is to provide an idealised version of what a woman should look like. Over a period of time, seeing models with the same look and the same presentation suggests a stereotype of the kind of person women should identify with.

Textual analysis: *Empire*

This issue, December 2001, benefits from having a subject then very much in the

Fig 12.5   Empire, *December 2001*
Source: Peter Mountain courtesy of *Empire* magazine

popular consciousness as a Harry Potter book had just been released as a film. After the books and booking of cinema tickets, consumers eagerly sought any publicity or review material. *Empire* offers an 'exclusive on set access' using a bright yellow star shaped and red type strapline. It offers a 'first' look at films such as *Ocean's 11* etc. There is a preview of the Oscar's at the bottom of the page as Tips for Oscars 2002, which took place three months later in March 2002.

The puff under the masthead announces: 'The UK's No. 1 film magazine'. Above the masthead is (apparently) a confessional gossip-related story/interview with the actor Billy Bob Thornton. The gold background with red and white CAPITALISED type on a triangular pug (at the right hand top corner) indicates that the magazine is bursting with reviews: 50 PAGES OF REVIEWS.

The masthead including the EMPIRE magazine is in full capitals with shiny white relief and black shadowed effect, with the bright red letters bold, structurally strong and prominent. This typeface and design concept conveys the idea of the big picture and the drama of the epic scale of Hollywood cinema films and mass audiences.

The still from the Harry Potter film's promotion department is simply meant to provide the instantly recognisable central figure and icons (glasses/owl) of the film. The words 'Harry Potter' are in a gold serif giving a special sense of the literary source of its inspiration.

The two other images promote (top left) a male action genre film and (foot of page banner) Nicole Kidman's role in the thriller *The Others* and a personal view of *Sixth Sense*. The maleness of the rest of the front page is counterbalanced by the promise of a female actress film review, portrait and interview.

Advertising

Unlike newspapers, magazines aim to make a profit through a mixture of cover price and advertising. 66% of business magazines are given free to people who match the publisher's criteria. In this case, revenue comes mostly from advertising. Approximately 78% of revenue comes from display advertising. Magazines have a ready-made pre-defined target audience, so they provide an effective point of contact for advertisers and their target consumers. The following rates for advertising are printed in the *British Rates and Data*.

J-17: April 2002 standard advertisement rates:

The cost of the advertisement is more when the position is a favourable place like the back cover of the magazine where people will see it if is lying on a table or in a dentist's waiting room, for example. The right hand side is deemed more favourable than the left.

Title	Right of page	Back page
FHM	£17,250	£38,000
J-17	£8,700	£10,440
Empire	£6,700	£8,800
MixMag	£3,850	£7,650

Table 12.3 *Rates for advertisements in Emap; selected titles*
Source. www.emapadvertising.com

The rates above for *J-17* can be compared with those of *Empire*, which is for 16 to 30 year olds. The reason for the difference in cost is that *J-17*'s average readership figures (Jan–June 2002) were 737,000 compared with 519,000 for *Empire's*. Readership is an industry estimate that records how many people in the UK read an average issue of a magazine. (The National Readership Survey is conducted by NRS Ltd to provide industry estimates of over 200 major consumer publications.) A magazine may reach homes

where there is more than one person, or public areas where several people read them. These figures are important to advertisers who want to be sure they can target their potential product sales to the right people and achieve high circulation figures.

Editorial

In each edition of a magazine, the editor introduces the contents in an editorial feature near the front. An editorial is usually an opinion or an account of the magazine's current position or views on current issues. The by-line indicates that it is the editor's view. He or she speaks to the reader in an informal, chatty manner, often signing off with a handwritten signature.

The editorial for *J-17* notes the problem of trying to write anything not serious after the bombing of the New York Trade Centre Towers. However, the tone is sombre and offers the contents of the magazine as a way of thinking about something lighter. The tone is reassuring and confidential.

The editorial for *Empire* includes a picture of spectacles (Harry Potter's) and enthusiastic support for the film and observes its popularity. The tone is familiar and friendly as though talking to you on the street.

Mode of address

The mode of address is the manner, tone and attitude adopted by the magazine when speaking to the reader. In teenage magazines today, the mode of address is meant to be friendly, in a sisterly or brotherly way. This differs from talking down to the reader, or talking at the reader as if by a news presenter.

ACTIVITY 5

Compare and contrast the types of teenagers referred to in the editorials of two women's magazines, such as *Bliss* or *J-17*.

1. Are the two magazine editorial profiles you have chosen different in any way?
2. How do you think their descriptions of the potential readership will attract advertisers?
3. Suggest two or three advertisements that would fit into each of these magazines.
4. Do you think the real readership is the same as the one presented by their profiles? Explain your reasons.

ACTIVITY 6

In groups discuss which magazines you or your family purchase.

Are there any magazines which everybody reads? Are there magazines which only one person reads? Construct a survey of ten people in a particular group, for example, girls or boys aged 11 to 14 years or girls or boys aged 14 to 19 years.

1. Find out what magazines they like and why.
2. Is there a common response? Are there any big differences in responses?

(**Discuss**)

Study a range of magazines targeted at teenagers aged **11 to 19 years** and young adults aged **15 to 24 years**. For example, for women: *More, Sugar, J-17, Smash Hits, Marie Claire, New Woman* or *Red*. For men: *WWF, Hip-Hop, NME, The Face, Loaded, FHM* or *Men's Health*.

Discuss the range and variety of interest in the contents, for the audience of each magazine:
a front cover (images, headings, puffs, straplines, and price)
b the contents page (inc. images)
c the advertisements.

Female magazines: facts

Percentage of female readers of each 'sector' of magazines

▮ Women's weekly titles, including celebrity and gossip (e.g. *Woman's Own*, *Bella*, *Take a Break*, *Hello!*): 55%
▮ Women's titles, including lifestyle and fashion monthly (e.g. *Marie Claire*, *Cosmopolitan*, *Vogue*, *Harpers & Queens*): 14%
▮ Women's monthly titles, home interest (e.g. *Good Housekeeping*, *Woman & Home*): 11%

ACTIVITY 7

Discuss which of the following statements about the absence of a teenage male lifestyle magazine you agree with or disagree with.

1. Ed, age 13 years
   'Basically there's the *Beano* and pornographic magazines and not much in between. I'd like to see stuff on fashion, a problem page, articles about the army, things like that. *FHM* is good, they have pictures of girls without being hardcore porn and *Tropical Disease of the Month* is wicked.'
2. Jonathan, age 13 years
   'Loads of people would read a general magazine if it wasn't too expensive. They should have interviews with famous people and pictures of girls on the front. Some boys might find it too girly and that

might put them off. I wouldn't mind a problem page, so long as it wasn't too disgusting. I only read football magazines – other things like music mags and mags with picture of girls are aimed at people older than me.'

3. William, age 16 years
'I think there should be general magazines for teenage boys, but I am not sure how many people would read them. My friends read *FHM* and *Loaded*, probably because of the naked women. If there was stuff available on things like drugs and more emotional subjects they might read it – but they wouldn't admit to it.'

4. Mark, age 15 years
'I read *Dream*, it's music with a bit of fashion. There doesn't really need to be a magazine for teenagers because they are catered for by men's magazines and specialist magazines.'

5. Emily, age 13 years
'Boys read football magazines and car mags. I get *J-17*, *Sugar*, *Bliss*, *Big*, *Top of the Pops*. They should do something like that for boys because they don't get stuff like gossip and things in the soaps and music and advice. But they're probably happier with football.'

ACTIVITY 8

Invent a new magazine for boys which targets 11 to 19 year olds. It is to be called *17 Plus*, to attract all males in that age range. Create the following:

1. A mock-up for a front cover, including price, masthead, headline, straplines and layout. There is no need to write any of the articles.
2. Contents page.
3. A list of ten assorted advertisements.
4. Outline what your leading feature and image will be, for the front page.
5. Write your editorial letter introducing the magazine.

Magazine ownership

Publishing companies are now often large corporations who own several businesses; some media related and others in completely different business areas, such as the leisure industries.

Despite the downturn in advertising sales, the global giant AOL-Time-Warner bought the biggest British publishing company, IPC Magazines, for £1.5 billion. Most leading magazine titles are owned by a small number of companies. In the consumer sector, IPC Magazines is currently the largest publisher. Reed Business Publishing is the leading business publisher. Both companies are owned by Reed Elsevier Ltd. Other major magazine publishing companies include BBC Magazines, Condé Nast, D.C. Thompson, Emap, G & J (UK), H. Bauer, The National Magazine Company and Reader's Digest. HarperCollins is owned by Newscorp, which is the same company that owns the film company, Twentieth Century Fox and *The Times* and *Sun* newspapers.

ACTIVITY 9

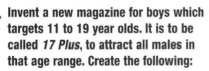

Research one of the companies listed in Figure 12.5 and find out what they own. What titles do they publish, how much do they cost and what are their best sellers? Most companies have Internet sites to look at, and *The Media Guide: A Guardian Book* is an alternative source of information.

Case Study: Emap

Emap started life as a local newspaper company and acquired a stock exchange listing in London in 1947.

Emap's description of itself follows:

'Emap plc is a media company whose purpose is to create entertainment and information which can be delivered to every home and business within defined communities. Emap's business activities focus around three main areas:

- Over 150 top selling consumer magazines in the UK, France and around the world.
- Over 200 business to business events, magazines and conferences, many of them market leaders, including Smash Hits Poll Winners Party.
- 18 UK radio stations, including Kiss FM and 6 digital music stations and six rapidly growing TV channels.

In addition, Emap is very involved in new media: Websites, email marketing and mobile messaging. It employs around 5,500 people based in over 50 offices in the UK, Europe and around the world.

Emap has a large portfolio of brands. It has a strong competitive position within each of its businesses:

- consumer magazines – number two in the UK
- consumer magazines – number three in France
- radio – number three in the UK
- business to business – number two in publishing, number one in exhibitions in the UK.

There are four main networks of media products and linked media:

Emap Performance – Radio Stations, Music TV Stations (The Box, Q, Magic, Kiss, Kerrang!, Smash Hits), the music magazines (Kerrang!, Q, Smash Hits, Sneak, and the music websites (aloud.com,kissonline.co.uk, mixmag.net, mojo4music.com, q4music.com, smash hits.net, the box.co.uk, kerrang.com).

Emap Elan – Lifestyle magazines and websites FHM, FHM Collections, The Face, POP, Arena, Arena Homme Plus, Top Santé, Closer, New Woman, Heat, J-17, More, Period Living, and Bliss etc.

Emap Esprit – Health, Nursing, Parenting and websites

Emap Active/Auto – Motoring magazines, Bike magazines. Outdoor and Sport etc and websites.

Emap Advertising acts as a point of contact to work across the range of media in its portfolio. The multi-media nature of some brand names works to provide advertising possibilities. Kiss, Q, Kerrang and Smash Jits are now all multi-media existing as radio stations and programmes; online sites, text message services and events such as the Smash Hits Poll Winners Party and Q Awards.

Smash Hits is the most famous and established fortnightly pop magazine; first to break new acts, in fact it's the UK's pop bible.

'The *Smash Hits* reader is obsessed with Pop Music and simply has to know everything about the latest bands. The readers love and trust *Smash Hits* because it's the ultimate fix for everything a 12-year-old girl needs to know on Planet Pop! Our early teenage readers are not just chart followers, but pop obsessed.'

Median Age (7–19) 12
7–19 Readership 1,304,000
Source: Youth TGI

Emap Radio's 18 radio stations have been grouped into 3 radio brands – the Magic Network, Big City Network and Kiss. Each of these brands is targeted at a specific lifestyle within the broader age band of 15 to 44-year-olds. The stations are represented by Emap Advertising in London and Manchester, as well as local sales teams at each station.

Their portfolio of radio stations, concentrated in the North East, North West, Yorkshire and London, makes them the third biggest independent local radio group in the UK. In 1999, Emap Radio reportedly has a 16% share of independent local radio listening hours (Source: RAJAR Q2 2002).

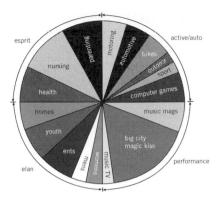

Fig 12.6 *Emap's cross media operations*
Source: Emap 2002

Internet music website

The Broadcasting Bill created the opportunity for EMAP to enter other broadcasting areas. This resulted in the acquisition of The Box in 1996 – a unique interactive music television channel controlled entirely by the viewers.

In 2001 Emap recorded pre-tax losses of £527 million. The main problem was the purchase of Emap Petersen, an American publishing house specialising in cars, guns and ammunition magazines. As a result of selling off Petersen, Emap began to streamline its operation but still is involved in a variety of media and cross-industry businesses.

The industry magazine, *Mediaweek*, described Emap's survival through the 'repositioning of weekly celebrity title *Heat*, which deflected from some of the group's problems. Emap had the inspiration to change its focus toward the women's weekly market and had one of the year's success stories on its hands. In February's ABCs it recorded a massive 137% circulation rise, year on year and, by August, was still rising, up a further 147%. Like the other mag success story of the year, *Glamour*, the title succeeded by growing the market and targeting an upmarket audience which had previously shunned women's weekly titles. Its original take on the celebrity market has taken

it into the Premier League of magazine brands and the title is now branching out across other media, with Heat TV in the pipeline.'

Emap also invested in the French magazine sector hoping to increase its European base.

Producing covers: student work

Study the examples of covers created by Media Studies students in Figures 12.7, 12.8 and 12.9.

Figure 12.7

This student was asked to create a new artist and to produce artwork for two different music magazines. She chose to invent a hip-hop artist and placed the image in two contexts; first, a street indie magazine and second, what the student regarded as a more mainstream magazine, *The Face*.

To produce the image, she took photographs against appropriate backgrounds, having

Fig 12.7

Source: © Rachel Stone

Fig 12.8

Source: © Sara Morland

Fig 12.9

firstly planned out ideas in drawings. Once developed, she enlarged the photographs using a software programme called Photoshop (could use a photocopier for this).Then she cut out (could be scanned) the masthead of the two magazines. Next, she created straplines and cover lines and placed them over the background images.

Figures 12.8 and 12.9

The same process was carried out by another student for the fictional solo artist, Jade. She is seen to be more at home in the version of a dance, music and club magazine, *Mixmag*, whereas she has been made to appear more glamorous for a glamorised version of the more mainstream music magazine, *Vox*.

Specimen unseen print question: OCR

These Tasks are not actual examination questions. The questions are the sole work of the author and are devised to match the style, mark allocation and format of the relevant question papers from AQA and OCR. They are designed for examination practice. The Tasks are designed to follow the examination paper timings and mark allocations. It is essential that candidates check the specified topics set for the year of their examination, by the examination board. For previous examination papers contact the examination board direct.

Study the two extracts (earlier in the chapter) *J-17* November 2001 (page 187) and *Empire* December 2001 (page188).

Answer all questions in full sentences giving specific examples from the extracts, as appropriate.

a) Which features of these extracts identify *J-17* as an example of the teenage magazine genre? **(6 marks)**

b) The front covers of *J-17* and *Empire*

magazines are designed to attract an audience by creating an impact. Giving two examples for each, explain how this impact is constructed by the choice of:

i) the vocabulary (words and phrases)
(8 marks)
and
ii) design and typeface **(8 marks)**
and
iii) the choice of photographic images
(8 marks)

c) Using at least two examples, one from each magazine, explain the concept of an EXCLUSIVE. **(6 marks)**

d) What kind of audience do you think would buy *Empire* magazine What would be their lifestyle and media interests? **(12 marks)**

e) With detailed reference to other magazines you have studied, compare how each represents the genre differently.
(12 marks)

 Extension Tasks

1a **Research** the following magazines and assess who their target audience is (for example, ABCs, age, gender) and what their readership profile is (for example, lifestyle):
- *FourfourTwo*
- *F1 Racing*
- *Ebony*
- *Amnesty International*

b **Analyse** the magazine's areas: editorial page, front cover, contents and advertisements: attitude, lifestyle and messages.

2 **Design** a TV and radio campaign for launching a new teenage male magazine. The advertisement should be no more than 15 frames of a storyboard. The radio advertisement should be about one minute. Provide a short explanation of how the campaign will reach its audience and persuade them to buy the magazine.

3 **Create** a fanzine web page for the Internet, or a mock-up for one. Research existing web pages for ideas about design and layout. Design features that allow the person browsing to interact. Define the area of interest and explain what type of audience is targeted. What images would you use to attract the audience?

 Examination Skills

Knowledge and Understanding

Students will need to have studied the typical features of design and layout of a magazine, ownership and the targeting and construction of audiences. A strong knowledge of typical content and an awareness of alternative approaches to production and layout will also be useful.

Textual Analysis

Students will need to demonstrate skills in interpreting images and text. They will need to be able to denotate and connotate the front page as a whole, and in its different parts: images, headlines, cover lines, masthead, etc. Attention should be paid to the use of colours, typeface and language on the front cover of a magazine. The institutional style, messages and values and audiences should be brought out by analysis of visual and written content and mode of address. For example, an analysis of *Cosmo girl!* (front cover) on page 185 could be:

Cosmo girl! features a full page image of music celebrities Destiny's Child. The characters look straight at the camera as though they want to appear friendly to the readers. The females' smiling looks suggest enthusiasm and awareness of how attractive they are. Their dress code reveals bare shoulders and suggests evening wear.

Practical Work

In the AQA examination, practical skills using knowledge of layout and typical content on cover and in content lists will be required. Questions on set topics such as TV talk shows may, for example, require the student to create mock-ups of a TV listings page. Mock-ups (hand drawn, rough layouts) will be asked for, including: straplines, headlines and a rough idea of image size and typeface size, font style and colour. The use of promotional texts such as radio advertisements, full page advertisements in other magazines or television advertisements may be part of the creative element of an AQA style question. Institution and audience should be defined by the visual, typographic and colour styles. Contents lists, straplines, mastheads and the tone and manner of address should convey the type of institution and its intended audience.

13 Advertising: standards and controls
Who's in control?

What you will learn

In this chapter you will study where advertisements are placed, their different purposes, and the creative approaches that producers adopt. A contemporary advertisement is contrasted with an historic example. The case studies provide analysis of audience responses by the industry regulators: the Advertising Standards Authority, Independent Television Commission and the Radio Authority. The main assignment is to produce a mock-up and a pitch for an advertisement brief, in the role of a creative advertisement agency.

KEY WORDS

- representation
- bias
- sexist
- racist
- ageist
- controls
- positioning

TECHNICAL WORDS

- creative dept.
- media planners
- copy
- advertorial
- masthead
- tag line
- camera ready
- typeface
- demographic
- psychographic

What are advertisements?

One definition of advertisements by the Advertising Association is:

> Advertisements are messages, paid for by those who send them, intended to inform or influence people who see them.

There are three points to consider in this definition. Firstly, all advertisements contain a message which may be expressed in words as a slogan – for example, 'Kill Your Speed'.

Secondly, advertisements are paid for by advertisers. The cost of an advertisement in glossy magazines, for example, means that advertising is a major source of income (approximately 40%) for magazines. Advertising also provides money for the television channels which carry the advertisements. Advertising is therefore a commercial business, as opposed to 'free' publicity created by press releases or photo opportunities.

Thirdly, advertisements have a purpose to persuade or raise awareness of the existence of their product in the people whom they target. The advertising for the new *Star Wars* film, released in 1999, was claimed to have achieved a massive 80% public awareness, months before its actual release.

Who advertises?

In the UK a range of advertisers exist, many of them are small businesses who try to promote themselves. Bigger companies will buy in an advertising agency to create the messages in the relevant media. Famous advertising agencies such as Saatchi and Saatchi, and Bartle, Bogle and Hegarty became successful over a period of years and command respect from companies looking for national coverage and high impact campaigns.

The Government also spends considerable amounts of money on advertising. By 1989, the Government had become the nation's largest advertiser, as a consequence of its record spend on advertising in excess of £98 million (M. Scannell, 'The impact of marketing and public relations in modern British politics', unpublished Ph.D. thesis, 1991). In September 1989, the advertising campaign to promote the privatisation of electricity cost £76 million. The highest commercial advertiser spent no more than £12 million total in that year.

Government advertisements fall into two types: information (for example, tax returns or child benefit) and persuasive (for example, to warn the public not to drink alcohol and drive).

Other groups of people who advertise include some political parties and also pressure groups, such as Amnesty International, Oxfam or the National Society for the Prevention of Cruelty to Children. Individuals also advertise their second-hand goods in newspaper or magazine 'classifieds', usually for free.

Advertising media

More than half of the money spent on advertising in the UK is spent on the press – newspapers, magazines and trade directories. The second most important advertising medium is television, accounting for 27% of advertising money. TV advertising is more expensive than in newspapers, therefore only the bigger companies can advertise on TV regularly.

TV	27%
National Papers	18%
Magazines	16%
Local Papers	16%
Direct mail	11%
Radio	7%
Outdoor	5%
Cinema	0.5%
Total	**100%**

Table 13.1 *Advertising Market Expenditure*
World Advertising Research Centre 2001

Direct mail

Direct mail is advertising material sent straight through the letter box into people's homes. It is usually described as 'junk mail', and 11% is spent on this type of advertising in the UK.

Others

Outdoor advertising such as billboards, bus shelters and buses account for 5% of the costs. Radio advertising is cheap and 7% of advertising costs are spent on this medium. Cinema advertising reaches a tiny 0.5%, though this is a relatively young audience.

Fig 13.1   Beckham and Police sunglasses product endorsement

ACTIVITY 1

1. **Watch** the advertisement breaks before and after the regional evening news. **Make a list** of all the advertisements in these breaks. How many are about national products? How many are products or services from local companies? How many trailers or 'teasers' are there for programmes on that channel later? Are there public information programmes produced by the Government?

2. Now watch the advertisements in a break during a soap opera (6.30 to 8.30 pm) **Compile a list** of advertisements. **Compare** the breakdown of these types of advertisements with those in your first list. Do the two lists differ in content and if so, how do they differ or not? Do they suggest a different type of person is watching for each slot in the schedule? If so, who are these people?

Study the list of advertising media below:

Billboard	Leaflet
Brochure	Magazine
Catalogue	National press
Cinema	Packaging
Circular	Point of sale
Direct mail	Poster
Directory	Press general
Electronic mail	Regional press
Facsimile	Transport
Mobile phone	

Write down three advantages and disadvantages of the following: television, newspaper, radio, billboard, direct mail.

Advertisement production

Creative department

An advertising agency's creative department actually produces the advertisements. The department is run by the agency's creative director. There is often a series of creative teams, each consisting of a copywriter and an art director. These two work together on words and pictures. Some agencies have their own art studios, though most now have artwork created by outside studios. Illustrations, photographs and typesetting have to be produced and checked ready for printing by the team. If the advertisement is a television promotion, then actors, actresses and props have to be organised for the television studios.

Copy

Copy is the term used for all the words in print or voice-over, and the printed words in television and cinema advertisements. When the copy is put together with the artwork, the printed material is then described as 'camera ready'. This means the artwork can be photographed for the final film negative before printing many copies in the chosen format.

Editorial

An editorial is usually a leading article and has the writer's by-line attached to the top of the piece. An editorial can be any piece of writing in the newspaper or magazine that expresses the paper's viewpoint. Editorial pieces are usually confined to the main feature articles and the headlines. There is also often an editor's comment column inside the paper.

Advertorial

An advertorial is a mix of an advertisement and an editorial. The use of advertorials is very common in local newspapers. In exchange for purchasing advertising space for a product, the paper will provide free space to the advertiser, in an article about the product itself. The article will never be critical about the product; if anything it will be positive. The newspaper gains advertising revenue and the producer of the goods gains free advertisement space.

Estate agents, for example, who wish to sell an expensive house, will often be regular buyers of newspaper space to advertise their properties. The articles next to these advertisements appear to be neutral at first, when talking about a 'charming new housing estate'. However, when you read to the end of a piece, it is clear from the telephone number and the contact name of the estate agents that the piece has been used to promote the properties on behalf of the estate agent.

Media planners

Media planners help advertisers place their advertisements in the best slots in the breaks between television programmes. They preview as much of the television programmes as possible, by looking at the television listings and watching what is in the programmes they are going to advertise alongside. The media planners then purchase blocks of time from the TV broadcasters. Advertisements shown only regionally are much cheaper than a guaranteed slot in the national independent network.

Summary of production process:
- Strategy development.
- Copywriting.
- Design and art direction – creating image and layout.
- Production of print adverts, including illustration and photography.
- Production of TV and radio spots.
- Media buying.
- General coordination, planning and budgeting.
- Public relations.

Advertising campaigns

In 2001, advertising in general slumped on television and in magazines. Radio and internet advertising increased. In a time of uncertainty, inventive cross-media branding and marketing were called for.

Revlon Charlie Deodorant

The twelve shots of the playful antics of people in a photo booth provide the message that in a tight space it's still cool to be physically close to your friends and remain friends because of the (apparently) obviously very effective smell-preventative deodorant sold by Revlon. The deodorant not only works but it also suits attractive young men and women with individual styles (denoted by the various hairstyles) and of different races.

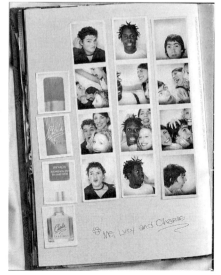

Fig 13.2   Revlon Charlie advertisement
(see colour section)

ACTIVITY 2

Research other perfume/deodorant advertisements.
Design a perfume advertisement for men. Write an analysis of its meaning and why it will appeal to both men and women.
Create a slogan, storyboard images, script and sounds for an advertisement. Film it if you have the resources.
Write an evaluation (500 words) of what the processes of research, design, scripting and filming were about.

Advertising controls

The Advertising Standards Authority (ASA)

The Advertising Standards Authority was established in 1962 to provide independent scrutiny of the system of self-regulation of advertisements. Self-regulation meant that the industry itself checks its own standards. The aim is to ensure that the system operates in the public interest. The ASA is independent of the Government and the advertising business.

Sponsorship

Television sponsorship has increased considerably as rules have relaxed about what can and what cannot be shown. Beamish Stout sponsors *Inspector Morse*, Stella Artois sponsors *Film Four* and Cadbury's Chocolate sponsors *Coronation Street* on ITV. Masthead programming is now allowed on all ITC licensed services other than Channels 3, 4 and 5. Masthead programming is programming that uses the editorial and production resources of a magazine title.

Fig 13.3   Mizz: *goes aromatic with Revlon*

Revlon cosmetics used a novelty technique for targeting a teenage audience. As part of one promotional campaign, the smell of perfume was sprayed on the cover of the Mizz magazine. Both the magazine and the cosmetics company aimed to benefit.

ADVERTISING CODE

Principles

2.1   All advertisements should be legal, decent, honest and truthful.

2.2   All advertisements should be prepared with a sense of responsibility to consumers and to society.

2.3   All advertisements should respect the principles of fair competition generally accepted in business.

2.4   No advertisement should bring advertising into disrepute.

2.5   Advertisements must conform with the Codes. Primary responsibility for observing the Codes falls on advertisers. Others involved in preparing and publishing advertisements such as agencies, publishers and other service suppliers also accept an obligation to abide by the Codes.

2.6   Any unreasonable delay in responding to the ASA's enquiries may be considered a breach of the Codes.

2.7   The ASA will on request treat in confidence any private or secret material supplied unless the Courts or officials acting within their statutory powers compel its disclosure.

2.8   The Codes are applied in the spirit as well as in the letter.

Fig 13.4a   ASA Code guidelines

Source: © The British Codes of Advertising and Sales Promotion, CAP

ALCOHOLIC DRINKS

46.1 For the purposes of the Codes, alcoholic drinks are those that exceed 1.2% alcohol by volume.

46.2 The drinks industry and the advertising business accept a responsibility for ensuring that advertisements contain nothing that is likely to lead people to adopt styles of drinking that are unwise. The consumption of alcohol may be portrayed as sociable and thirst-quenching. Advertisements may be humorous, but must still conform with the intention of the rules.

46.3 Advertisements should be socially responsible and should not encourage excessive drinking. Advertisements should not suggest that regular solitary drinking is advisable. Care should be taken not to exploit the young, the immature or those who are mentally or socially vulnerable.

46.4 Advertisements should not be directed at people under eighteen through the selection of media, style of presentation, content or context in which they appear. No medium should be used to advertise alcoholic drinks if more than 25% of its audience is under eighteen years of age.

46.5 People shown drinking should not be, nor should they look, under twenty five. Younger models may be shown in advertisements, for example in the context of family celebrations, but it should be obvious that they are not drinking.

46.6 Advertisements should not feature real or fictitious characters who are likely to appeal particularly to people under eighteen in a way that would encourage them to drink.

46.7 Advertisements should not suggest that any alcoholic drink can enhance mental, physical or sexual capabilities, popularity, attractiveness, masculinity, femininity or sporting achievements.

46.8 Advertisements may give factual information about the alcoholic strength of a drink or its relatively high alcohol content but this should not be the dominant theme of any advertisement. Alcoholic drinks should not be presented as preferable because of their high alcohol content or intoxicating effect.

46.9 Advertisements should not portray drinking alcohol as the main reason for the success of any personal relationship or social event. A brand preference may be promoted as a mark of the drinker's good taste and discernment.

46.10 Drinking alcohol should not be portrayed as a challenge, nor should it be suggested that people who drink are brave, tough or daring for doing so.

46.11 Particular care should be taken to ensure that advertisements for sales promotions requiring multiple purchases do not actively encourage excessive consumption.

46.12 Advertisements should not depict activities or locations where drinking alcohol would be unsafe or unwise. In particular, advertisements should not associate the consumption of alcohol with operating machinery, driving, any activity relating to water or heights, or any other occupation that requires concentration in order to be done safely.

46.13 Low alcohol drinks are those that contain 1.2% alcohol by volume or less. Advertisers should ensure that low alcohol drinks are not promoted in a way that encourages their inappropriate consumption and should not depict activities that require complete sobriety.

Fig 13.4b ASA Code guidelines
Source: © The British Codes of Advertising and Sales Promotion, CAP

How much control does the ASA have?

A number of sanctions exist to counteract advertisements and promotions that conflict with the Advertising Codes:

1 The media may deny access to space.
2 Adverse publicity may result from rulings published weekly by the ASA on its website (www.asa.org.uk).
3 Trading sanctions may be imposed or recognition revoked by the advertisers, promoters or by the agency's professional association.
4 Financial incentives provided by trade, professional or media organisations may be withdrawn.

The ASA deals with the following:

▎ Advertisements in newspapers, magazines, brochures, leaflets, circulars, mailings, catalogues and other printed publications, facsimile transmissions, posters and aerial announcements.
▎ Cine film and video commercials.
▎ Advertisements in non-broadcast electronic media, such as computer games.
▎ Viewdata services.
▎ Mailing lists, with the exception of business to business.
▎ Sales promotions.
▎ Advertisements and promotions covered by the Cigarette Code.

The Committee of Advertising Practice (CAP) is the self-regulatory body that devises and enforces the Codes. CAP's members include organisations that represent the advertising, sales, promotion and media businesses.

Broadcast commercials are the responsibility of the Independent Television Commission and the Radio Authority.

Independent Television Commission (ITC)

The ITC monitors television advertisements and decides which advertisements should be withdrawn, according to the ITC Code of Advertising Standards and Practice. In 2001, the ITC received 7,554 complaints about advertisements virtually the same number as in 2000. The most serious sanction imposed by the ITC was a fine of £100,000 on LWT.

An example of a complaint received about an advertisement was for an RSPCA parody of a toy commercial which viewers thought capable of encouraging rather than preventing animal cruelty.

ACTIVITY 3

1. Select two magazines, one aimed at a female reader and one aimed at a male reader.
2. How many advertisements include images of women? What ideas about women do they represent? Repeat the same for the adverts aimed at men.
3. Do you think the representations are realistic, idealised or restrictive?

Complaints

An important aspect of the ASA's work is dealing with complaints about advertisements from members of the public, consumer groups and competitors. The procedure has stood up to scrutiny in the courts and is designed to balance speed with fairness to all sides.

Complaints received

During 2000, the Authority's staff received 12,262 complaints relating to 8,457 advertisements. 937 complaints were carried forward from 1999, relating to 677 ads. The numbers of new complaints received showed an increase of more than 4% compared to 1999 – although these concerned a smaller number of advertisements. There were 810 complaints about 587 ads that were being dealt with as the year ended and these were carried over into 2001.

Complaints resolved

During 2000 the ASA resolved more complaints in comparison with 1999 – but that these were about fewer advertisements. The number of complaints resolved increased by 2% to 12,389, although these complaints related to 8,547 advertisements – a reduction of just under 1% from the 8,617 ads that generated complaints in 1999.

A total of 1,662 advertisements required investigation, with these generating a total of 4,313 complaints. 1,031 of these advertisements were formally investigated and 631 were dealt with informally.

In total, 1,329 ads were found to breach the Codes – or 15.5% of all ads dealt with in 2000.

ACTIVITY 4

Research recent asa.org.uk complaints. What reasons are given for the complaints and what are the ASA's judgements?

Advertisement	No. of complaints	ASA decision
Yves Saint Laurent Beaure Ltd	948	Upheld
Npower	219	Not justified
Elida Faberge Ltd	217	Not upheld
NTL Group Ltd	175	Upheld
Benetton (UK) Ltd	144	Not upheld
Marks & Spencer plc	124	Not justified
Huntingdon Life Sciences Ltd	93	Not upheld
Keep the Clause	88	Not justified
Conde Nast Publications Ltd	84	Not upheld
Gossard (UK) Ltd	76	Upheld
Total	**2,168**	

Not justified are those, after consideration, the ASA Council has ruled that the complaints do not justify investigation under the Codes. In these cases no adjudication is published. However, further details of the above cases are available on the ASA's website or from the communications team.

Table 13.2 *Top 10 complaints in 2000*
Source: Adapted from asa.org.uk

Offence

Research into advertising in the UK carried out by the ASA draws the following conclusions. The British public found the main causes of offence to be:

- Setting a bad example to children.
- Being disturbed or unsuitable for children.
- Featuring bad language.
- Being shown in the wrong place, so that children can see it.
- Being in bad taste.

- Being sexually explicit.
- Containing violence.
- The portrayal of women.
  Source: Adapted from ASA Annual Report 2002

Taboo subjects

Taboo (or completely 'no-go') areas for advertisers include death, religion and bad language.

Case examples: complaints made to the ASA

Studying test cases on the regulation of the advertising industry can reveal how commercial factors work to combine messages and values for the purposes of selling products.

ACTIVITY 5

1. Read the examples of print-based advertisements which follow. Discuss the contents of the advertisements as they are described in the wording of ASA's adjudications and verdicts.
2. Study the verdicts. What is your opinion of the verdicts? Give reasons for your answer.

Complaint: **Objection to an advertisement, in the *Dandy*, for Cheestrings, that was in the form of a comic strip. The page was headed 'ADVERTISEMENT' and stated "Cheestrings. Present Strings at a Birthday Party" in the top left-hand corner. The complainant objected that, although the page was headed 'ADVERTISEMENT', to a child it was not clearly differentiated from the editorial content of the comic.**

Adjudication: Complaint not upheld. The advertisers said the advertisement was designed to convey the message that Cheestrings could be used in an alternative, fun way and was one in a series that had run in the *Dandy* and *Beano* comics. They said they designed and researched their advertisements with both parents and children, which had shown that children of six to 12 years old could easily distinguish the advertisements from the editorial. They pointed out that the regular editorial features and characters would be familiar to readers and believed that the 'Strings' character would not be confused with *Dandy* characters. The Authority considered the advertisements would be recognised by children as advertisements and were unlikely to be confused with the editorial content of the comic. It did not object to the approach.

Source: ASA

Complaint: Objection to an advertisement in the *Guardian* for *Q* magazine. The advertisement was headlined 'Jesus! It's Madonna WORLD EXCLUSIVE INTERVIEW!'. The complainant objected that the reference to Jesus was offensive.

Adjudication: Complaint not upheld. The advertisers apologised for the offence they had caused and said they had withdrawn the advertisement. The publishers did not comment on the complaint. The Authority considered that, although the advertisement's play on the names Jesus and Madonna was unlikely to cause serious or widespread offence to readers of the *Guardian*, it asked the advertisers to take care when using this approach in the future.

Source: ASA

Case examples: using the ITC's Code of Advertising

ACTIVITY 6

1. Read the following complaints about advertisements.
2. Discuss and write down what you thought were the reasons for the complaint. What were the reasons for each verdict?

Nature of Complaint

Advertising for the *Mirror* claimed 'Tomorrow, the *Mirror* is just 10p' and repeated variations of that claim a number of times. The complainant objected that he had been charged more and, when he contacted the Mirror Group, had been told that the offer applied only at selected outlets. He had not seen any qualification on the commercial.

Assessment

The ITC found that the advertising had run only in certain regions and that it had carried superimposed text which read 'Price reduction only in restricted parts of Yorkshire, Tyne Tees, Granada & Ulster TV regions. Usual price 32p. No purchase necessary. Details from Mirror Group offices.' The agency explained that the 10 pence price was only available from independent newsagents in the regions listed or from newsagents belonging to groups whose shops were all within those regions. (In other words, if even one branch of a chain was outside the four regions, none of the branches would have sold the paper for 10 pence.) However, the text was not held on screen for as long as the ITC's rules require, was in small type and for part of the time was against a confusing background of newsprint. The ITC judged that the text was too hard to read.

In any case, the ITC judged that, even if it had been legible, the disclaimer had not given viewers a sufficiently accurate indication of the availability of the offer. Given the absolute nature of the main claims, the ITC concluded that the advertising had been misleading.

The advertising ran for a short time only.

Decision

Complaint upheld.

Source: ITC

Nature of Complaint

Advertising for Sky's Movie Channels featured ordinary people quoting famous lines from various films. One was 'You're only supposed to blow the ****** doors off' (Michael Caine in The Italian Job). Some complainants objected in principle to the use of swearing in television advertising. Others were concerned about scheduling when children were likely to be watching.

Assessment

The ITC recognised that, for some viewers, any swearing in advertising is unacceptable but did not consider that most viewers would find this use of a relatively mild swear word inherently offensive, particularly since it was used in a relevant context. The ITC did, however, accept that parents were entitled to expect that television advertising should not appear to endorse or encourage swearing and, for this reason, instructed the BACC to restrict the commercial to post-9pm.

Decision

30 complaints upheld on grounds of inappropriate scheduling

18 complaints not upheld

Source: ITC

Case Study: alcohol

ACTIVITY 7

1. Study the Advertising Standards Authority's guidelines concerning advertisements about alcohol on page 198.
2. Read the Advertising Guidelines and the specific guidelines for alcohol printed by The British Code of Advertising and Sales Promotion on behalf of the ASA on pages 202 and 203.

Analysing Still Advertisements

For any print advertisement, there are three areas that can be analysed:

▍ Languages and categories
▍ Audience
▍ Messages and values

Study the leaflet in Figure 13.5 and answer the following questions relating to it.

Languages and categories

How is the meaning presented in Figure 13.5? What effect does the presentation have? What does it mean and what type of advertisement is it?

Text

Consider brand name and slogan when analysing advertisements. How does the slogan in Figure 13.5 relate to the image and the graphics? It is also important to consider typefaces, point size and the use of upper or lower case letters.

Fig 13.5   A leaflet linked to several advertisers through film promotion tie-ins

Source: Nestlé

Technical codes

How was the leaflet made? Analyse the image in Figure 13.5 in terms of: lighting, cropping, enlargement, colour and text (typeface and point size).

Audience

Who is the leaflet in Figure 13.5 directed at and how has this been achieved? Who produced it and for what reason?

Messages and values

What is the overall message of the advertisement in Figure 13.5?

*Fig 13.6   Celebrity endorsement of a
campaign can heighten its profile*

Advertising

The most commonly used typefaces are:

▌ Futura
▌ Franklin Gothic
▌ Bembo
▌ Garamond
▌ Goudy

It would be useful to study some
advertisements to see which typefaces are
used.

Target audience

In defining a product there needs to be
research into who will buy it. Questionnaires
will aid this process. Refer back to
demographic groups in Chapter Three.

Research questionnaire one

Use the following check list to produce
a questionnaire for a chosen target
audience.

1 Demographic group:
▌ Sex
▌ Age range
▌ Cultural or ethnic group
▌ Marital status
▌ Household size
▌ Occupation type
▌ Home owner or renting
▌ Income range
▌ Other

2 Psychographic
The most important values are:
▌ Home, family, career, spirituality,
adventure, honest, spiritual, status.
▌ Hobbies, interests.
▌ Greatest concerns, for example, crime,
the environment.
▌ Religion.
▌ Political affiliation.
▌ Spending habits.
▌ Amount of spare time.
▌ Voluntary work.

Research questionnaire two: media usage

Use this checklist for a telephone
interview for a face-to-face
questionnaire.

Name and age

1a TV (yes/no)
  At these times/days. . . . .
  b List all TV channels and programmes
  you think your target audience
  watches.
2a Radio (yes/no)
  At these times/days. . . . .

b List all radio stations or types of radio stations.

3a Newspapers (yes/no)

b List newspapers you think your target group reads (daily, weekly, local, regional or national).

4a Magazines (yes/no)

b List all magazines you think your target group reads (regional and national).

5a Does your target use the Internet (yes/no)

At these times/days.....................

6a Music – what type of music does your target group listen to?

b In which medium do they listen to music (Radio, CD, Audio-cassette, TV programme)?

7 Of the above media which media do you think are best for reaching your target group? List all that apply, but star those which are outstanding.

Positioning

In advertising psychology, every person can be 'positioned' in terms of their attitude. For example, a 'couch potato' or a 'get up and go' person. Review also Chapter Three for ideas on audiences. You need to define your typical consumer's attitude before deciding where and how to construct the images. Draw up a list of statements or points based on the information in Questionnaire Two, and decide which media will suit them best. If they do not watch TV, then there could be a great deal of money saved.

Changing audiences, changing tactics

Two recent elements of modern life have changed the way advertisers try to reach their audiences:

▌ the advance of new technologies such as the mobile phone and the internet

▌ the decline in the fortunes of conventional advertising formats such as the between programme television advertisement or the traditional magazine advertisement

Mobile phone take up has been so phenomenal that advertisers now send advertisements through **text messaging**. Telephone messages carry **direct advertising**, sales, and **indirect advertising** through promises of prizes etc. One aim is to persuade the phone user to give their name and contact details so that they can go on a mailing list for future promotions. Once an advertising agency has a list of people, they can send offers to the audience according to their age, consumer product preference and time of consumption. For example, Clinique, a face product company, targeted an audience of 15–24 year olds on their phones via a So Solid Crew fan club text message.

Specific targeting of a particular age or of interest groups is called **niche marketing**. A niche is a segment of the total mass audience, e.g. heavy metal, rock male teenagers or club-going flat-owning professional female under 24-year-olds.

Ambient advertising

Advertisers think hard about **how** and **where** to catch the consumer; so they personalise their advertisement to be seen or heard. This is known as ambient advertising – the aim is to find somewhere in the consumer's personal space; traditionally the place for this would be billboards and street locations. The aim is to assess an audience's specific consumer habits and preferences, e.g. shopping in Oxford Street and clubbing in Soho on a Friday evening. By targeting people's lifestyle as they are going about their business through their phone or internet connection is a stage beyond hoping they will read an advertisement in a magazine or watch an advertisement on television.

Banner and strip advertisement

Banner advertising is where there are blocks of promotional text on an **internet site** dedicated for some other purpose. For example, on an internet site you will often find advertisements popping up, or scrolling across the screen or simply occupying a banner heading across the top or side of the page. This is one way of funding a website, for example, web-based versions of newspapers in California can be read for free because they are subsidised by advertisers buying the spaces around the edges of the text.

TV sponsorship and strip advertisements

Many programmes are sponsored by advertisers and advertisements are often split into segments throughout an advertisement break. Animated Tizer fizzy drinks logos appears throughout *CD:UK*.

Advertising slogans

Here are some popular slogans:

- L'Oreal – Because I'm worth it.
- Kit Kat – Have a break, have a Kit Kat.
- Honda – First the man, then machine.
- Galaxy – Why have cotton when you can have silk?
- Levis – Original.

Watch and make notes on the key slogans of some television advertisements, and collect some magazine slogans which you find effective.

Celebrity approval

ACTIVITY 8

Channel 4 launched E4 using the comedy act of the character 'Ali G', a pseudo-gangster white rap artist from Staines. His popularity fitted the teenage to young adult demographic of the channel.

Research and discuss
Research some advertisements or public health messages that use a celebrity.

Discuss
a) Why were they chosen?
b) What age group do they appeal to and why?

Analysing television and film advertisements

ACTIVITY 9

1. **Watch** an advertisement and draw the main shots (frames). Use simple line drawings – you do not have to be an artist. Write down the script and the elements of the *mise-en-scène*: lighting camera shot size, angle and movement.
2. **Analyse** the advertisement: denotation and connotation of image and sound.
   Denotation: What is in the frame?
   Connotation: What do the sounds, shots and signifiers suggest to you? How do these ideas relate to wider ideas in society?

OXO: a case study of historic and current representations of the family in television advertisements.

ACTIVITY 10

Study a current OXO advertisement on television or the contemporary one on the website: www.oxo.co.uk under Television Advertising.

MESSAGES AND VALUES

What image of a **family** is **represented**?

1. Explain what each **type of character** is:
   a) children
   b) a mother and
   c) a father
2. Describe how the advertisement **narrative** brings out what their attitudes are to being a parent or a child. What can the children do or not do?

MISE EN SCENE

3. Describe what the house looks like? Does the furniture tell you anything about who they are and, for example, how well off they are?
4. Study
   a) the lighting
   b) camera movement, framing and angles and
   c) editing techniques. What kind of mood and story do they convey?
5. What is the SPOKEN message of the advertisement, usually from the voice off screen?

ACTIVITY 11

Now study the OXO family from the two previous eras:
   a) 1960s
   b) 1980s
on the website: www.oxo.co.uk. How is the image of the family different in each of the 1960s and 1980s eras?

Apply the same questions you answered for the contemporary study to the 1960s and 1980s advertisements you study (see below). Bring out what the differences are in:

a) techniques of persuasion for example, (The advertisement is trying to get me to laugh at the mother outwitting her children and husband to make me think that OXO is a fun item to consume)
b) design and style
c) images of a family
d) messages

MESSAGES AND VALUES

What image of a **family** is **represented**?

1. Explain each **character type** in turn: a) children, b) mother and c) father.
2. Describe how the advertisement **narrative** brings out what their attitudes are to being a parent or a child. What can the children do or not do?

MISE EN SCENE

3. Describe what the house looks like? Does the furniture tell you anything about who they are and for example, how well off they are?
4. Study
   a) the lighting
   b) camera movement, framing and angles
   c) editing techniques. What kind of mood and story do they convey?
5. What is the SPOKEN message of the advertisement, usually from the voice off screen?

Other old and new advertisements to compare:

At www.adflip.com there are a multitude of historical examples of advertisements. By **brand** e.g. Revlon or by **product** e.g. lager, you can trace the changing techniques, designs, messages and values of still advertising. Good examples are:

Coca Cola (old and new posters)

Compare advertisements for representation

Fig 13.7   Don't drink and drive: use of female look similar to a teenage girl's magazine to create a shock public message

Source: Central Office of Information

of women in the 1940s compared with in the 1980s. Follow this up by looking at how television advertisements have changed, for example the old global advertisements were designed to be seen all over the world, showing either images of American street youth lifestyles or 'teach the world to sing' multi-ethnic images of youth. In the early 2000s, Coca Cola's marketing strategy was changed to allow local creative advertising companies to produce, on their behalf, culturally specific images of different types of people, for example a UK council flat in which father and son bond through Coca Cola.

PG tips

Humour: old advertisements of chimpanzees and new ones using Aardman animated animals.

Benetton

Historically controversial: multi-coloured jelly babies, recently born babies, HIV carriers and death row prisoners.

Specimen examination question: AQA

These Tasks are not actual examination questions. The questions are the sole work of the author and are devised to match the style, mark allocation and format of the relevant question papers from AQA and OCR. They are designed for examination practice. The Tasks are designed to follow the examination paper timings and mark allocations. It is essential that candidates check the specified topics set for the year of their examination, by the examination board. For previous examination papers contact the examination board direct.

Paper Two controlled text (4hrs)

Advertising Brief
From: The Government's Central Office of Information
To: Agency

Produce a competitive bid for a £2 million campaign to prevent drinking and driving in the over 45 year old age bracket. Research has shown that younger generations have, on the whole, responded well to not drinking and driving. However, there is a hardcore group of men who do not heed any warnings, maintaining the 'there's nothing wrong with one for the road' attitude. The TV advertisement will only run once over two weeks, and is best placed in the run up to Christmas. The poster or posters can accompany the timing of the television drink and drive advertisement warning.

Previous campaigns have tended to show the effects of the accidents and portrayed the victims as they are today. The images have been hard-hitting. Do the public need a new approach?

TASK 1

a Describe what you think are the key features of Government advertisements?

b Government advertisements are often produced by advertising agencies. Describe the process of creating an advertising campaign for a client.

c What are the advantages and disadvantages of television, radio or posters in launching an effective media campaign?

(30 marks)

TASK 2

Either

a Draw, design or describe a cinema trailer in storyboard format (not more than 10 frames). Make sure you fill in all the storyboard frames and annotate them indicating a soundtrack, lighting, camera movement, voice-over and props.

(25 marks)

TASK 2

or

b Design a poster campaign. Make sure you design and annotate the image, layout and typeface. Consider the target audience – if they are over 45 years old, how will you interest them without making it easy for them to reject the message?

(25 marks)

TASK 3

You will need to use the radio to help promote your campaign.

Either

a Create a radio advertisement to go out on local radio, lasting 30 seconds and drawing people's attention to the campaign (30 seconds equals 90 words maximum). Remember to use other sound effects as well as voices.

or

b Suggest other ways in which you might promote your campaign.

(30 marks)

TASK 4

Write a letter to the Central Office of Information explaining:

■ The key features of your campaign and the ideas and effects intended in the sound and images and text used in the poster or trailer.
■ The characters or figures, and the types of males they represent.
■ The forms and conventions you have used.
■ The precise method of targeting the audience – messages in typed text and in visual codes.

(15 marks)

Specimen Examination Question: OCR

Answer questions 1 and 2

1. With detailed reference to specific examples from more than one medium, explain how **two** particular campaigns targeted their audiences. **(30 marks)**

2. With detailed reference to specific examples you have studied, discuss how attitudes to women, men or race have changed, at different times by analysing advertising of the period. **(30 marks)**

 Extension Tasks

1 **Research** the responses to any advertisements you think are controversial, such as Benetton, Tango or Hooch. Produce a demographic and a psychographic questionnaire to use before asking questions. Analyse (300 words) your findings and explain what it is that people object to or why they do not mind.

2 **Produce** an advertisement for a film trailer on the radio (30 seconds) for a new audience.

3 **Research** the ITC (http://www/itc) and ASA websites (http://www.asa.org.uk) and study the previous year's findings for a particular product (perfumes) or a criteria (language). Report your findings on paper or in another medium, such as news print or radio.

4 **Make** a new advertisement by redesigning an existing print advertisement product, to target a new audience.

5 **Select** any magazine and carry out an analysis of how many advertisements contain males or females as the main figures. How are they represented?

6 **Research** advertisements on www.adflip.com that has an advertisement print archive for a range of historical examples.

Examination Skills

Specimen Question: AQA Knowledge and Understanding

Examiners are looking for a good degree of knowledge about regulation and control by the main governing bodies: ASA, ITC and the RA. There needs to be a good understanding of the process, as well as the huge financial implications of advertising in any medium which carries it. Strong understanding and application of the audience concepts of demographic and psychographic will produce the best answers.

Textual Analysis

There should be sound denotation and connotation of an advertisement. The best approach is to describe and then analyse the ideas associated with the image, its construction and the connection with the words. The time and the place where these advertisements can be seen or viewed can greatly affect their impact.

Task 1 asks you to identify typical features of government campaigns. The truth is, that tactics have changed over the years. With Aids health promotions, the initial method was to stereotype girls and boys into fixed roles and behaviours. The Aids television and poster advertisements of the mid-80s depicted boys who 'coped' with their heroin addiction by saying 'I can handle it', in a kind of macho stance. Girls were shown as being body conscious, so all reference to drugs was about how bad it makes you look ultimately.

With drink advertisements, there have been at least three types of tactics in the annual campaign against drinking and driving. The first was to show that the driver might be killed in a horrific car crash. The second was to show the effects of driving on the victim's family. The third was to show the enduring effects on the victim of the car crash, after being severely injured by a drink driver.

Specimen Question: OCR Knowledge and Understanding

The following points may be made:

1. a. An account of the chosen advertising campaigns
    b. Information regarding the producers
    c. Analysis of the construction of the campaigns
    d. Identification of the target audiences and methods used to target them across more than one medium.

2. a. The selection of appropriate examples from campaigns
    b. The analysis of methods of representation of people, places and issues related to time periods
    c. Analysis of visual/verbal/written presentation
    d. Interpretations of the representations and analysis of historical context.

Practical Work

The composition of words into slogans and catch phrases is one half of the task of producing a poster. The creation of an image is targeted at the audience, but also builds the imaginary audience into the image itself. The layout, design and the typeface all require thought and considered selection. The image itself needs to cover gesture, poses, expression, clothes and props. An awareness of who owns the product and how the producer includes a logo is also desirable.

14

Sport
Game, Sex and Match

What you will learn

This chapter covers sport, media, money and technology. The massive amount of money that can be made from sport has changed the way sport is run and the way it has been experienced over ten years. Now, with the introduction of new technology, there are new ways of viewing and paying to be sports spectators. This chapter is about how spectator sports are presented, including sporting events, game shows, confessional shows and quiz shows.

KEY WORDS

- spectator
- spectacle
- pay-per-view
- subscription
- digital
- personalities
- celebrities
- 'live'
- pre-recorded
- audiences
- virtual reality games

TECHNICAL WORDS

- highlights
- photography
- replay
- commentary

Why watch sport and games?

Action and violence

The 1975 sci-fi film *Rollerball* is set in the future, where sport is completely dominated by media. Violence is banned from society, except in sport. The rollerball game is a violent cross between ice-skating and American football. All the action and violence of the rollerball game is captured on camera and the audience watches as avidly as if it were the National Lottery. In the film, the television audiences enjoy the cruelty of the physical combat and some of the casualties in the game die. This is reminiscent of sports in Roman times, when if gladiator fights did not end in several deaths, the spectators were disappointed.

Drama

Some of the reasons why people watch television sport are no different than when watching a television drama. Most sporting games involve a contest between two sides: teams or individual competitors. There is conflict, tension and drama, and by the end of the match one side wins or there is a draw. Some individuals are singled out as heroes, and there are often villains to criticise.

In the 1998 football World Cup, the England football player David Beckham became the English side's public villain for being sent off and reducing the team to ten men, and therefore potentially allowing England to lose. Michael Owen was seen as the hero because he was only eighteen and he scored a spectacular goal. Sporting commentators use dramatic language, which makes the event

Fig 14.1   *David Beckham: the media must have their 'villains' ...*

Source: EPA Photo/AFP/Gerard Cerles

sound like a story or a film narrative, using phrases such as a 'fascinating spectacle', 'a fight to the finish' or a 'gripping finale'.

The spectator who uses radio or television enjoys sport because of the skills of the team or the individual, the drama and changing fortunes, the attack and the counter-attack.

Sports media

Which media can audiences view or obtain information from about sport?

Some examples are:

▌ Television
▌ Newspapers
▌ Radio
▌ Teletext
▌ Fanzines
▌ Books – autobiographies, novels
▌ Advertising
▌ Sponsorship
▌ Films
▌ Internet
▌ In person

ACTIVITY 1

1 Study a TV programme listings page from a newspaper or magazine. How many different types of sports can you identify?
2 Compare the BBC's sports output with that of Sky Sports 1, 2 and 3.
3 How many hours for the different types of programme format can you identify over a period of one week?

	BBC (hrs/week)	Sky Sports (hrs/week)
Live events		
Pre-recorded events		
Chat shows		
Documentaries (pre-recorded)		
Quiz shows (pre-recorded)		
Others		

4 How much of BBC1's sports output is live?
5 Is there a difference between Sky's and BBC1's types of sports television programmes?

Fig 14.2   . . . and their heroes
Source: © Empics/Michael Ashton

Sport	Annual income men (£)	Annual income women (£)
1 Formula One	8.1 million	n/a
2 Football	2.0 million	n/a
3 Tennis	1.9 million	1.5 million
4 Horse racing	1.1 million	1.1 million
5 Athletics	up to 1.0 million	up to 1.0 million
6 Snooker	500,000	13,000
7 Golf	470,000	90,000
8 Cricket	300,000	n/a
9 Rugby	72,000	n/a
10 Rowing	2,000	2,000

Table 14.1   *Salaries of those at the top of their profession*

BSkyB

As a commercial provider, BSkyB sells advertising space in order to fund sports programmes and staffing. The influence of BSkyB on sport has been dramatic.

In 1989, BSkyB was created as the first UK satellite station. It began with five channels and increased to over 40 by 1996. In 1994, BSkyB paid over £300 million for exclusive rights to the Premiership football league. This effectively ended the BBC's control of broadcasting all the top live football matches.

BSkyB's investment has totalled £1.5 billion since it started investing in sport in 1989, when it started its satellite Sports Channel. Initially, the subscription fee for Premiership viewing was over £5.99 but by 1999 this rose to £24.99.

In 1999 however, the Football Premiership turned down Rupert Murdoch's bid to renew total exclusive rights to broadcasting top level football.

Sports issues

The effect of corporation takeovers on sport could be to bring it increasingly under the control of a few companies who have media ownership. Investments have been made in the following ways:

- High salaries earned by top players, agents and managers.
- Ten new stadiums built between 1989 and 1999.
- International sports stars joining football clubs in other countries (Chelsea's own football team has nearly 90% of foreign nationalities).

Sporting values

Fair play and gamespersonship are values associated with sport. As in cowboy films the audience expects to see that the baddies are punished and the virtuous are rewarded. The sporting world is now highly professional and in some sectors like football, at the top level sports people are very well paid.

Audiences also watch the way that sports stars behave in private and in public. There are numerous newspaper reports about corrupt footballers, managers, and officials and their sex lives, because they are in the public eye and these items sell newspapers.

More specific sports world issues such as performance enhancing drugs, violent fans and who owns teams, are also covered in TV documentaries and radio features.

Celebrities

Athletes and commentators at the top of their profession are now seen and heard as frequently as soap stars and politicians, in advertisements, on television, on radio, and in magazines and newspapers. Eric Cantona, the footballer and poet, promoted EuroStar travel to France. In real life Cantona attacked a spectator who was calling him racist names by jumping into the crowd. The EuroStar advertisement's image of the poet and peaceful man was quite different from his previous image as a kung fu kicking footballer. Gary Lineker, in contrast, is known as a clean, honest player, who jokingly promotes Walkers crisps by stealing crisps from other famous people. Vinnie Jones appeared in the British film, *Lock Stock and Two Smoking Barrels* (1998), because his already established 'tough guy' image suited the crime theme in the film.

Real life

The ordinary spectator gains enjoyment from watching live TV because it is one of the forms of television in which one cannot predict what happens next. This expectation of surprise and real life drama is shared by other 'live' programme formats, although these can be pre-recorded. These programmes also involve a kind of game: including contestants, presenters as 'referees' and studio audiences as 'spectators' with voices.

Game shows and chat shows

Chat shows, confessional TV shows such as *Kilroy*, *Ricki Lake*, *Vanessa*, *Trisha* and *Oprah Winfrey*, and quiz shows such as *Who Wants to be a Millionaire?*, involve strong elements of tension and surprise because they are or appear to be depend on human success or failure.

Structure

The programmes are not scripted, or so we are led to believe. After they have been recorded live, edited and shortened to fit the programme length, they still create the sense that no one can tell how the participants or members of the 'crowd' will react at any given time. Similar to sporting events, in confessional TV shows or competitions, such as *Blind Date*, the viewer is presented with a contest between the participants which depends testing the knowledge, skill or calmness of the participants who are placed under pressure. The difference is that for most sporting events the professionals play to earn a living, whereas in confessional or quiz shows, ordinary members of the public perfom for the thrill of being on television or to win prizes.

Budgets

Game shows can afford to give away large prizes because there are no lavish sets or 'stars' to pay for. The budget is mainly spent on the prizes, the staff salaries and the presenter(s). A presenter like Angus Deaton on *Have I got News for You?* can be paid around £18,000 per show.

The crowd as 'performer'

Confessional TV shows also get the studio audience involved in cheering, booing and commentating, so that they become part of the action. This can be likened to televised sport for mass audiences. In confessional television shows such as *The Jerry Springer Show*, the audience is encouraged to respond to what the programme guests say.

Sometimes this can lead to fights between members of the audience. This makes the programme appear more unpredictable and even adds to its appeal, although programmes are rarely broadcast if matters get out of hand. In contrast, other programmes with big audiences such as the *National Lottery* have audiences who only clap or cheer when they are told to by the studio managers.

ACTIVITY 2

1. **Study** a number of chat shows, confessional shows and programmes which involve participants and an active studio audience.
2. **Examine** where the cameras must be positioned in order to film the presenter, the audience and the participants.
3. To what extent is the audience allowed to speak out and do its own thing? How much time does the programme spend on shots of the audience, and what they do and say?
4. Is what you are seeing the whole event, and if not, how much of the real event might have been edited out? How can you tell?
5. **Study** the camera positions and sound coverage of the audiences and participants in a sporting event like Wimbledon, American or English football. Are there differences of approach in how the crowd is used? How is the crowd used to create atmosphere? Are they just used as background? Do members of the public get asked their views on the game?

Real danger

Whether pre-recorded or live, game shows and sports programmes promise surprises and even danger. Both sporting professionals and members of the public perform on their 'stages' before our eyes. Most television programmes are shortened and edited before they go out on air, however, live radio and television offers the danger, the thrills and the mistakes, the recoveries, the jubilations and disappointments of real life.

> Watch a sport on TV where there is a high chance of failure, such as a motorbike rally, skateboarding, skiing or horse jumping. Study how the commentator talks about failures or disasters. To what extent does the commentator have to make the accidents sound less bad than they actually appear on screen?

Theatre of cruelty

Some sports programmes emphasise danger or pain, such as wrestling or extreme sports. These tend to be broadcast on dedicated channels or shown only occasionally. In wrestling, the loser is often seen to be hit over and over again, in different ways. This is part of the show, in which the audience is seen to enjoy the spectacle.

Wrestling is an unusual sport as most of the action is faked. Even though the audience is aware of this, they enjoy the sight of strong men or women 'acting' out a body contact fight. It is disputed that much of a wrestling show is arranged in advance, including the final outcome. Ringside audiences and fans of *WWF* (*World Wrestling Federation*) claim not to mind whether a match is fixed or not.

Extreme sports

Extreme sports programmes cover activities such as tobogganing, skateboarding or bungee-jumping, and these have a greater factor of risk and failure built into them. Twenty years ago these sports would not have been considered worthy of attention. However, thirty years ago snooker and darts were not considered worthy, but now they are highly popular television sports.

Sporting programme content

Title sequences

Most television sports title sequences convey considerable energy and wit. The pace of the editing for the title sequence of *Match of the Day* is quick and dramatic; the camera work is varied with sweeping pans and zooms, together with a soundtrack which is highly energetic and dramatic. The shots are of famous football players waiting in the changing rooms or displaying their skills in scoring goals, and shots of mass cheering from the grounds.

ACTIVITY 3

Study a number of sports programme title sequences. See how they create a sense of audience expectation for their particular sport:

1. Denotate and connotate their images and sounds.
2. Look at the following elements and analyse how they are presented.
   a Drama
   b Characters
   c Celebration or disappointment
   d Sound voice-over
   e Soundtrack music and effects

Highlights

Much of television sports programming is prepared earlier than its time of transmission. The highlights of each game on *Match of the Day* last between fifteen minutes and half an hour. How far do you think these programmes represent what actually happened in the game? What do you think was left (edited) out? Why do you think these sections were edited out?

ACTIVITY 4

1. Go to a game of sport: for example, volleyball, swimming competition, football or rugby. Record it on video or audio-tape. Make a shot list and create a rough edit plan. The edit plan shows the shots in the order you want.
2. **Edit** your footage down to ten minutes. What did you leave out and what did you keep in?
3. Was there a need for a voice-over? How does the target audience for the product affect what is said in the voice-over commentary?
4. How could you make your final video sequence video or audio-tape look and sound professional?
5. How would you film a long-distance running race, bicycle race or ski jump, using only one camera? What difference would having two cameras make?

Replays and slow motion

Action replays are an essential part of modern sports programmes. They allow audiences to see action again, which they cannot see if they are at the ground or track (although many stadiums do have large screens to replay scenes). Cricket also uses the 'third umpire' to judge whether a player is run out or not. It is important to be able to view a sporting event from as many different angles as possible.

Studio critics are asked to commentate over a replay so that the whole sequence can be enjoyed and analysed over again. Use of the replay of the goals and, for example, the idea that goal scoring in football is the best part of the play, have been criticised for making games seem more exciting than they really are. In the real game there often long periods when the play is not exciting. Boredom, however, is not an experience programme makers want their audiences to have. The TV audience is therefore always given a highly selective view of what actually happened.

Technical elements
Cameras

Most large sporting events use more than one camera to record the event. In football matches there are two goals to record, plus the two lengths of the pitch. In reality there are many more angles to cover.

Voice-over

Like any piece of live radio or television sport (swimming, acrobatics, hockey, rugby league), the action is presented through the voice-over of the commentator. Commentators provide background information about the players or the athletes, and warm the audience up before the game or race. Once the game is under way, the action is dramatised by the increasingly excited voice-over. This keeps the tension flowing until there is a surprise, a goal or a win; the voice is then jubilant, and then quiet and calm again. Some sports, such as cricket, do not lend themselves to fast talking and the tone of the voice is more reflective and casual.

Fig 14.3   Gary Lineker – a well-known and popular sports presenter
Source: © BBC Photo Library

ACTIVITY 5

1. **Watch** a ten minute section of a football, tennis or swimming match with the sound turned down. See how much you can understand without the commentary. What can't you understand without the help of the commentator? Is there any advantage in not being able to hear the commentator?
2. **Review** the discussion in Chapter Eight about presenters' clothes, tone of voice, use of language and content. How do sports commentator's present them-selves? Are they emotional and do they get carried away? Are they quiet and more informative, and less inclined to show their personal bias? Which style do you prefer: emotionally charged or calm and informative?
3. **Listen** to a BBC Radio 5 sports programme or any local sports commentary live and watch any television commentator on the same sport. What do the presenters do differently on the radio in terms of:
- content
- explaining visual detail
- expressing their own reactions
- soundtrack effects

Personalities

Radio and television presenters provide the links between the sport and the commentaries, conducted in interviews with studio experts. Presenters become personalities and their image is created to make audiences identify with them and the channel they work for. Famous football presenters like Desmond Lynam are well-known for their smooth and calm manner.

The voice of Murray Walker, the motor car racing commentator, who, after many years, moved from BBC1 to ITV, has become associated with the world of motor car racing.

Finance and the sports media

Sport is a very profitable industry. It is now possible to pay for some television sports channels by subscription or on a pay-per-view basis.

Publishing

Men's enthusiasm for football is expressed in different media, notably, through comedians such as David Baddiel and Frank Skinner. There are many autobiographies on famous football clubs and stars, and now there are books about female football fans also.

Sports fanzines

The biggest area of writing has been by the fans, in the fanzines. The format used to be A5 and the 'zines were photocopied and stapled together. Now the Internet has drawn in the 'zines onto web sites, and so the format has changed. The editorials of 'zines tend to be outspoken on the fans' point of view of their club. They often criticise the management or the players. 'Zines express personal opinions, and so the rules of professional journalism do not always apply.

Fig 14.4   An example of a sports fanzine
Source: www.borobarmy.com

Home viewing
Subscription

Subscription television is where a customer pays a regular amount of money on an annual basis and in return is provided with all the services on that channel.

Pay-per-view

Pay-per-view occurs when the viewer pays a one-off amount to watch an event. Popular sports, especially boxing, which have a wordwide interest but that people cannot afford to travel to, are obvious targets for pay-per-view. The promoters know this and can make the live boxing fight exclusive to paying viewers. The rest of the viewers have to wait for the highlights after the event has finished on the same channel, or watch on other channels.

		Date	Revenue £ million
1	Evander Holyfield v Mike Tyson	June 97	1.99
2	Lennox Lewis v Mike Tyson	June 02	1.80
3	Mike Tyson v Evander Holyfield	Nov 96	1.60
4	Mike Tyson v Peter McNeeley	Aug 95	1.58
5	Oscar De La Hoya v Felix Trinidad	Sept 99	1.40
6	Frank Bruno v Mike Tyson	Mar 96	1.36
7	Evander Holyfield v George Foreman	April 91	1.36
8	Mike Tyson v Razor Ruddock	June 91	1.23

Table 14.2 *World's top pay-per-view sports events*

Advantages of pay-per-view

In the UK football is one of the sports where fans often live a long way from the place where their team plays, or the home fan does not want to travel a long distance for away matches. Many Londoners support Northern teams and the opposite also applies. Approximately seven million English and Welsh fans claim to support Manchester United, Liverpool or Newcastle. 95% have never visited a football ground and would prefer to watch it at home. Pay-per-view is aimed at the viewer who does not want to subscribe all season, but might want to watch the occasional match at home.

Disadvantages of pay-per-view

The disadvantage of pay-per-view is that supporters have to pay to watch a match they might previously have watched for free on other terrestrial channels. The long-term view is that, although large clubs will prosper, the smaller clubs will suffer. Smaller clubs with low attendance rates will not be selected over those with high attendances, as this would not make much money. The rich clubs will get richer and the poorer clubs might not even survive.

New technology and the future

Current satellite systems and the new digital boxes which come with the next generation of video recorders and televisions allow the viewer to press a button and pay to view there and then. The pay-per-view customer can also, with some packages, choose which camera angle and position they want to watch from. TV companies now use many cameras at the ground and the viewer selects where they want to view different sections of the match from. Formula One motor car racing crosses many countries every year and this is a typical example of being able to see a 'live' broadcast of an event.

In Spain on 14 March 1999, Canal Satellite Digital broadcast the football clash between Barcelona and Real Madrid. This game attracted 295,000 paying customers. The game reportedly generated an income of £2.5 million, of which £1.15 million was divided between the two clubs. Canal Satellite deployed 150 personnel, 18 cameras, six commentators and an airship for the match. However, restricting the game to pay-per-view customers caused a storm of protest among the public. Politicians promised to change existing regulations to protect games of 'national interest'.

In the UK, there are approximately 18 million football fans in England and Wales. Pay-per-view is predicted to bring in £280 million for Premiership clubs by the 2003–2004 season. Clubs could also earn a further £240 per fan from selling a 'television season ticket', offering a package of 60 live games per season. That compares with the £135 million the entire Premiership received from Sky Sports for live rights in 1999.

'Free to air'

The problem with one company achieving great success is that other companies may lose money. The other major issue is then whether any major sports events will be seen on 'free to air' channels. Free to air is the term given to non-commercial stations such as BBC1. The BBC traditionally broadcast all the big events 'live' every year, however, Formula One, football and rugby union are now often shown on other channels. Among the events that the BBC have held onto are Wimbledon and the Oxford versus Cambridge boat race.

In the USA, one solution has been to allow all American football games to be shown free on television, funded by expensive advertising between the breaks. Television rights and merchandising are shared equally around the National Football League's 30 teams.

Digital Disaster

Two great disasters struck sport, and football, in particular, in 2002.

The first was when ITV Digital (Carlton and Granada) announced in 2002 that they could no longer support the televising of football as they could not gain enough viewers. The overinvestment of money for ITV Digital has led to great uncertainty about the future of several football clubs as they are paying their players large sums of money to stay with them. ITV Digital have not been able to develop fast enough against slow takeup and strong competition from Sky, who already have 5 million subscribers, but it took them ten years to build that base. The Premier division clubs should sustain themselves but the lower division clubs who have spent a great deal may have to close down.

The second major disaster was when the German media giant announced it was going to go bankrupt. As they had bought the rights to the World Cup in 2002 and Formula One, the prospects for fans of both sports looked bleak.

Both these incidents remind us of the downside of global media sponsorships where the smallest clubs and sports activities become the main victims when things go wrong.

Sports simulation: AQA

Your Premier division football club, Grandchester United, is about to be taken over by Glaxa, a large insurance company. Glaxa are working with Earth, a large cable company. Earth have a very large share of the UK cable market. This will mean that you will only be able to see the matches on television on a pay-per-view or subscription basis. You could always buy an expensive season ticket and go to the matches but you can't always get to the away matches. On the other hand, the club has a shortage of European players, so the takeover would enable you to buy some world class players.

However, you have decided to launch a media campaign to resist the takeover, arguing it is in the interests of the club's fans to prevent the takeover occurring. Answer the following tasks in order.

Paper Two controlled text (4 hrs)

TASK 1

a Explain the typical features of presentation in BBC's or ITV's television sports programmes? Comment on aspects of the following: studio, presenters, live action, graphics and special effects. Refer to one or more types of sports.
(30 marks)

TASK 2

Either

a Script a local radio news item about the problems of the potential takeover bid by Glaxa. Include both positive and negative points of view. (1–2 minutes long: average 3 words per second.) Use the radio script pro-forma provided.

or

b Design (in a sketch) a web page for a club fanzine called *On the Spot*. Your page should include a space for the club's fans to express their points of view. Explain the details of your page, in writing.

(20 marks)

TASK 3

Either

a Produce a local evening newspaper (regional newspaper) item: indicate contents of a photo (a very rough sketch), caption, headline, and text of 100 words (the masthead is not necessary). The editor's view of the issue may be biased in one way or another.

or

b Design a poster which expresses your views on whether the club should be taken over by Glaxa or not. You have paid for advertising space in your local paper for a full page spread. Include a slogan, written text and images.

(30 marks)

TASK 4

Write a letter to the fans in the club's fanzine explaining why you think Grandchester United will not benefit from the takeover by Glaxa and Earth. Explain the points for and against, and argue why you think your point of view is best.

(20 marks)

 Extension Tasks

1 **Research** broadsheet and tabloid newspapers for examples of stories in the main section on sporting personalities. How are they presented? What angle do they take? Produce a fanzine version of the same event: describe layout, content and images.

2 **Watch** another country's presentation of a sporting event, for example, Italian football. Study the commentator and commentary style, the content and tone, the camera positions, and movements and shot sizes, the use of crowd's participation, the studio experts, the soundtrack and the title sequence.

3 **Video** a table tennis match from the viewpoint of one player. Evaluate its strengths and weaknesses. To what extent can you produce something of interest, which is not conventional, using two or three cameras?

4 **Video** a football match that is also going to be broadcast on the television. Record your own commentary at the same time. Compare the results with that of the televised commentary. Is your version of the match similar or different to the television or radio commentary? How would you improve yours or their commentary?

Examination Skills

Knowledge and Understanding

To answer a question on sports and the media you should become familiar with the main organisations and media products involved in the big money business of sports media (the BBC and other international organisations such as Bertlesmann and American news companies). There should be a good knowledge of the different ways in which live and pre-recorded television sports events are sold, presented and distributed. The range of media, sports journalism and radio, for example, should be studied to gain an understanding of forms and conventions of sports presentation, reporting, commentary and analysis. Alternative media products such as fanzines and community cable should also be explored. Terms such as pay-per-view and subscription will need to be used to indicate some of the different ways in which sport is financed and consumed. There should be an understanding of the relationship between the sponsors and the sporting organisation's commitments to advertise products. Students should understand the different presentational formats and styles of reporting in all media.

Textual Analysis

The analysis of television and radio sport should tackle standard conventional formats of programmes. The title sequences, presenter, commentator, the crowd and the participants are all actors in the sporting 'drama'. Discuss the denotative and connotative associations with sounds and images. In radio, the structure and the format of the sports programme should be studied: music, interviews, reports and commentators. Identify institutional elements of branding, logos or lettering, voice or soundtrack.

Comment on Task 1: TV Sport presentation styles

The studio presentational style of Gary Lineker on BBC1's Match of the Day football programme is relaxed and yet authoritative. He usually wears a jacket and tie and looks straight to the camera for the links. He is usually accompanied by two or three 'experts' who are often ex-players. They are usually seated behind a desk, making them appear more authoritative. The same format also applies to the commentaries on tennis or Olympic sports. The anchor presenter makes comments, provides information and tries to tease comment and predictions out of the studio panel. There are often links to the pitch where an on-the-spot commentator gains, in close-up or medium shot, immediate post-match reactions from the players and the managers. Throughout the game, the crowd is usually seen and heard in the background 'en masse' but not usually interviewed as individual commentators.

Practical Work

Producing simulations of professional products for sports requires careful thought. The use of a commentator is a convention which could be broken. With one camera, the use of zoom, pan and movement tracking around the game should be used carefully, to sustain interest. The edited version should demonstrate a logical sequence, for example, the football in the goal mouth comes after the person kicks the ball, not before! Radio lends itself more easily to the constraints of non-professional sports reporting. Utilise the soundtrack of the crowd and the participants of the game itself.

15 Local and community radio

'Listen to the radio, it's better than your stereo'

What you will learn

In this chapter you will learn about national, local, community and alternative radio; digital radio; what is meant by 'access' programming; and commercial and public service broadcasting, licences and regulation.

KEY WORDS

- access
- analogue/digital
- commercial
- public service broadcasting
- regulation
- Radio Advertising Bureau (RAB)
- the radio industry's audience monitoring body (RAJAR)

TECHNICAL WORDS

- DJ
- franchise
- jingles
- idents
- posse
- satellite
- speech
- sound bite
- terrestrial

ACTIVITY 1

Research Task

Find out information about radio stations in your area, from the radio stations, internet, local papers or library etc.

Gather information and write notes using the following questions as a basis for your findings.

- What is the range of local radio stations in your area?
- Do you have a town, city or regional radio station?
- Which of these stations are regional eg all Birmingham or county?

- Which of your local stations are for a restricted area ie just the town or city?
- Which local stations are commercial and which are not for profit, e.g. BBC radio or a festival radio station?
- Is there a school, college, student radio station in your area?
- Are there any community radio stations?
- Do you have a hospital radio station?
- Are there any pirate (illegal) music stations?

⚠ ACTIVITY 2

Research Task

Obtain a programme schedule from a radio station, internet or the local paper of one radio station in your area.

Languages and categories

Listen to the programmes and make notes on the general style of the station from the programme schedule.

1. What is the range and type of programmes on the radio station? Note down what type of speech programmes there are: for example, is it all music introduced by a DJ or is it a mixture of chat, phone-ins and celebrity interviews and mainstream pop, or is it street/dance club music and interviews with artists etc?
2. Target audience
   Who is the station aimed at: age, gender, race, religion; specialist or general interest?

Format

Generally speaking radio can be divided into music-driven programming and speech-oriented formats.

Music based narrative

There are two main formats

▌ **DJ** (disc jockey) plus music – they mix these items with phone-ins, quizzes, requests and interviews with celebrities or local people.

▌ **Posse** plus music – this involves banters between DJs between music, news bulletins and traffic reports. Radio presenters allow listeners to listen in to their jokes and chat about what they did last night etc.

Danny & Nicky in the Morning

Every weekday morning between 6 and 9am, you can listen to 'Danny and Nicky in the Morning' on Southern FM. It's the Number 1 show in Sussex, thanks to the mixture of humour, hits and top competitions.

Congratulations, you've found the official home of **'Danny and Nicky in the Morning'**, Sussex's most listened to **'Breakfast Show'**. On this page you'll be able to catch up with all the madness of **Southern FM** in the morning.

Danny Pike, Nicky Keig-Shevlin and **Moody** the producer wake up Sussex with **'Today's Best Music'**, loads of fun, contests, you on the phones and e-mail, plus all the essential News, Sport, Weather and the only airborne traffic reports in Sussex from **Paul Williams** in the **'Southern FM Sky Patrol'**.

Danny, Nicky and **Moody**, are responsible (or should that be irresponsible!), for more chaos in the morning, than anyone in Sussex. If you wake up dazed and confused, this is the show for you!

Source: Southern FM.com (part of Capital Radio Group Plc)

Speech/talk based narrative

- **Magazine** format mixes interviews, music, competitions, and phone-ins, documentary inserts.
- **News bulletins** are often more frequent on radio than television and use the same type of formats: wrap, clip and two-way elements. **Wraps** are a news item which moves from the bulletin reader to the reporter to a clip of reality and then back to the reporter. **Clips** are items which move from the bulletin reader to a clip of actuality. The actuality could be a famous person or a voice of a person in the street (vox pop).

BBC World Service specialises in themed reports from around the world such as music. If you are British and abroad then specialist news digests can keep you in touch with news 'back home'.

There are three basic elements to radio:

- Words
- Sounds
- Music

Sound bites

Most radio is served in short clips and **jingles** (short musical sequences to identify a brand or station) and **idents** (short sound sequences providing an identity for the station, e.g. the sung "BeeBeeCee Radeeyoh Twoo"). These are often called sound bites as they are easily digestible. Music singles are usually not longer than 3 minutes. When people are interviewed it is important to record sentences that don't go on for ever. Professionals who are publicists talk in short quips, knowing that their words will be edited as soundbites. Two responses often used if people have achieved some success are: 'over the moon' or 'delighted'.

Alternative radio tries to break with the sound bite culture. Chris Morris broke conventions on his programme **Jaam**, played late at night/early morning, combining atmospheric music with dreamlike voiceovers with no clear beginnings and endings over a two-hour period.

Industrial sales

Sales of CDs have declined recently but the average UK listener tunes in for 25 hours per week. This figure is compared with 22 hours three years ago (RAJAR).

Advertising sales on commercial television have also dropped considerably prior to 2003. Radio has actually grown a little, up 0.5% during the first part of 2002, despite a world economy dip (RAB).

London hosts over a quarter of the total radio industry. Some national radio stations based in London, such as Capital Radio, broadcast and own franchises such as Heart 106.2 and the Galaxy Brand.

Fig 15.1   National and local radio

Corporate radio

Some local radio stations are also national franchises, such as Galaxy and Heart. A franchise is where a local operation is run by a group of people but owned by a parent company. The franchise will run the operation in the style required by the owner. The owner of these two stations is Capital Radio, which owns large stations in metropolitan areas. It had revenue of £64.9 million in 2001. They took over independent London station Xfm and regional stations Century and Beat 106, First Oxfordshire Radio Company and Bucks Broadcasting Company Limited. They also own Border Television plc and restaurants. Their analogue stations cover 58% of the UK population in most metropolitan areas. Chris Tarrant is one of their major London presenters. They hold 29% of national radio advertising.

The main audience for Century is 15–24 and in some areas for Beat, for example, it is the mid-30s audience. Its content is mainly music, with interviews of popular artists, and some live sessions. In 2002 it had an aggressive policy to change its over forty years audience to a thirties one so as to attract more lucrative advertisements.

Community

New Style Radio Station – Birmingham, half speech and half music. The speech content consists of health, education and employment, Caribbean news and features. In contrast Buzz, based in Birmingham, which broadcasts commercial black music, was bought up by London-based Choice and is now less oriented to Birmingham itself.

Hospital and college

Many large cities have a radio station on their hospital or college campus and these provide useful training grounds for future careers.

Access and community

Two examples of access stations who reach a specific interest group in the community.

- Desri, Southall, London reaches a Punjabi audience and broadcasts music, speech, and celebrates cultural events.

- Glynn Taff Tenants and Residents Association works with Glamorgan University and provides information about rights, advice and music.

Alternative and pirate radio

Pirate radio stations are illegal stations which operate without a licence, from the IRA, to broadcast.

A famous radio station called Radio Caroline broadcast from a small ship off the Essex coast in the late 1960s. There are probably about 200 pirate radio stations. Web based sites are also examples of new outlets for alternative radio stations.

Public Service Broadcasting

The concept of public broadcasting is defined as broadcasting that serves the needs of the public, as opposed to the advertisers or shareholders. PSB mixes high quality programmes that inform, educate and entertain at times to meet the needs of different audiences. Many local stations obtain licences so that they can service a particular need. For example, a music or cultural festival.

Restricted Service Licence

For a short period of time, say six weeks, it is possible to obtain a restricted service licence (RSL).

This allows a radio station the opportunity to broadcast for a specific purpose for around 6–10 miles radius.

You need to apply to the IRA (Independent Radio Authority).

Communications Bill 2002

Many voluntary groups fear that the new legislation may affect how much space there will be for ordinary people to have stations that represent their views. If there is too much commercially-led radio and television it may just be mainly celebrity-led pop chart music stations. Information about health, housing, employment, civil rights is cheaply provided by radio and yet it is more easy to finance a station using popular chart-based music. All radio and television stations are supposed to provide general public information to the public, for example a quota of news as part of their licence agreement. New legislation may not insist on this quota.

BBC radio

Through the licence fee the BBC produces local radio programmes. In every region the BBC has a local version and their remit is to provide a service for the public. Since 1995 the BBC have also been broadcasting digital radio. This means they have been able to transmit a signal by compressing signals through computer technology.This has involved installing modified transmitters to reach radio sets. The listener has to have a digital radio, a satellite box or cable or internet connection, www.bbcradio.co.uk, to receive it. The effect of this technology has been to increase the number of signals and programmes that can be transmitted. It is now possible to receive over twenty channels via satellite on television, including a range of ethnic and music tastes.

From a national base BBC has reached local communities through new programming such as Ixtra – contemporary black music, including UK garage, Hip-hop and R'n'B. BBC Asian Network broadcasts news and current affairs to Asian communities. Network Z will broadcast archive comedy, drama readings

From Radio 2 and Radio 4. There are stories, games and competitions. Some of this content is targeted at children and some is targeted at adults in different strands.

ACTIVITY 3

Practical

Make a speech and music based audio-recording for a radio item on 'what youth want for the future of our local radio' in your area. Consider which local radio station programme would be the best on which to transmit your documentary.

Try to imitate the programme's style and format. You could turn the recording into a campaign item to have more radio for your age group, music style etc. How will you organise the structure of your radio piece? For example, will you do a series of street interviews cut into a studio based session with 'experts'. Or, will you just present one voice giving a scripted argument, like an election broadcast to the listener, promoting your views with your passion and persuasiveness? See pages 72-73 for layout guidance.

Specimen Examination Question: AQA

Topic (for examination 2004)

TASK 1

What are the main features of local and community radio?

Give examples from your own study and discuss both programme content and the way stations are organised and financed.

(25 marks)

Fig 15.2   A studio at Capital Radio

You are a local group who wish to create a new radio station for 12–24 year olds in your area. It is called **Radi Radio** and will transmit for a 6–10 mile radius. Initially, you are going to run a pilot using a restricted service licence (RSL).

You need to apply to the IRA (Independent Radio Authority). To succeed you will have to compete against two other proposals. One is sport based, **Sporto** and the other, is more like Radio Two for the over-30s – it is called **Startunes**.

Read their programme specifications and use the headings to create your own profile using the same headings e.g. Content, Style etc.

(25 marks)

Sporto

Content: mainly live reporting of sporting events in the area. The airtime is therefore mainly during the day, though if there is an event happening in another time zone, such as football in Japan or boxing in Las Vegas, then Sporto will cover it.

Style: Chatty presenters, some renowned ex-sports people plus professional critics.

Advertising: A good deal of advertising, from local and national companies.

Sponsors: Nike are the main sponsors, along with an as-yet unspecified drinks company.

Presenters: Local professionals and sometimes key sporting personalities.

Target Audience: aged 18–39

Startunes

Content: 50 minutes of 70s and 80s music an hour

Style: chat based, competitions, phone-ins and music.

Advertising: local companies mainly, but also national products such as travel, car and house insurance, home improvements like doubleglazing.

Sponsors: Commercial group

Presenters: professional middle aged DJs well known for their sports interests and local newspaper articles.

Target Audience: 18–39

TASK 3

a Devise a catchphrase for the station's jingle, lasting 10 secs, that will convey a sense of style to your listeners. For example, 'Surf one o seven point two (107.2FHM) – the smooth way to start your day'. Explain what type of music, instruments you will use to accompany this catchphrase.

(10 marks)

b Write a radio advertisement using the programme sheet (page 254) for playing on the new station every fifteen minutes on its first day of broadcast. Include: programme content, presenter profiles, news of competitions etc, services such as traffic or news bulletins, and the unique selling points of your station. Indicate music and sound effects where relevant.

(15 marks)

TASK 4

a Design a web page for your new station including: a logo, programme content, advertisements (if necessary), other special features such as competitions, DJ biographies etc.

(15 marks)

b Write a letter to the Independent Radio Authority explaining the reasons why you think **Radi Radio** should be given a full licence. Try to justify your bid by discussing the following:
– audience figures
– services to the public
– commercial benefit to local businesses
– financial success
– name famous and local worthy people who support your cause.
– the reasons for the urgent need for a radio station like this in the area.

(10 marks)

 Extension Tasks

1 Research the history of radio time lines on: radioauthority.org.uk

2 Obtain a copy of The Radio Magazine from radiomagazine.co.uk (free to schools)

3 Listen to radio stations on satellite or cable television and analyse the different styles of music channel.

4 Study student radio – studentradio.org.uk and find out what type and content of programmes they run.

Examination Skills

Knowledge and Understanding

In order to carry out the tasks in the specimen paper you will need to have studied a range of local and community radio stations, including programming schedules and programme formats and content, the financing through sponsors, advertising or public service licence. It would be advisable to obtain glossy brochures, audience demographics for potential advertisers and station magazines as well as listening to the radio programmes and studying the web sites and newspaper programme schedules.

Practical skills

You should try to obtain news and music programme sheets from the radio stations and learn how to layout speech, and instructions for sound and music. Studying jingles and idents will help to keep the programme flowing as well branding the station with a particular style or sound and mental image.

It would also be helpful to study advertisements for local radio in print media: newspapers, free weeklies, bus shelters and buses, and the station website is usually very informative in how the station perceives itself. Layout for web sites and radio news and magazine formats should also be studied and practised, in case these are practical tasks asked for in the examination. Cross media texts such as advertising and news media are now part of all GCSE rubrics.

16 New media and old

Into the Net and onto the ROM

What you will learn

In this chapter you will study the past and present of media technologies and their applications. A number of questions about the future and present are asked: what can technology now offer, for whom is it produced, who owns it and how can it be used? Who controls the content of the Internet?

KEY WORDS

- standalone
- networked
- on line
- E-mail
- digital
- analogue
- interactivity
- convergence
- regulation and control

TECHNICAL WORDS

- satellite
- cable and terrestrial
- Rom
- Ram
- DVD
- World Wide Web
- Internet
- Intranet
- nonlinear editing

To boldly go . . .

At the turn of the twentieth century, in 1900, the world had just begun to experience the wonders of film. At that time, no one quite anticipated the major impact cinema would make on our everyday lives. In fact, the invention of the submarine and the expansion of cities were viewed as greater subjects of interest. In a similar fashion, the turn of the twenty-first century has seen major technological changes which have affected all the traditional media sectors.

Communications media were separate until recently. Today, the television, cinema, music, radio, print (papers, magazines and comics), computer games and software, on line computing, advertising, and news gathering industries do not exist in isolation. With the invention of the computer, digital technology and new ways of using the telephone, new technologies are now transforming each medium.

Computers

There are three forms of computer systems:

- standalone
- networked
- on line

Stand-alone

First, there is the standalone computer, which uses discs, CD-Roms and hardware disc drives. Most people use computers for word processing and need to keep their information stored on separate discs from the hard drive. The hard drive is the internal processor that runs any programmes sent to its memory.

The computer's RAM (random access memory) is activated by a 'floppy' programmed disc, containing information and interactive material. The ROM (read only memory) part is memory that can only be read from. Microwaves have computer chips which are run on ROM, so that instructions work when the power is switched on. Most computers now accept CD-Roms, which allow image and text files and multimedia texts to be easily read.

Networked

The second type of computer is the networked computer, where information can be sent from one computer to another when they have been linked up. Many schools, colleges and workplaces are networked so that information can be easily circulated. A small group of computers can be linked and closed off to other computer access. This is called an 'Intranet'. In businesses, many professional accountants or legal professionals will set up their closed circuit of computers into a Intranet, to maintain confidentiality.

Internet

The third type of computer system is the global Internet. The Internet is a collection of computers linked together around the world. The World Wide Web (WWW) is a collection of machines running software for sending graphics across the Internet.

As an Internet user, you give yourself a name which becomes your URL (Uniform Resource Locator). For example, a typical address would be: http://www.yourname@aol.com.uk. The address can also be contacted to activate your web page if you were to create

one. Some people create more than one address if they wish to discuss different topics, for example, *Titanic*, sci-fi films or Indie music. The address length is less daunting than it seems, as the structure of the different segments of the URL can be broken into four parts:

▌ **http** equals hypertext (special code to enable transfer from part of the web to another)
▌ **www** equals World Wide Web
▌ **yourname** is the network name you have
▌ the last section tells you the Internet service provider, for example aol (America Online) and the country or place you are sending the message from.
▌ **co(m)** equals company, and the uk equals United Kingdom (au = Australia, etc.).

The Internet is now a major form of communication and information exchange, as it is immediate and cheap in comparison to phone bills. The E-mail (electronic mail) messaging system has created a whole new phenomena of newsgroups, chat groups, net 'zines and personal communication links between people who have never met each other, from all over the world.

ACTIVITY 1

Research
What is your experience of/consumption of/access to new technologies? (for example, phone texting, DVD recorder, internet music downloading, digital radio or television)
Develop a research project investigating a particular new technology e.g. digital television, MP3, third generation mobiles, DVD sales.
Buy some DVD and MP3 magazines for general background and use as source material.
Try news site archives like bbc.co.uk and guardian.co.uk and key in some terms

(Digital TV for instance), see what you can find.

Suggestions for research questions:
a) When will analogue television end?
b) What is the future of free music from the internet? Present it to the class.
c) Will mobile phones take the place of walkmans?
d Is the arrival of DVD the end of VHS?

Convergence

Traditional media companies have joined up with computer on line services, software companies and telephone companies. This means that, with a few exceptions, a few large companies now control almost every aspect of media production, the products, the means of distribution and the point of sale. The word convergence describes how the different media meet in one point.

In the home, the broadcast media of television and radio will link with the fax, the phone call and the electronic message, through one central point – the computer screen. From one screen people will be able to interact with:

- television and radio and television
- information
- home banking
- shopping
- games and events
- E-mail

Big businesses are investing in as much of the following as possible:

- Newsgathering media, TV stations, information and news suppliers, newspapers.
- Telephone services.
- On line computer networks and software.
- Broadcasting networks and systems of delivery.

- Copyright purchases of photographic and moving images, music, arts.
- Rights to events, such as world boxing matches, UK football, American football and basketball.

The company that wins the race to control all of these sectors could become extremely rich and powerful.

Your local newspaper may belong to one of the bigger organisations, such as Trinity International Holdings or NewsQuest. The television franchises are owned by a small number of organisations who also own papers and radio stations.

ACTIVITY 2

Research your local TV company and radio and newspaper companies. What is the parent company called? What else do they own in other media and other businesses?

Formats

Film

Film conventionally used 35 mm celluoid to project images onto cinema screens. However, film can now be distributed in various formats. Today it can be:

- Transferred onto digital versatile disc (DVD).
- Bought as video tape in 'sell-through' shops like Woolworths.
- Broadcast via satellite, cable or terrestrial aerials on television.

Television

Television is broadcast in three 'live' forms:

- satellite
- cable
- terrestrial (aerial)

Satellite channels can be used by subscribers

on a monthly rental or pay-per-view (i.e. pay for a particular event like a boxing or football match). You need a satellite dish to receive signals from a satellite station, which is located in space. Cable television links with a central relay system – to install this roads have to be dug up and the cables attached to the house's video player or television.

Television programmes can also be sold and packaged in video tape format. The arrival of digital broadcasting means that many more channels, widescreen pictures and interactive services such as banking are available.

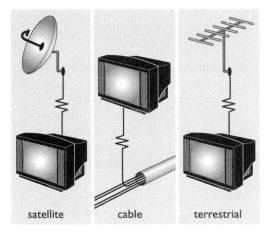

Fig 16.1   Satellite, cable and terrestrial

Digital technology

Digital technology has only just begun to enter into the world of television. It is more efficient than analogue broadcasting as you can transmit up to six channels in the space which used to be taken up by one.

Until now, radio and television have used 'analogue' broadcasting, which converts signals into waves. The waves are transmitted through the air from large transmitters in high positions and are received by television aerials. Digital broadcasting uses computer technology. It converts sound and pictures into a series of digits which are transmitted through the air using modified transmitters, and are then received by television aerials.

By using digital technology, around 200 TV channels will be made possible. Digital technology allows high definition television, widescreen pictures, CD quality sound, and 'near video on demand'. This is where a film is shown at a different start time on several different channels, so that the viewer can choose a convenient time to start watching. To receive digital television the viewer needs to buy or rent a set-top box decoder which is placed next to an existing video player.

Using digital cameras to film

Storing film/video and sound information digitally in computer memory means that editing can be more flexible. This process is known as non-linear editing.

In the past, the usual career path into film production has been the scriptwriter trying to persuade producers to give them enough money to make a film. More film makers are now using cheaper and more sophisticated digital camera technology to produce their own films, to demonstrate their talents. This demands more active and practical involvement in the process of production by the producers.

Music

Music can be played on audio-cassette, CD-Rom, mini disc, television and the Internet. Vinyl records are now often collectors' pieces. DJs (disc jockeys) and MCs (master of ceremonies) of dance and club music use vinyl to mix sounds, but this is a relatively small market. Digital versatile discs (DVDs) play either sound only, or with images, and can hold an entire film on one side. Once these become recordable, they should replace CDs as the main format.

Record companies have exploited the fact that people want to have the best sound quality possible, and for many years vinyl and audio-cassettes have been thrown away as the CD version of the 'back catalogue' has replaced them. The scramble over how to record and distribute music is still highly competitive, as it was when Sony won the battle of the walkman. However, in the early 1980s Sony did lose the battle over betamax, as VHS video tapes became the public standard.

Radio

Radio conversions from analogue to digital will increase the number of stations well above the current. However, franchises for the development of digital 'multiplexes' where joint bids are made, has not been a success as yet.

BBC news is now bi-media, meaning that its reporters have to use the same material and work in both televison and radio. ITV's regional output remains television-based only.

The digital age

Global Ownership

The ownership of the world's media has become a battle of a few company giants, such as News Corp, Time-Warner Inc. and Bertelsmann MG. These companies seek out the rights to music, film, publishing and televising sporting events to increase their profitability.

Company	Revenue ($)
Walt Disney Company	−158 million
Bertelsmann MG	873 billion
Viacom Inc.	−224 million
Time Warner Inc.	−4.9 billion
The News Corporation	−401 million

Table 16.1 *World's largest media owners (2002)*
See www.mediachannel.org for up-to-date figures for global media ownership revenues and profits.

Company	Turnover (£)
Reed Elsevier	713 million
Pearson	2.47 billion
Granada	1.81 billion
United Business Media	412.8 million
Carlton	214 million

Table 16.2 *UK's media owners largest (2002)*
Source: Interim reports, various

UK ownership of digital broadcasting

The current UK ownership of digital broadcasting is split three ways, however, there are links between them.

The UK digital highway is shared through six multiplexes. Multiplexes combine all the inputs into one signal. Viewers then access the bundle of signals according to which supplier they use. A different decoding box will also be needed for each supplier. The revenues for the suppliers will be made from selling TV set-top boxes, the programme subscriptions, the pay-per-view programmes.

Sky Digital

Sky Digital is owned by BSkyB. Sky Digital transmits on 200 channels and carries BBC1 and BBC2 and Channels 4 and 5. In addition to the usual Sky channels, Sky Digital will also screen Manchester United football matches.

ITV Digital

New bidding for the right to occupy the space left by ITV Digital is contested by BSkyB and the BBC.

Cable and Wireless

Cable and Wireless is a cable channel that aims to provide Sky Digital's programmes on its network.

BBC

The BBC, with the international company Flextech, have their programmes shown on Sky and Online Digital.

Equipment

Seven manufacturers are developing television sets with an integrated set top box: Toshiba, Panasonic, LG, Grundig, Amstrad, Sharp and Samsung.

Shopping

Today, there is much talk of a revolution in information, entertainment and financial systems and how this revolution will change our lives. Already it is possible to buy goods through a home computer and shop in a 'virtual space' on screen, which looks like a shopping area. The purchasers select goods by clicking on the mouse. The on line computer and the television set are two pieces of modern technology that link TV, computer games, teletext, E-mail, films and sport on demand.

Convergent services

Examples of the way computers, media and telephones have crossed over are:

▋ Internet services are delivered to TV sets via systems such as Web TV.
▋ E-mail and World Wide Web access via digital TV decoders and mobile phones.
▋ Web-casting of radio and TV programming on the Internet.
▋ Music publishing on the Internet.

Example 1: Music

The rock artist David Bowie produced an album that he then placed on the Internet as an on line CD. Both audience participation and commercial gain could result from this arrangement. This is what he believes could happen in the future:

> The users can decide on the packaging themselves. Hundreds of ideas have come in, of photographs, tickets, and memorabilia collected by fans of the tour I just did. Users could download a selection of these images and make their own booklets, printing it out, putting it in a case and eventually downloading the album itself from the internet.
>
> Source: David Bowie, interviewed by Emma Brockes, the *Guardian*, 15 January 1999

Individual music artists who wish to publish on the Internet run the risk of upsetting their record companies. However, the cost of buying a CD could become far cheaper if local stores were sent the soundtrack down the Internet. They could then write their own discs, thus reducing packaging costs. The discs would consequently be cheaper.

In March 1999, Sony began distributing music via satellite to specially designed television set-top boxes. Subscribers to Sony's multi-channel digital satellite service can download CD-Roms to mini discs, CD-Rom or re-writable DVD. The competing format is MP3, a particular type of compressed information file that compresses the information so it can be transferred more easily. Customers will need specially designed set-top boxes to download MP3 files.

Example 2: Television

Television formats have also been transferring onto the Internet. In 1999, Mark Lamarr, a music and television comic, for AOL (America Online) reproduced the 'chat-with-celebrities-net-show' formula that Oprah Winfrey ran successfully in the United States.

Example 3: Radio

Blur 'web-broadcasted' a 45 minute Radio 1 concert on their official website.

Example 4: Advertising

In March 1999, BSkyB failed to win access to the new digital service of ITV 2 on satellite. This was a disappointment to them, as they could therefore not gain the additional advertising revenue. ITV could regard this as a potential loss to BSkyB.

Shortly after the case of BSkyB and ITV, Granada and Carlton were warned by the ITC for refusing to carry an advertisement for Sky premiere's football channel Sky Sports:

Example 5: Film and DVD

The new DVD format is now set to surpass VHS in the US. In the fourth quarter of 2001, when *Shrek* was released it sold 2.5 million copies in three days. With a retail value of more than $50m, the release demolished a record set only two weeks before by *Star Wars: Episode 1 – The Phantom Menace.* That DVD sold some 2.2 million copies, with a retail value of $45 million in its first week.

Blockbuster has already eliminated 25% of its VHS library to make room for the 'high growth, high margin' digital format. The discs take up much less space than the video tapes and they last longer and contain more material.

The rental companies like Blockbuster can make more money out of DVDs. People prefer to buy DVDs than rent them, so Blockbuster is selling more DVDs as well as renting them. The sale of DVD players is also rising, so the market is able to expect more DVD sales. Is this the end of the VHS?

ACTIVITY 3

Research the query: do you think you will have a VHS video player in three year's time?

Example 6: Game consoles and networks

Console games

Fig 16.2   Xbox

Global sales of games will total $17.5 billion in 2002.
This figure is comparable to the film industry's box office takings of $20 billion.
The figures for DVD and video sales are $31 billion.
The takings for music CDs are over $33 billion.
(Forecast sources: Goldman Sachs, *Screen Digest*, IFPI and Merrill Lynch.)

According to one forecast, sales of games will overtake music CDs by 2005.

Console sales will exceed $45 million in 2002, bringing in a further $8.7 billion.
(SoundView Technology Group, San Francisco.)

Console sales are fiercely fought over between the three main producers:

Sony - PlayStation
Microsoft - Xbox
Nintendo – Gamecube
Each of these has drastically reduced their prices to entice customers to buy their product.

The average cost of making a computer game is $2–5 million. A successful title can earn $200–300 million, as much as a blockbuster movie.

New trends indicate that more adults are playing games:

60% of Americans play games, either on consoles, handheld devices or PCs.
Of these gamers, 61% are adults and 43% are women; the average age is 28.
Source: Interactive Digital Software Association

There is massive interest in network gaming online. However, the stand alone consoles need to have plug-in adaptors to link their boxes to networks, so it will take about three years before most consoles are sold with one built in.

Different types of games are:
■ Fantasy role playing, e.g. *Pimkin*, *Sim City*
■ Beat 'em ups, i.e. fights testing speed of reaction
■ Speed and navigation control games – *The Simpsons*, Grand Theft Auto.

Speed of development depends on how soon people have the high-speed broadband internet connections in their home. This is likely not to be in place till 2005.

ACTIVITY 4

What type of computer games do you play?
What type of technology do you play on?
a) consoles b) handheld devices, e.g. mobile phone c) PCs
Name some titles of games you play
How would you describe their type:
a) fantasy role play b) fight/action 'beat 'em ups' c) speed and navigation controls d) other

Example 7: Multimedia

Previously, television production companies would offer broadcasting, video production and post-production facilities. For example, the production company Victoria Real has five trading areas:

1 Broadcasting and video production – television and corporate videos.
2 Post-production facilities – television, film and graphics.
3 Interactive programming and advertising – interactive television.
4 World Wide Web – web pages.
5 Real products – software products.

The idea of a television company now seems old-fashioned. With the rise of video games, interactive television and CD-Roms, an approach to the information world is no longer confined to a series of half hour television programmes. Different levels of involvement and more direct electronic forms of text, visual and aural communication are now possible. On the other hand, the chance to explore the Internet across nationalities may not seem so exciting if we have to pay a high price for it. Another doubt is whether the drive towards convergence actually means sameness and not the diversity we might have hoped for.

Regulation and control

The content of all digital services must comply with published codes on programme content, advertising and sponsorship, technical standards and subtitling. Therefore, new digital television services will still have to comply with the controls, according to whether they are terrestrial (land-based), satellite or cable. The BBC, ITV, Channel 4 and Channel 5 have to follow guidelines on the number of hours they broadcast of factual and fictional programming, and community and public information services.

17 How much do I know?

Use the following questions to test your knowledge of important facts from each chapter.

Music: Chapter 6
1 Who are currently the five major companies in the music industry?
2 Name two labels from each company.
3 Who still continues to buy vinyl records?
4 Name two departments in a typical major music company.
5 What is the playlist?
6 What is synergy?

Film: Chapter 7
1 What is a unique selling point (USP)?
2 Name five major studios.
3 Name two distribution companies.
4 What is the BBFC and what does it do?
5 What is a shot-reverse-shot?
6 What is a tag line?

Television and Radio News: Chapter 8
Television:
1 What is the watershed?
2 What is the ITC?
3 What is the BSC?
4 What does 'hammocking' mean?
5 Name six news values?
6 Name one supplier of news.
Radio:
1 What is the RA?
2 Which TV channel organises its news teams to produce television and radio from the same material, i.e. a bi-media approach?

Newspapers: Chapter 9
1 What is a masthead?
2 Name six newspaper companies (note that this is not necessarily the same as the title of the newspaper).
3 Give five reasons for declining circulation figures of national newspapers.
4 What type of power does the PCC have, to control the press?
5 Describe a constraint which newspapers have in their reporting from courtrooms.
6 What is the ABC and what does it provide?

TV Hospital Dramas and Documentaries: Chapter 10
1 Name at least two hospital dramas.
2 Describe what happens in a cliffhanger.
3 What is a serial?
4 Name two types of filming techniques that are associated with making documentaries look real.
5 Describe three ways in which documentaries differ from dramas.
6 Name a documentary programme series from one of the TV channels.

Reality Television: Chapter 11
1 What are ratings?
2 Name one lifestyle television programme.
3 What is a schedule?
4 What is **inheritance**?
5 What is **pre-echo**?
6 Give three typical features of talk shows.

Magazines: Chapter 12
1 What is currently the top selling TV and radio listings magazine in the UK?
2 Which publishing company also owns Kiss FM?
3 What is the word given to describe an article written by the editor, which passes comment?
4 What is a niche magazine?
5 Name ten typical features in the contents of a magazine.

6 What is the circulation figure of a magazine (as opposed to its readership figure)?

Advertising: Chapter 13

1 Name six places where advertisements can be found.
2 What does the ASA do?
3 What is BRAD?
4 What does the ITC monitor?
5 What is an advertorial?
6 What is copy?

Sport: Chapter 14

1 Name two television programmes, of any type, which have sponsorship logos in their title sequence or in the break points of a programme.
2 What is subscription TV?
3 What is the difference between live and pre-recorded highlights of a sporting event?
4 Name two UK newspapers owned by the owners of Sky Sports 1, 2 & 3?
5 Which company currently owns the rights to televise Formula One car racing?
6 Why is sport such a lucrative money maker for television companies?

Local and community radio: Chapter 15

1 What does IRA stand for?
2 Which body issues commerical radio licences?

3 Which body measures radio audience figures?
4 What advantages does digital radio have over analogue?
5 What is pirate radio?
6 What is an RSL?

New media and old: Chapter 16

1 What does www mean?
2 What do the initials DVD stand for?
3 What is a back catalogue (music industry)?
4 Explain what pay-per-view means.
5 What is the benefit of an ISDN line?
6 When did the BBC start its first regular TV broadcast service?

Media studies concepts

Demonstrate your understanding of Media Studies concepts by writing your definitions of each of the following:

1 Languages
2 Categories
3 Producers
4 Audiences
5 Messages
6 Values

18 Resources

Your learning resources centre or your local library should have most of the following newspapers and books.

General: all media

1 'Media Guardian' section of *The Guardian* on Monday – articles, facts and figures. Covers soaps, advertising, newspapers, magazines, documentaries, dramas, institutions, future of broadcasting.
2 Media section of *The Independent* on Wednesday.
3 Media sections of Sunday broadsheets.
4 Review section in *The Guardian* on Friday – useful for latest film, video and music reviews.
5 'The Editor' – a supplement in *The Guardian* on Saturday – the world's media, surveys of news coverage, media Internet sites, magazine reviews.
6 *The Media Guide: A Guardian Book* – published every year. Contains a directory of who is who in media businesses and statistics on films, television, advertising, newspaper circulation and magazines.

Researching information

When asking for information from organisations, remember that most of the people who answer the phone are very busy and are often part of small office teams. Ask precise questions, such as: 'Can you send me your information/press pack or annual report about your organisation?'. If more than one person in the class is covering the same topic get one person to write on behalf of everyone else and share the copy.

Advertising

1 Advertising Standards Authority (ASA) – 2, Torrington Place, London WC1E 7HW. Website: http://www.asa.org.uk

2 Independent Television Commission (ITC) – 33, Foley Street, London W1P 7LP. Website: http://www.itc.org.uk
3 Advertising Association – http://www.adassoc.org.uk
4 Wired Advertising Research Centre – http://www.ware.com
5 Archive of advertising slogans and posters – http://www.emediaplan.com
6 Advertising archives– http://www.advertisingarchives.co.uk

Book publishing

Major book publishers now have their own websites. You can look at these to see how they design web pages and promote their books. Some feature an organisational map of what departments and businesses they own, and sometimes an end of year accounts report.

Film

1 *The BFI Film and Television Handbook* – a yearly review of film box office and television viewing figures. Published by the British Film Institute, 21, Stephen Street, London W1P 1PL.
2 *Sight and Sound* film magazine – published monthly by the British Film Institute. Serious film reviews and full synopsis, credits and reviews of all film and video releases. Website: http://www.bfi.org.uk
3 *Empire* and *Total Film* are mainstream magazines which contain information, gossip and reviews on film releases.
4 British Board of Film Classification (BBFC) 3 Soho Square, London W1V 6HD.

Film Internet sites:
Ain't it cool news – http://www.aint-it-cool-news.com

Bollywood – http://www.alt.movies.Indian

The Cinema Connection – http:/media.socialchange.net.au/CinemaConnection/

Cinema Sites – http://www.cinema-sites.com

Filmworld – http://findafilm.com/html/thisweek.html

Hollywood On-line – http://hollywood.com

Internet Movie Database – http://www.imdb.com

Motion Picture Release – http://www.tvgen.com

Moviefinder – http://moviefinder.com

Premiere magazine – reviews and news from America – http://sites.premiere.com

Hollywood Reporter magazine – reviews and news from America – http://sites.hollywood.com

Yahoo Entertainment Movie and Film Links – htttp://www.yahoo.com/Entertainment/Movies…and…Films

Hollywood film studios all have their own sites.

Music

1 British Phonographic Industry (BPI) – 25, Savile Road, London W1X 1AA. Website: http://www.fbpi.co.uk
2 On line music – TOTP Charts (BBC Online site) and Pepsi Charts (Channel 5).
3 Music press – magazines such as *Smash Hits* or *Select*.
4 Music Internet sites:
There are a wide variety of dedicated sites to bands and performers.

General music information and links to other music sources of information – http://dotmusic.com/artists

The Knowledge (independent labels/artists) – http://www.knowledge.com

Some music magazines also have websites (*NME*, *Q*, *Rolling Stone*).
The major music companies all have websites promoting their products (EMI, Virgin).
The Recording Industry Association of America – http://www.rios.com
http://www.worldpop.com
http://www.mtv.co.uk
http://www.Q4music.com
Artists such as Peter Gabriel or David Bowie are creative artists as well as musicians, and often also have their own sites –
e.g. http://www.DavidBowie.com

Newspapers

1 Audit Bureau of Circulations (ABC) – Black Prince Yard, 207–209 High Street, Berkhamstead, Herts HP4 1AF. Website: http://www.abc.org.uk
2 Campaign for Press and Broadcasting Freedom – 8, Cynthia Street, London, N1 NJ
3 Newspaper Society – Bloomsbury House, 74–78 Great Russell Street, London WC1B 3DA.
4 Press Complaints Commission (PCC) – 1, Salisbury Square, London EC1 8AE.
5 Newspaper and magazine Internet sites:
http://www.dailymail.com
http://www.independent.co.uk
http://www.mirror.co.uk
http://www.telegraph.co.uk
http://www.pa.press.net
http://www.the-times.co.uk
http://www.record-mail.co.uk
http://www.reednews.co.uk
http://www.guardian.co.uk
For links to UK local newspaper websites, check out the sites of publishers such as Emap, Reed,Thompson and Northcliffe.

Magazines
http://www.emap.co.uk
http://www.ipc.co.uk
http://www.bigissue.com

Radio

1 IRN – radio and news agency. 200, Grays Inn Road, London WC1 X 8XZ. Website: http://www.irn.co.uk
2 Radio Authority (RA) – Holbrook House, 14, Great Queen Street, Holborn, London WC2 5 DG. Website: http://www.radioauthority.org.uk
3 Radio Advertising Bureau. Website: http://www.rab.co.uk
4 Radio Internet sites:
http://www.spinner.imagineradio.com
http://www.radio.yahoo.com
http://www.radio.lycos.com
http://www.rollingstone.com
http://www.capitalradio.co.uk
http://www.atlantic252.com
http://www.bbcradio.co.uk
http://www.studentradio.org.uk

Multimedia: games consoles etc

http://www.playstation.com
http://www.xbox.com
http://www.gameboy.com

Television

1 British Broadcasting Corporation (BBC) – covers BBC radio and television. Portland Place, London W1A 1AA. Website: http://www.bbc.co.uk
2 *Broadcast* magazine – contains audience ratings by programmes, films, children's TV, drama, sport, plus channel-by-channel overview.
3 Broadcasting Standards Council (BSC) – 7, The Sanctuary, London SW1P 3JS.
4 Independent Television Commission (ITC)
5 ITV (Network Centre) – 200, Grays Inn Road, London WC1 8HF.

Examination Boards

1 Assessment and Qualifications Alliance (AQA) – Devaf Street, Manchester M15 6EX. Website: http://www.asa.org.uk
2 Oxford and Cambridge Royal (OCR) – 1, Hills Road, Cambridge, CB1 2EU. Media Studies Subject Officer: Birmingham Office, Mill Wharf, Mill Street, Birmingham B6 4BU. Website: http://www.ocr.org.uk
3 Welsh Joint Education Committee (WJEC) – 245, Western Avenue, Cardiff CF5 2YX. Website: http://www.wjec.org.uk

Glossary

The conceptual glossary which follows contains media studies terms. Technical terms are explained in the text of each chapter (see also Index).

Anchor Words or captions used to 'hold down' the meaning of a photograph create an 'anchor'. Without captions or words, the meaning of an image is more open to interpretation.

Audience In media studies, the term audience is used to describe more than the common sense idea of a group of people who sit in the cinema seats. An audience can also be defined by different criteria: social, demographic, psychographic or cultural. Audiences are targeted by media producers and can also be constructed. Audiences have different uses, needs and expectations of media.

Category The media can be divided into different categories by technological differences, including radio, film, television and magazines. Media can also be labelled in terms of their form, for example, documentary, fiction, news or light entertainment. They can also be labelled in terms of their type, genre or style, for example, horror or crime films, or quiz and soap opera TV programmes.

Code A code is a system of meaning which is understood within a social group or a society. In the western hemisphere, values and ideas about society are conveyed in the audio-visual media. For example, Rembrance Day, marking the end of the 1914–1918 war in the UK, is represented visually by poppies and barbed wire. In film, the haunted house settings provide the visual code for the horror genre.

Connotation Connotation is a secondary level of meaning by which codes and conventions are interpreted. It is different from denotation, which describes factually what is in the image.

Connotative meanings link ideas associated with the image from outside the text. See also denotation.

Construct All fiction or factual media products are artificially created. Therefore, all media texts are constructs. What the media depict is only a representation of imagined or real life. There is no such thing as a natural 'effect'.

Conventions A convention is any agreed or established way in which the elements of a medium's language is combined to create meaning or an effect. A typical convention of game shows is to include bright flashing lights and showbizzy sets, and a loud participating audience. A typical convention of a horror film is to see an open window, the curtains blowing and the moon covered by a dark cloud.

Denotation Denotation is the common sense descriptive level of meaning in an image or sound. See also connotation.

Genre The term genre is usually associated with different 'types' of film – adventure, comedy or western, for example. The word can also be applied to television, for example, game shows, thrillers or soaps.

Icon Originally an Eastern European Christian painting depicting God or Jesus. Today, the term icon is used to describe someone or something which has achieved almost god-like status. In the world of politics or music the fans often 'worship' their idols so much that these people become icons.

Ideology The system of beliefs found in the values and messages of a media product. These values might be found in the messages which makers of the products want to convey: 'buy these trainers, be cool'. The product might reflect the values of the society and the time in which the product was made, for example patriotic second world war films.

Institution Institutions are organisations which produce media texts, with production facilities, finance, distribution, exhibition, technology, and associated messages and values. It is a term used to describe not only large organisations such as the BBC, but also social institutions such as the church or the state. The term also applies to the different producers in the production process. For example, an advertising agency produces an advertising campaign for the Government's Central Office of Information.

Languages Languages are the forms and conventions belonging to each medium. For example, in film, the formal elements include the visuals (type and size of shot, framing and composition and lighting) and the soundtrack (speech, sound effects, atmospheric sound and music).

Mass Mass media texts are deliberately designed to appeal to the widest number of people.

Mise-en-scène A French term, meaning everything which is placed in and associated with the frame (shot) of the camera: props, dress, scenery, camera angle, shot size and movement, lighting, colours, acting.

Narrative The structure of the story line or organisation of the media product. The plot of *Cinderella* is usually told as the fairytale describes the events. The narrative is how the events are told. It is also possible to talk about the narrative structure of non-fiction texts such as television news programmes.

News values The factors and criteria by which news producers decide the selection and order of

the news. The word is a media studies term not used by the professionals in everyday discussion.

Niche Niche audiences are small and select in terms of social or interest group. For example, the financial news section of a television breakfast news programme is aimed at business men or women. A niche audience is a small segment or corner of the whole market.

Polysemic A visual image which contains several meanings, especially if there is no caption or heading to anchor it.

Producers The makers of the media texts include not only the artists, directors and production crew but also the people who plan, distribute and market the film. For example, a television programme broadcast by the BBC might be made by an independent television company on behalf of the BBC.

Representation A media text contains representations of people, events and places which the producers have produced to communicate with their audiences. The media text is by its very nature a constructed, second-hand and partial version of real or fictional life. A media text contains dramatised action or actual events through its medium. For example, television and its means of presentation is broadcasting.

Sign A sign is an element of the image which contains a reference to some other idea in reality. For example, the British flag connotes national identity. The term 'signifier' is used to describe the object which contains a 'sign' of meaning.

Text All media products which can be interpreted and 'read' are defined as 'texts'. Films, posters and trailers are all media texts which belong to the cinema industry. Toys used for tie-in product merchandising are not media texts.

Appendix

TASK
NUMBER

**STORYBOARD
SHEET**
**Directions, dialogue,
camera, music,
special effects (sfx)**

Do not write
in this margin

PRODUCTION SHEET

MEDIA: FILM, TELEVISION OR RADIO

Special instructions Vision	Special instructions Sound	Dialogue	Other information Setting, interior, exterior, action	Timing

Index

Page numbers in *italics* refer to illustrations.